Structuring International Economic Cooperation

Structuring International Economic Cooperation

Gavin Boyd

St. Martin's Press
New York

© Gavin Boyd, 1991

First published in the United States of America in 1991

Printed in Great Britain.

ISBN 0–312–05802–0

Library of Congress Cataloging-in-Publication Data
Boyd, Gavin.
  Structuring international economic cooperation / Gavin Boyd.
    p. cm.
  Includes bibliographical references and index.
  ISBN 0–312–05802–0
  1. International economic cooperation. 2. International economic
relations. I.   Title.
  HF1418.5.B72 1991
337—do20   90–19782
                                                           CIP

Contents

Preface

This book is intended to assist understanding of the vital need for wide ranging economic cooperation between the major industrialised democracies, and especially between the USA, Japan, and Germany. The need arises because very large interdependencies are linking the advanced market economy states in ways that cause each one's policies to affect, directly and indirectly, the growth and employment rates, the inflation levels, and the trade flows, of the other countries. The interdependencies, accordingly, have to be managed, in the common interest. Governments can attempt to manage them with emphasis on asserting their own interests, very competitively and even aggressively, depending on available leverage. There is a danger that this will become a common trend, but it must be averted, especially because the smaller and less advanced countries will be seriously affected. The basic purpose of the cooperation that is clearly needed will have to be the promotion of general growth with equity.

Questions about the range of cooperation have to be considered because trust in the effectiveness of market forces can justify claims that governments should confine themselves to minimal supportive and regulatory functions. Alternatively, governments can be seen to be assuming necessary functions for the orchestration of economic growth, especially through consultations with firms, and the fostering of cooperation between firms. With this perspective, important requirements for harmonising industrial and foreign direct investment policies can be identified. These requirements can be recognised with an awareness that governments tend to experience losses of economic sovereignty as national firms move into international operations and become footloose, while independently shaping economic structures in home and host countries. These losses of economic sovereignty can have increasingly significant consequences for overall growth rates, employment levels, trade balances, and the management of monetary and financial affairs. International economic cooperation, then, can be seen as a process through which governments can cope more effectively with what are often regarded as problems of domestic management.

Much of the policy literature on international economic issues neglects the significance of global trade and production activities by multinational corporations. This neglect can be responsible for distortions and biases in the perspectives of political decision makers, many of whom operate on the basis of quite simplified understandings of economic processes that affect constituency attitudes. In the USA Congressmen are well acquainted with the commercial issues posed by the nation's large trade imbalances, but in many cases appear to be unaware that American firms have been maintaining their shares of world markets through overseas production, although in ways that are becoming difficult to quantify because of the complexities of international ownership and of corporate linkages.

A considerable volume of the international economic policy literature is also deficient because of insufficient concern with the dynamics of policy communities in the major states. These have to be understood in order to appreciate factors responsible for higher levels of macromanagement in some states than in others, and for diverging orientations toward questions of trade, monetary, and financial cooperation. There is a danger that macromanagement problems caused by failures to cooperate will contribute to unfavourable changes in the dynamics of policy communities, increasing economic nationalism instead of moderating it in line with the growing requirements for collaboration. Processes of political change and continuity thus have to be considered in discussions of foreign economic policies.

Questions of international leadership are given some attention in the economic policy literature, mostly with reference to the USA, but this large and difficult subject now has to be opened up with some appreciation of the potential of the European Community. The deepening integration process in Western Europe is assuming global significance, not just because of a rejuvenation of neofunctional logic but also because capacities for a more assertive role in world affairs are being developed. With enlightened leadership these capacities could be used for an ambitious program of Trilateral economic cooperation, and to assist the development of a Pacific economic community, comprising the market economy states of East Asia and North America.

The preparation of this book was aided in many ways by collegial encouragement and support while I was a Visiting Professor in the Political Science Department at Rutgers University, Newark, New Jersey, during 1989/90. I am especially grateful to the chairman, Yale Ferguson, for stimulating discussions and numerous kindnesses received during that year. The writing of several chapters benefited from discussions in a Rutgers faculty colloquium and at meetings of the International Studies Association, the Pacific Asian Management Institute, the European Studies Association, and the American Political Science Association. I am especially indebted to Colin Dodd, Dean of Commerce at Saint Mary's University, Halifax, Canada, for assessments of issues in international finance offered during numerous exchanges related to conferences on Pacific economic cooperation.

Gavin Boyd

1. States, Policies, Firms and Markets

A multicountry world economy is being constituted by high volume trade and transnational production. These processes are expanding principally because of the integration and diversification strategies of American, Japanese and European multinationals, which are influenced in complex ways by the policies of governments. Vast prospects for growth are evident as the benefits of specialisation in the service of world markets are increased, under competitive pressures, through the technological and managerial capabilities of firms operating on a global scale. However, international structures to bring corporate strategies and government policies into harmony in line with widely shared common interests are lacking.

Imbalances, strains, and inequities are features of the structural interdependencies linking industrialised democracies with each other and with developing countries. The expansion of operations by international firms, while resulting in great efficiencies, drives less competitive enterprises into decline, and leads to a growth of oligopoly power. Governments, depending on their relationships with firms and their policy orientations, in some respects aid this process but in other ways attempt to hinder it, with consequences that reflect differences in macromanagement capabilities. The increases in oligopoly power, as they are used, tend to produce very serious problems of market failure, the gravity of which can be added to by administrative support of the expanding firms, and also by administrative neglect of the disadvantaged enterprises, which confront increasing difficulties because of the shifts in market power. The relatively liberal world trading system has been weakened by the attempts of governments to enhance national growth by favoring or opposing changes in the operation of markets, through direct and indirect methods of managing trade, and through the use of inducements and pressures in the implementation of foreign direct investment and industrial policies. While GATT's significance as a forum for the negotiation of trade liberalisation measures has declined, problems in the global monetary system have tended to have negative effects on the overall realisation of gains from international trade and transnational production. Volatility in global financial markets, while intensifying competitive pressures in product markets, has had dampening effects on corporate planning for trade and direct investment.

The rising levels of all the imbalanced and strained interdependencies in the emerging multicountry world economy, and its problems of market failure, set requirements for comprehensive international cooperation. This is primarily a challenge for the larger industrialised democracies, as their policies and the activities of their firms have the most extensive effects on the world economy. Their present patterns of cooperation on trade, monetary, and investment issues are quite limited, and are not expanding to meet the needs of the international system of production and exchange. The efforts of their administrations to enhance national competitiveness in world markets produce conflicting results, evident especially in trade surpluses and deficits, and the disparities in gains are tending to make shifts toward more cooperative policies less feasible politically.

The need for wide ranging international economic collaboration may be disputed on the basis of liberal economic theory, which is a source of expectations that if governments allow broad scope for market forces overall levels of efficiency and welfare will be raised. The principal task, then, is considered to be general trade liberalisation, for which governments are to eliminate subsidies to their firms and confine themselves to minimal administrative functions. Large differences in the international competitiveness of firms, and of countries, however, would persist, especially because of marked contrasts in degrees of social and political integration within states and in the macromanagement capacities of their administrations – even if it were agreed that governmental involvement in the guidance of industry and commerce would be reduced. Disparities in the spread of gains from liberalised trade would probably be large, and indeed would probably increase, as stronger firms in the better managed states would become more competitive. Disparities in the spread of gains would also tend to be large for noncompetitive reasons, as the terms on which national markets would become more open would be determined to a large extent by the bargaining leverage of the major states.

Liberal thinking also has to take account of other difficulties. The many cultural and institutional factors responsible for high levels of integration and competitiveness, notably in Japan and West Germany, are not negotiable. Nongovernmental institutional arrangements linked with official structures, such as the involvement of West German banks in industrial management, virtually substituting for industrial policy, are also not negotiable. The monetary authority of a very independent central bank is also not negotiable, as is evident in the West German case, although the use of this authority for neomercantilist purposes can have very significant effects on trade.

The forms of international economic cooperation that are becoming necessary will have to take account of diverse uses of macromanagement capacities in the more integrated states, and will have to provide for enhancement of the macromanagement capabilities of the less integrated national political economies. Enhancement of those capabilities for more competitive involvement in the world economy is being urged in much policy literature, but what the international political economy needs is not just evenly matched competition between the major industrialised states but a functional and equitable balance between competition and cooperation between firms, in a context of harmonised national policy environments.

International economic cooperation that goes well beyond trade liberalisation and which involves overcoming macromanagement deficiencies in the less integrated industrialised democracies will be difficult. To understand the problems that must be anticipated it will be necessary to examine processes of continuity and change in the major advanced states with international leadership capabilities. Trends in the evolution of these states will have to be taken into account if directions are to be set for political designing aimed at the promotion of comprehensive international economic cooperation. Trends in the activities of firms will also have to be considered, because corporate managements will have to be drawn into the necessary forms of international collaboration: national economic structures, it is clear, will continue to be shaped more and more by the production and marketing decisions of large enterprises. National economies are already being linked more by multinational firms, through their internalisation of markets, than through the operation of market forces in arm's length trade.

Continuity and Change

Processes of continuity and change in advanced national political economies involve multiple forms of reciprocal causality. These invite contextual analysis because in each state the configuration of cultural, institutional, and functional elements, refracted in political psychology and political sociological perspectives, is distinctive. Yet the understandings sought must also be comparative, because of instructive similarities between the characteristics of leaders, interest groups, political parties, administrative structures, and policy styles. In addition, developmental insights are necessary, because most forms of competitive political advocacy, although having sectoral appeals, invoke the public interest. Political continuity tends to reflect broad consensus about macromanagement for the common good, while change often manifests dissatisfactions with the overall performance of a government as well as its effects on specific and localised constituency concerns. Citizens become active in democratic politics not simply as individual utility maximisers but with some sense of community identification and some concepts of moral values relating to tasks of governance.[1]

In the Group of Five major industrialised democracies there are contrasts between high continuity and low continuity states. Those in the first category – Japan and Germany – are more integrated national political economies under effective macromanagement, although with neomercantilist orientations. In the second category are less integrated national political economies – the USA, Britain, and France – in which political processes are quite conflicted, to the detriment of administrative performance. Collective choice in the first group of states is more functional, and sustains consensus. Over time, the contrasts between the two types of states tend to become sharper, as disparities resulting from successes and failures in managing asymmetrically interdependent growth increase, while reinforcing factors making for continuity or change.

Firms benefit substantially as components of the more integrated national political economies. Supportive policy environments and corporate links aid managerial and technological innovation, thus enhancing competitiveness. Broad policy consensus sustains stable fiscal and monetary restraint, for noninflationary outward oriented growth. Domestic prosperity secured through competitiveness in foreign markets thus strengthens interest group and popular support for the ruling parties. Administrative capacities to cope with stresses in the international trading and monetary systems are therefore quite strong.[2]

Policy environments and corporate links are less supportive for firms in the more internally divided states. Corporate planning has to reckon with greater uncertainties in markets and administrative measures, greater exposure to stresses in the global trading and monetary systems, and heavier costs of government, in part because of welfare burdens resulting from slower growth. Incentives to gain strength and independence through ventures into overseas operations are thus very strong. Distributional as well as growth issues are posed more sharply in the political processes of these states, because of the effects of weaker and less consistent macromanagement, especially when pressures of political competition push administrations into expansionary policies, and when these necessitate deflationary measures after their political benefits have been attained. Currency depreciation tends to result from trade deficits, attributable both to losses of competitiveness and the extensive movement of firms into overseas operations, as well as to the inflationary consequences of expansionary policies. Currency appreciation however tends to be forced by high interest rates related to large scale government borrowing and to periodic deflationary measures.[3]

The evolution of national economic structures tends to be more dynamic and balanced in the more integrated states, under processes of administrative guidance based on corporate involvement in policy communities. Concepts of optimum national economic structures tend to be more specific and more influential in policy processes, and associated with these concepts are notions of optimum structural interdependencies that shape foreign trade and foreign direct investment policies.[4] These are especially evident in Japan, where they derive much operational significance from the nation's acute resource deficiencies. In the less integrated industrialised democracies, in which policies are shaped reactively by pluralistic policy communities, *ad hoc*, particularised, and sometimes conflicting ideas about the requirements of politically significant industrial sectors tend to be operational.

The macromanagement capabilities of the more integrated states are tending to become more advantageous because of the increasing shares of their firms in global markets, and because of the cumulative effects of failures by the less integrated states to solve the coordination and control problems that arise as their national economic structures become more complex and are subjected to pressures for rationalisation only by market forces. Governments in these less integrated states seek wider cooperation from firms and interest groups, for improved performance, but tend to be handicapped by executive, bureaucratic, legislative, and interest group pluralism. For the international political economy, then, the principal result is that the more integrated states tend to become, in effect, more actively neomercantilist, while the less integrated states are increasingly disadvantaged. Differences in size, however, may enable a less integrated state to exert greater leverage on trade issues by threatening to restrict access to its large market.

The variations in policy and performance, and in capacities to bargain over terms of market access, have to be seen in the somewhat hierarchical pattern of relations between the major industrialised democracies. This pattern has evolved with changes in asymmetries as rapid growth has moved Japan into great prominence, while Germany has become established as the dominant member of the European Community, and the USA has adjusted to a contraction of its shares of world trade and production, but has become virtually locked into deficit financing on a scale that is increasingly difficult to sustain. Overall, political economy factors are the most important explanations of these changes, but in the USA leadership policy preferences have been exceptionally potent, drawing attention to the significance of political psychology variables, notably beliefs, values, and perceptions of national interests. The most pervasive factors operative in each state however have been cultural, affecting the political sociology of intra-elite and elite-societal relations. The manipulation of political business cycles is restricted by cultural factors, consensus, and institutions in the more integrated states, but value orientations in the less integrated advanced countries in effect allow considerably wider scope to attempt such manipulation in their political processes. The effects, of course, can be very damaging, as happened when President Nixon initiated expansionary measures to influence electoral choices while the Post World War II system of fixed exchange rates was crumbling in the early 1970s.

Strong States

Positive developmental effects of the main forms of reciprocal causality in more integrated industrialised democracies tend to ensure political continuity. Problems of advanced political development, many often identified as problems of governance, are avoided or overcome because community oriented values in the culture assist the building and maintenance of institutions, and practices of consensual decision making, while macromanagement achievements reinforce consensus and facilitate diffuse leadership. The policy style is rational rather than cybernetic, engaging with fundamental long term problems in the public interest that tend to be neglected by the conflicted short term decision making in more pluralistic states. Resources for the support of political activity are spread unevenly in the more integrated as in the less integrated states, but with less divisive consequences because of all the factors working for the maintenance of social partnerships.

The Japanese political economy's levels of integration and performance are high, and these have extremely important implications for the evolution of the international political economy because dynamic outward oriented Japanese growth increases marked asymmetries in the nation's interdependencies. The level of integration is due primarily to strong orientations toward group and community values that sustain a relatively egalitarian pattern of social stratification in which class differences are blurred while a very large middle class expands with the changing occupation system of a postindustrial society. The main institutional expression of the culture is a strong bureaucracy, whose economic agencies provide extensive informal administrative guidance in consultations with business associations and firms. These give managements experiences in policy learning, and officials experiences in strategic planning, in solidarity building contexts, reinforcing ties within the corporate community and between it and the administration. The entire process is conducive to high levels of X efficiency, that is pervasive integrative task orientation, with a very functional balance between competition and cooperation. The Japanese polity thus illustrates to an extraordinary degree the significance of cultural factors in policy communities, which have been rather neglected in the analysis of decision making networks.[5]

The high degree of integration in the Japanese system reflects a strong tradition of communal solidarity in coping with a hostile environment. It also reflects intensely felt imperatives for domestic cohesion to ensure superior competitiveness in the markets of foreign countries with which interaction is difficult because of the very distinctive and exclusive qualities of Japanese culture. Associated with these imperatives are others that are more compatible with the nation's need for harmonious interdependencies with trading partners. These are imperatives to orchestrate the development of a balanced economy operating on the expanding frontiers of technology – an optimum national economic structure, with optimum external trade and transnational production links, less and less handicapped by resource deficiencies. Japanese elites, concerned at the political costs of aggressively competitive involvement in foreign markets, show awareness of the necessity to strive for the goodwill of trading partners, but also reveal compulsions to maximise the nation's competitiveness and further strengthen its positions in global markets, despite the antagonisms that tend to be aroused. The two contrasting orientations affect administrative and corporate responses to a difficult issue now assuming prominence: how to accommodate inward foreign direct investment that has to be accepted from the USA and West European countries where Japanese firms are engaged in large scale production ventures.[6]

Broad elite policy consensus is associated with the high degree of integration in the Japanese political economy. This sustains a superior level of macro-management which aids the political fortunes of the ruling Liberal Democratic Party much more than the quality of economic performance assists its conservative counterparts in other industrialised democracies. The principal opposition party, the Japan Socialist Party, is an extreme left organization that attracts the support of only a modest part of the working class, and that lacks appeal in the nation's rather egalitarian society. The dominant role of the ruling party however is made possible to a considerable extent because voter support is encouraged by intensive election campaigns, financed by very large corporate donations to the organization's leading figures, in consideration of administrative favours. The Japan Socialist Party and other opposition groups do not have access to such substantial resources. Financial scandals which occasionally affect the status of the ruling party can draw some voter support to the opposition groups, but the realignments tend to be fragmented, as ideological differences prevent the formation of an effective opposition coalition. Ideological rigidity has prevented the Japan Socialist Party from evolving an appeal that could draw substantial support from the large middle class, and in recent years the leftist image of the party has been a disadvantage because of changes in both China and the USSR.[7]

The Japanese political economy's capacities for broadly consensual macro-management, adapting to the strains of the external environment, are likely to remain very potent, over the mid term. The rising structural interdependencies caused by the expansion of trade and overseas production, however, entail vulnerabilities. A severe recession in the USA could make the continuation of rapid export led growth very difficult. Popular dissatisfactions could then increase the significance of the opposition parties. Over the long term moreover the positions of those parties may be strengthened by social and economic changes related to the large scale movement of Japanese firms into overseas operations. This may significantly reduce manufacturing in the home economy, increase unemployment, and contribute to the emergence of a *rentier* society. Japanese economic ministries have a vital responsibility to provide administrative guidance that will ensure substantial growth in the domestic economy, but this is likely to become increasingly difficult as the nation's international firms gain strength through global operations and develop linkages with other transnational enterprises.

The culturally based emphasis on consensual decision making affects leadership political psychology much more than elite behavior is shaped by cultural influences in other advanced states. There are strong constraints on assertive leadership. Policy has to be defined in terms of mainstream orientations of large policy communities, in which middle level officials operating with considerable autonomy formulate proposals for endorsement by peak business associations and senior administrative officials. While high level attempts to give forceful direction are inhibited, consensus formation depends on the convergence of incremental forms of advocacy. The area of established consensus remains large, especially because of the reinforcing effects of successes in macromanagement.

The core of the stable consensus is a commitment to a macro oligopoly policy, in which the principal components are a strategic trade policy, linked with industrial, technology, and foreign direct investment policies; and fiscal, monetary, and financial measures, which support infrastructure development while restraining consumer demand yet limiting currency appreciation. Positions gained in foreign markets by Japanese firms through intensely competitive exporting are expanded through overseas production activities, especially in the USA and the European Community. Linkages with US and European firms are meanwhile extended, especially for market sharing and technology exchanges. The policy mix has to be managed by coping with upward pressure on the Yen resulting from trade surpluses. This pressure is resisted through mainly informal financial controls, and is moderated by the balance of payments effects of large scale outward investment, including purchases of US government bonds as well as the establishment of overseas production bases in the USA, the European Community, and Third World locations. Domestically, further growth of oligopoly power in the Japanese economy appears to be an element in the consensus, in so far as market strength at home is seen to be necessary for national firms seeking maximum competitiveness in world markets.[8]

Continuity in the policy mix is challenged more by external than by internal factors. The macro oligopoly orientation has major political costs not only because of accumulating trade surpluses but also because high degrees of cohesion within each Japanese economic presence are considered threatening in host countries. The decline of less efficient firms in host countries, moreover, can be readily attributed to Japanese competition when popular bias is being encouraged by political journalism, as has been happening in the USA. The political costs of the macro oligopoly endeavour have been growing both because of the disruptions of foreign markets and foreign media bias. Severe US discrimination against Japanese trade and outward direct investment may be provoked. A more fundamental problem however is that the costs could be greatly increased by a drastic slowing of growth in major trading partners to which Japanese neomercantilism would have contributed.[9] A macro oligopoly policy, it can be argued, has to be implemented with prudence, so as to limit risks posed by the interaction of political and economic factors in the trading partners whose markets are deeply penetrated.

Germany

The only major industrialised democracy that can be compared with Japan because of political continuity based on cultural factors and prosperity secured through neomercantilism is Germany. The degree of integration in the German political economy is not as high as Japan's, and German external involvement through trade and transnational production is relatively restricted, but entails fewer political costs, although large trade surpluses are accumulated. The costs are in effect kept low by holding a dominant position in the European Community, and, mainly because of that position, Germany is better placed to provide leadership in the international political economy.

The level of integration in the German political economy is high because of strong orientations in the culture toward community and national values. These are conducive to the growth of consensus and cooperation, but without the restraints on individual assertiveness that are pervasive in Japan, as decisive leadership is recognised to be vital for collective achievement. German structures are more hierarchical than those in Japan, and their functions tend to be more influenced by leadership political psychology factors, which usually vary across wider ranges. Yet processes of political cooperation are in certain respects more extensive in Germany, as policy communities function within a system of *cooperative federalism*, and there is broad collaboration not only between the levels of government but also between the two major parties, the Christian Democratic Union and the Social Democratic Party. These two parties differ significantly in ideology and class support, and the contrasts represent a potential for change through shifts of power, but they share a substantial area of policy consensus relating to the basic tasks of managing an established social partnership of government, capital, and labour for continued export led growth.[10]

Overall, German macromanagement is less successful than Japan's. The principal deficiency is a failure to promote employment, and related to this is a somewhat class biased welfare policy. In a political sociological perspective, instead of the solidarity, social security, and exceptionally high productivity associated with Japanese style industrial management, there is a somewhat polarised pattern of industrial relations which tends to strain the nation's social partnership. Corporate adaptation to slow growth in trading partners and to slow growth in the home economy – attributable in part to strong monetary and a considerable degree of fiscal restraint – has been less paternalistic and inventive than managerial strategies in Japan. Assessment of the large market failure represented by the currently high level of unemployment – about 10 per cent of the work force – has to take into account fairly extensive exploitation of the state's unemployment benefits, but the elements of government failure and corporate failure are substantial.[11]

Political economy management, in which the very independent central bank plays a large role through monetary measures, serves neomercantilist objectives not only by restricting the growth of internal demand but also by keeping the currency somewhat undervalued, thus in effect limiting imports. The similarity with Japanese internal demand management however involves more significant external accountability, for while both states have to respond to US concerns, Germany also has to make its policies acceptable to other members of the European Community whose growth prospects are affected. Advantages are derived from the dominant position in the Community through the trade surpluses accumulated by neomercantilism, which have increased the competitiveness of German industries, and from an informal partnership with France in Community leadership, but Community resentments at the deflationary bias in German policy represent a significant political cost. These resentments will tend to increase if Germany has disproportionately large shares of the gains from fully liberalised trade after complete market integration in the Community, scheduled to be achieved by 1992.[12]

Corporatist interest representation, involving strong peak business and labour organisations, is the main process tending to produce political continuity. This is more inclusive than the Japanese pattern of nonelectoral representation, because of the scope for autonomous labour involvement. Its influence tends to promote convergence between the two major political parties, while its continuation benefits from their forms of collaboration in the system of cooperative federalism. It is more vulnerable to economic strain than the Japanese pattern, however, both because it is somewhat less productive and adaptable, and is influenced negatively, to a degree, by the significant ideological and class based differences between the two main political parties. The vulnerability to strain, moreover, is tending to increase, because of the persistence of high unemployment, and because there is growing assertiveness by a leftist movement within the Social Democratic Party. A challenge from a rapidly growing radical environmental party, the Greens, is also tending to exert pressure for change on the Social Democratic Party's orientation. The Greens represent a political expression of a shift toward what are politely called 'postmaterial' values among considerable sections of the younger population.[13]

The established pattern of electoral representation favours the Christian Democrats, as they benefit more than the Social Democrats from corporate support of their campaign activities, and are aided by the ideological and class affinities of the small conservative Free Democratic Party, their coalition partner at the federal level. The Christian Democrats are also assisted by the status which they have acquired as the ruling party managing a general improvement of relations with East Germany, other East European states, and the USSR, through 1989 and into 1990, with a supportive attitude toward reforms in the Communist regimes. Dramatic manifestations of unrest and of economic stagnation in those regimes appear to have indirectly weakened the appeal of the Social Democratic Party, despite the serious level of unemployment and the prospect that that party, if in power, would adopt a relatively expansionist policy in order to stimulate domestically based growth.[14]

Electoral choices are not only individual and group responses to the sectoral and national results of macromanagement: leadership images, ideology, and nationalism influence popular attitudes, and, with the political changes in East Germany during 1989, the element of nationalism has become especially potent because of German reunification. Impressions and expectations produced by reforms in the USSR, pressures for democracy in East Germany, and the interaction of German diplomacy and Soviet behaviour related to the reunification issue have entered into the processes of German collective choice. The effects seem likely to continue favouring the Christian Democrats, who are in a position to hold the initiative because of identification with the pressures for change in East Germany.

German policy communities function with a distinctive ethos of collaborative problem solving in the public interest, tacitly understood as the continuation of export led growth, with substantial industrial policy responsibilities virtually delegated to the banking system. The policy mix is thus more concerned with fiscal, infrastructure and overall regulatory matters than is the case in Japan, where administrative guidance of corporate planning remains a vital element of macromanagement. Because of the highly independent role of the central bank, monetary matters are not dealt with in the formal areas of competence associated with the policy mix, but the small banking elite who constitute an autonomous policy community operate in line with the preferences of financial and industrial interests committed to neomercantilism.[15]

A macro oligopoly policy orientation is thus effective, but its implementation is a less integrated process than Japan's, and because it is supported by less substantial and less effectively organised adaptive capabilities, the entire political economy is more vulnerable to stresses in the global trading and monetary systems. Yet Germany, it must be stressed, derives substantial advantages from its dominant position in the European Community, where advances toward complete market integration in effect offer widening scope for German neomercantilism. In that context the prospect of increasing political costs can be seen to raise questions about the long term desirability of working toward more symmetrical interdependencies with other Community members, using methods of integrative rather than intensely competitive cooperation. The issue, however, is not prominent in German policy discussions, as these tend to be dominated by leadership concentration on enhancing growth through the established neomercantilist methods.

Less Integrated States

The less integrated large industrialised democracies, under less effective management, experience relatively more political change. Trends in their evolution thus have implications for the development of the international political economy that are different from those posed by the stability of the more integrated advanced states. Study of these implications has to begin with the USA, because change in its political economy evidences quite serious problems of macromanagement and has very wide effects in the global trading and monetary systems. The USA's international leadership is weaker than it was during the 1950s and 1960s when a relatively liberal pattern of global economic relations was being established, and the decline of the American role has been due to problems of advanced political development that have been major sources of pressure for change.

The United States of America contrasts with Germany and even more with Japan because of its vast size and resources, which have made possible growth that has been largely domestically based. The USA's structural interdependencies have thus been relatively smaller, and more manageable on that account as well as because of the leverage available because of the nation's ranking as the largest industrialised democracy. Territorial size and diversity has necessitated the development of a federal system of administration, but what has evolved is strongly pluralistic rather than cooperative federalism. This pluralism expresses an intensely individualistic culture that shapes institutions and processes. Power is distrusted, and institutions are structured with an emphasis on checking and balancing their authority. In the economy, individualistic rather than cooperative capitalism is a source of pervasive restraints on interventionist policies and of confidence in what has been called market justice rather than political justice.[16] There is distrust of concentrations of economic power, but this is given relatively weak political expression, mainly because of difficulties of aggregating interests on a sufficiently broad scale, as well as because of the lack of trust in administrative power.

The political economy functions in an institutional and policy setting that allows wide scope for market forces, and, while this reflects the individualism of the culture it also expresses general beliefs in the efficiency of those market forces. Extensive freedom for those forces however has left the way open for enterprises to acquire oligopoly power in the home market and move into international operations on a large scale, while loosening ties with the domestic economy. The USA has thus become a less and less integrated political economy, and this has happened while its structural interdependencies have been increasing through trade as well as through the transnational production undertaken by its international firms. Meanwhile problems of governance, associated with executive, bureaucratic, and legislative pluralism, have in several ways tended to give impetus to outward direct investment, and this has been encouraged as well by tax incentives secured several decades ago before the difficulties of pluralistic governance became very serious. In the recent history of the system all those problems have tended to become progressively more intractable, in part because of fairly common shifts from consummatory to instrumental values that have increasingly obscured the public interest.[17]

The problems of governance have tended to result in forms of government failure, and the most serious of these has been a large and intractable fiscal deficit. Heavy government borrowing to cover repeated deficits has to be made feasible by relatively high interest rates that exert upward pressure on the dollar while attracting foreign lenders. External debt service increases, but large balance of payments problems result from very substantial trade deficits. These are attributable to losses of competitiveness in foreign markets by US exporting firms, the substitution of overseas production for arm's length trade by US multinationals, and large scale penetration of the US market by Japanese, other East Asian, and European firms that have reached superior levels of productivity. Diverse restraints on imports by foreign states, notably Japan and Germany, have also contributed to the trade imbalances. Since the mid-1980s the US administration has sought to reduce the country's trade deficits by interventions in currency markets to hold the dollar at low levels, but it has been necessary to do this within narrow constraints. Upward pressure on the currency is exerted not only by interest rates related to government borrowing but also by monetary restraints intended to control inflation and prevent increases in production costs, as well as to limit the growth of consumer demand. Downward pressure results from the continuation of large balance of payments deficits, the inflationary effects of an expansionist fiscal policy, and losses of domestic and foreign confidence in the US economy, related especially to slow growth and instability in the US stock markets. Poor regulation of these markets, which invites speculation on a vast scale, is a consequence of the difficulties of pluralistic governance.[18]

Political change tends to be generated in the USA by the pressures of pluralistic competition. These increase because of distributional and growth problems posed by macromanagement failures and by the substantial outward movement of direct investment, which to a considerable extent results in the domestic market being supplied from overseas production. Issues of allocative as distinct from technical efficiency are presented by this trend, but are not engaged with because of the established emphasis on market forces and the difficulties of pluralistic decision making.

The French solution to problems of governance in a strongly individualistic culture has been avoided because of the pervasive distrust of power. Contemporary change in the American system has indeed weakened executive authority. Congressional assertiveness on trade issues has been the main factor, exerting leverage for protection of domestic markets disrupted by import surges, in a setting in which executive status has been weakened by perceived failures to promote balanced trade and industrial expansion. Congressional pressure, however, has not been a coherent force working purposefully for improved macromanagement, and legislative resolve to deal with the large fiscal deficits has been lacking. Presidential authority, exercised within limits set by Congressional activism and neglect, seeks to overcome those limits through populist strategies, so as to influence and identify with strong currents of public opinion. What is feasible in this regard and through administrative direction depends very much on the political and managerial capacities of the President, and these vary more than those of an executive head in a parliamentary system, especially one that is politically more integrated. Within the administration bureaucratic pluralism is a serious hindrance to consensus building and implementation, especially because of the diverging roles assumed by transient high level political appointees.[19]

The policy mix is restricted in scope and substantively is more difficult to define than that in more integrated states. The economy is managed with very heavy reliance on fiscal and monetary measures, operating respectively with expansionary and contractionary effects. Industrial policy is *ad hoc*, defence related, and on a small scale. Foreign direct investment policy is liberal, and external trade policy is a complex assortment of liberal and protectionist elements, reflecting the involvement of numerous bureaucratic agencies as well as Congressional groups. The weaknesses of aggregating functions, due to the absence of strong peak business associations and low levels of institutional development in the major political parties, make the evolution of a coherent and functional policy mix very difficult. Policy communities tend to function reactively, and the pressures of political competition under which they operate are responsible for mainly cybernetic rather than rational decision making.[20]

Foreign economic policy has been managed in the more distant past with confidence in the competitiveness of American firms, based on their strong positions in their home market. This confidence has diminished because US shares of world exports have declined, although US firms moving into overseas production have retained large shares of world markets. The fall in export shares, together with general awareness of trade advantages gained by firms in the neomercantilist states, has evoked demands from business and political groups for technology policies, subsidies, export promotion aids, and aggressive leverage on trade issues, to assist penetration of foreign markets.[21] The main executive response has been pressure on states with large trade surpluses to grant increased market access. The leverage against Japan has been stronger and more public than that against Germany. Monetary interventions to prevent rises in the dollar have had trade promotion objectives, and have indirectly helped to restrain demands for a more activist commercial policy. Such demands have focussed on the problem of securing wider access to the Japanese market, but pressure for this purpose has risked alienating Japanese investors whose cooperation is essential for US government borrowing to cover the budget deficit.

The gravity of the USA's macromanagement problems has tended to obligate concentration on the advancement of its perceived external economic interests, with more assertive use of its bargaining power, rather than on the provision of leadership for collective management of the international political economy by the larger advanced states. Because the fiscal deficit problem has remained politically very difficult, the use of monetary policy has become especially important for the executive in foreign economic relations, but within narrow limits set by domestic growth and external trade as well as borrowing requirements. What can be achieved in currency markets and with respect to the maintenance of domestic and foreign confidence, however, depends on cooperation between the Treasury and the Federal Reserve, and on interactions between currency, bond, and stock markets. An increasing difficulty is the erosion of exchange rate sovereignty, caused mainly by very high volume speculative activity. This increases the need for international monetary cooperation, but the urgency of the USA's problems has caused greater emphasis on the maintenance of monetary autonomy.[22]

Britain

Strong cultural affinities and the tradition of a special political and economic relationship link Britain with the USA, establishing a basis for cooperation that is unique in the context of relations between the five major industrialised democracies. Britain, however, is also a state experiencing problems of pluralistic governance, and its significance in the international political economy has been diminishing because of declining growth. Although a member of the European Community, moreover, Britain is on the periphery of the Franco–German partnership which dominates that grouping, and, disadvantaged on that account, has been tending to lose significance in the USA's external relations, while sharing less than could otherwise have been expected in the benefits of progress toward full market integration within that community.

Growth and distributional problems in Britain generate stronger pressures for change than those in the USA, but the difficulties of pluralistic governance tend to prevent effective engagement with those problems. The culture is less individualistic and there is more trust in government than in the USA, but class and class related ideological cleavages are more divisive, and there are generally lower levels of task orientation. Executive pluralism, attributable to the individualism of the culture, hinders the evolution of coherent and functional policies, especially because this problem is made worse by a type of generalist managerial culture prevailing at this level and by executive dependence on higher permanent officials who operate with cautious pragmatism under their changing political masters.[23]

The level of integration in the political economy is moderate to low. Strong peak business associations like those in Japan and Germany are not present; the aggregating potentials of the major political parties are weak, because of inadequate institutional development; and officials in the economic ministries are not able to foster broad cooperation by firms and labour organisations. Under Conservative administrations there has been emphasis on administrative aloofness from the operations of market forces, but with a hostility to organised labour and a severely deflationary bias in monetary policy that has been intended in part to weaken union influence by causing considerable unemployment. The socially polarising effects have been augmented by reductions in welfare spending.[24]

As distributional coalitions opposing technological change and hindering rises in productivity, many British unions have contributed to a general decline in the nation's industries. Abrasive management practices have also been responsible, and confronted with the problems of industrial decay managements have had strong incentives to invest abroad rather than in the expansion and modernisation of their British operations. High unemployment, by increasing the costs of government, and the high interest rates associated with the deflationary aims of monetary policy, have added to the incentives to move operations to foreign locations.[25]

Ideological differences between the two major political parties have been wide during the contemporary period of Conservative rule. The opposition Labour Party, under the influence of militant elements identified mainly with its industrial wing, developed a strongly leftist orientation, which was moderated slowly and only after three electoral defeats. The Conservative Party, under Mrs Thatcher's rather autocratic direction, became committed to the reinvention of *laissez faire* capitalism and to drastic reduction of the state's welfare responsibilities. On basic policy issues, then, the prospects for consensus became more remote.

Change in the British social structure effected through economic policy under the Thatcher administrations was intended to favour the Conservative Party's long term interests. The intended evolution of a post industrial society with a large middle class and a shrinking proportion of industrial workers was slow, however, and the breadth of the social base for Conservative support was diminished by the polarising effects of administrative bias against the unions and the underprivileged. The electoral challenge from the Labour Party meanwhile became more potent as its policy shifted toward the centre, and as the Conservative Party's image was affected by problems in its upper levels caused by Mrs Thatcher's dictatorial methods. Yet a possible shift of power to the Labour Party did not promise an alternative solution to the problem of economic decline. The Labour Party did not offer a credible prospect of social partnership for the support of an effective growth strategy, as its class and ideological biases remained significant, and the possibility of its return to power tended to increase the incentives for British managements to move operations to foreign locations.[26]

The persistence of growth problems and a failure to develop a more active role in the European Community have in effect kept Britain outside the two central processes of bilateral interaction, between the USA and Germany, and the USA and Japan, at the highest levels of the international political economy. These interactions occur at US initiative and, while they are not tending to become triangular, which would be advantageous for both Germany and Japan, they are assuming more significance as the levels of structural interdependence on which they are based continue to rise and as Germany and Japan gain greater prominence in global trade and production. Britain could become more actively associated with the US–German interactions if, with improved growth, a closer association with Germany could be developed, especially on the basis of rapport about the course of integration in the European Community.

France

For the present, France is Germany's only major partner in the leadership of the European Community, but stands apart from the German–US interactions. Although an active partner with Germany in Community leadership, France remains committed to a form of modified Gaullism which limits the scope for rapport with the USA, and for the United States has less significance than Germany because of lower ranking in the global pattern of trade and transnational production. Further deepening of the integration process in the European Community however will tend to bring France into closer association with Germany over a wide range of intra and extra community issues, including those in Atlantic trade and monetary relations.

France is in the category of less integrated industrialised democracies because of the divisive effects of an intensely individualistic culture, a deep ideological cleavage between conservative and Socialist political groups, weak institutions for interest representation, restricted opportunities for effective electoral participation, and the somewhat alienating consequences of exceptionally strong executive power. The economy lags behind Germany's, in size, productivity, and external market shares, and its growth tends to be hindered by the presence of a very large public sector, which expanded greatly under a Socialist administration during 1981. France, moreover, lacks a social partnership that could match Germany's, especially because firms in the private sector were alienated by the ideological hostility of the Socialist Party when it gained power in 1981.[27]

Growth and distributional problems generate pressures for change which strain the adaptive capacities of the political economy because of its lack of integration. Growth has to be sought in the increasingly competitive context of the European Community, and especially in unequal competition against Germany. Outside the Community the competition against Germany is even more difficult, and has to be managed while coping with losses of world market shares to US and Japanese firms that are more effective as rivals of German enterprises. France's industrial structure, while burdened with its relatively inefficient public sector, lacks firms that are sufficiently large and dynamic to adapt as effectively as those in Germany to the opportunities of full market integration in the European Community. Most of the leadership of the internally divided Socialist Party is unwilling to return the numerous nationalised industries to the private sector, and it is uncertain whether such privatisation would be politically feasible for a future conservative administration. Because roughly 30 per cent of the nation's industrial capacity is in the public sector, its drag on growth is substantial not only because of its own inefficiencies but also because of the extent to which these hamper private sector activity, as well as because of the burdens imposed on state finances on account of the soft budget constraints of the public sector enterprises.[28]

Distributional problems have special prominence, not only because of the difficulties of competitive growth but also because severe inequalities that were aggravated by the taxation policies of conservative administrations through the 1960s and 70s still influence class and ideological orientations associated with the Socialist Party. The conservative Gaullist party and its smaller ally, the UDF, are loose organisations, identified with middle and upper class interests, that are not able to offer credible prospects of building a social partnership for growth. The size of the middle class relative to the level of industrialisation is somewhat large, as there are numerous small firms, but the size of the industrial working class and its degree of alienation from what has been a socially irresponsible form of *laissez faire* Capitalism continue to benefit the Socialist Party.[29]

Alternations in power between Socialist and conservative parties with records of government failures in growth and equity seem likely to perpetuate France's low level of political integration and modest ranking for macromanagement. Associated with this prospect is the probability of marked changes in the use of executive power. A concentration of authority at that level and a drastic restriction of legislative competence have allowed wide scope for the expression of presidential policy preferences. These can vary greatly, especially because of the rather unstructured patterns of elite political socialisation in the weak organisations of the major parties. Effective direction of the political economy requires very active use of presidential power, and, while this may be exercised with major variations in style and orientation, substantively it may focus on preferred areas of policy and neglect others.[30]

Foreign economic policy is an area that can be affected by presidential activism or neglect. Under Mitterrand, since the mid-1980s, a Gaullist emphasis on asserting French independence and opposing advances toward a higher level of integration in the European Community has been replaced by support for progress toward monetary union. This is recognised to be necessary for adequate utilisation of the growth opportunities presented by full market integration. There is, moreover, the potentially more important prospect of leading a coalition of Community members for institutionalised fiscal as well as monetary cooperation through which Germany could be induced to show more consideration for the interests of other Community members in the management of its fiscal and monetary affairs. A further prospect would be the development of a Community structure in which influence could be exerted over future German external policies. At present the Community's system of political cooperation for the harmonisation of foreign policy objectives is relatively ineffective.[31]

Policy Continuities and Changes

Altogether, policy mixes in the more integrated and the less integrated major industrialised democracies evidence continuities and changes related to levels of macromanagement and to degrees of internal cohesion and unity within each of these advanced states. The policy mixes vary with respect to their sources in policy communities and the decision styles of those communities. On a more extensive scale, there are variations in scope and functional qualities. The more integrated states implement more comprehensive policy mixes, undertaking wider involvement in their economies, and for this rely considerably on informal methods of securing cooperation and on the supportive activities of autonomous institutions and associations. The less integrated states are committed to limited governance, because of concepts of authority based on strong beliefs in individual freedom. France, however, is an exception, because of the interventionist orientation of the strong executive, and the influence of ideology on the implementation of that interventionism. Functionally, the policy mixes of the more integrated states reflect rational rather than cybernetic decision making, with less significant political exchange aspects related to constituency concerns, fewer ideological cross pressures, and wider consensus on the relevance of economic ideas.

In political economy perspectives, political business cycle theory, partisan theory, and rational partisan theory have to be related to the contrasts between the more integrated and the less integrated states. Political psychology and political sociological factors become significant in this process as they assist understanding of the patterns of reciprocal causality responsible for continuity and change. Political business cycle theory depicts politicians in office seeking to maximise popular favour before elections by implementing expansionary measures, the inflationary effects of which have to be reduced afterwards by drastic deflationary policies. However, broad institutionalised elite consensus, to a large extent, prevents expansionary pre-electoral measures in West Germany and Japan. In the less integrated states tendencies to adopt such measures can be strong, because of weaker institutional restraints on the use of policy for political competition, but actual practice depends on leadership preferences, influenced by ideology, class sentiments, and economic ideas. Partisan theory, stressing preferences for low inflation and substantial unemployment or higher employment with higher inflation – related to ideology and class factors and to economic ideas – has more relevance for research on the less integrated states than on those with higher levels of consensus and performance. Rational partisan theory, noting the importance of leadership subjective preferences, gives attention to political exchange factors necessary for electoral success. Competitive utilisation of those factors is more evident in the less integrated states, but this is clearly influenced by the ways in which cultural factors produce flexible or intransigent types of individualism, as in the contrasts between the USA and France.[32]

Functionally, and with respect to political exchange aspects, policy choices are increasingly affected by the continuing rises in levels of structural and policy interdependence. Growth and distributional prospects depend more and more on national competitiveness and on administrative influence that can guide the activities of international firms as these affect the evolution of national economic structures. The fortunes of ruling and opposition political groups are becoming more closely linked, then, with what has been done or promised regarding national competitiveness. Hence policy mixes in the more integrated states tend to assume more distinct strategic qualities, especially concerning trade and foreign direct investment.[33] The pluralistic processes of the less integrated states give less coherent expression to imperatives for competitiveness, and tend to emphasise protection against advantaged trading partners.

An increasingly critical element in the policy mixes of the more integrated states is foreign direct investment policy, because of the very large and rapidly increasing volume of economic activity undertaken by transnational enterprises. Enlisting the cooperation of such firms, especially those that retain strong home country ties in the more integrated states, becomes necessary to serve the competitive purposes of industrial policy and trade policy. Tax and other inducements can serve this requirement, but the strongest factors that can be activated are culturally based affiliations, which are especially potent in Japan. For the less integrated states reliance on incentives is necessary in dealing with both national and foreign firms, but both have compulsions to limit exposure to the control and influence of governments in those states, because of the poor prospects for stable rapport about identities of interest. Most of the larger international firms that are beginning to dominate global markets are footloose, having American origins, and it is difficult for even the more integrated industrialised democracies – Japan and West Germany – to secure their cooperation with national plans for industrial development. Formal or informal restriction of their scope for operations thus becomes desirable for national competitiveness. At the same time enhanced administrative support for national firms becomes more necessary as these move into foreign operations and challenge the market positions of the footloose enterprises.[34]

Policy learning, associated with management of the policy mixes, is oriented toward enhanced national competitiveness in the more integrated states, and, accordingly, toward more competitive management of interdependencies. Continuity in both respects derives from stable perspectives and areas of consensus about the tasks of macromanagement. Policy learning conducive to integrative economic cooperation with other states thus tends to be excluded.

For German elites the imperatives for increased national competitiveness are evidently tending to become more evident as many of the large US multinationals expand their operations in the European Community and thus in effect enhance their positions in other markets. For Japanese elites, aware of the limited involvement of their firms in the European Community and the difficulties of enlarging that involvement, the prospect of large increases in the global strength of numerous US enterprises, through expanded European operations, is a potent challenge to increase national competitiveness.[35]

Policy learning in the less integrated states tends to be hindered by difficulties of agreement about perspectives, objectives, and methods. Enhanced national competitiveness is desired, but consensus on questions of administrative-corporate cooperation is lacking, and enterprise collaboration is not encouraged by the uncertainties of pluralistic policy making and the prospect of major shifts in power and policy as electors alternate in their choices between opposing parties. The movement of national firms into international operations, while facilitated by liberal policies with an individualistic basis, and in effect encouraged by the failures of pluralistic governance, tends to make policy learning to enhance the competitiveness of domestic firms more necessary but also more difficult. Protective trade measures tend to have appeal because of their political feasability, and policy learning limited to recognition of this can remain a potent factor in pluralistic policy communities.[36] In general the conflictual interactions within such communities, strongly influenced by political exchange concerns, tend to be cognitively restrictive.

The diverse policy mixes of the large industrialised democracies have to be managed while coping with forms of policy interdependence, which are significant within the contexts of influence relationships and interactions between governments. Vertical policy interdependence is evident between France and Germany, while mainly horizontal policy interdependence is apparent between Germany and the USA, and Japan and the USA, despite the efforts of US administrations to maximise available bargaining power in both relationships. Vertical and horizontal forms of structural interdependence are associated with vertical and horizontal policy interdependence, and tend to restrict policy options while providing incentives for cooperation. National competitiveness is sought to effect favourable change in the asymmetries of structural interdependence and policy interdependence. Interactions related to policy interdependence however can achieve more than what is possible through the use of bargaining power based on asymmetries in structural interdependence. There are potentials to communicate ideological beliefs, economic ideas, and proposals for community building.[37]

Trends in the interactions of the major industrialised democracies and in the management of their interdependent policy mixes tend to be driven by the effects of major asymmetries in structural interdependence. In the European Community large asymmetries are increasing within the vertical structural interdependence between France and Germany, and French endeavours to achieve competitiveness in manufacturing, for more balanced trade with Germany, are unsuccessful. The scope for productive interaction with Germany however is limited, in part because of stable features of the French policy mix, including the maintenance of the large and relatively inefficient state sector.

France thus has an interest in utilising the opportunities for coalition building that will become more significant if the European Community advances beyond full market integration towards economic union. Outside the European Community asymmetries in the more horizontal structural interdependence between the USA and Japan intensify their rivalries for increased national competitiveness, but interactions at the initiative of the USA focus on trade and monetary issues in a way that stresses the negotiability of Japanese rather than US macroeconomic policies. For the USA the issue of national competitiveness is politically intractable because of the tradition of administrative noninterference in the working of market forces, and also because gains in competitiveness by national firms facilitate their transitions into footloose multinationals.

Firms and Markets

The asymmetries in structural interdependence between the major industrialised democracies are being shaped increasingly by the activities of transnational enterprises. While the economic boundaries of the state have been extending in advanced nations, through administrative involvement in commerce, industry, finance, and infrastructure development, international firms have been reducing exposure to national regulation by expanding their global operations, yet have been contributing more and more significantly to the evolution of national economic structures, in line with strategies for widening shares in world markets. Great increases in efficiency result, because of the technological advances, the managerial capacities, and the financial resources of the transnational enterprises. National administrations however are challenged to consider options for further domestic economic involvement, and to plan for the development of optimum national industrial structures that will be sufficiently integrated to avoid losses of capacity and disruptions caused by foreign corporations.[38]

The largest assortment of international firms has emerged in a context of individualistic rather than cooperative capitalism. These are enterprises that gained extensive shares in the US domestic market and were thus able to support highly competitive operations in foreign markets, while losing ties to the home market in the USA and serving it in varying degrees from their external operations. Profits from these operations, acquired because of the inferior competitiveness of local firms, facilitate further overseas expansion, especially because of liberal US tax laws that encourage the reinvestment of profits gained abroad, and that in effect tolerate transfer pricing arrangements which limit tax liabilities. The main concentration of footloose international enterprises that have emerged from the USA, and that still have large operations within the United States, is in the European Community. The continuing expansion of their operations in its integrating market, by forcing numerous local firms into declines, is altering the pattern of market forces in the European setting. The economic boundaries of the state have been extended much further than in the USA by most Community governments, but these administrations lack the political will to introduce a common industrial and foreign direct investment policy, and indeed tend to compete against each other to attract US firms.[39]

Japanese transnational enterprises, retaining strong ties with the system of cooperative capitalism in which they have been based, constitute the second large assortment of multinationals, and it has a significant degree of integration because of their mutual links and connections with their home administration. This degree of integration, while conducive to high levels of X efficiency, and provides security for long term planning. In addition, it tends to augment the bargaining power of individual Japanese firms negotiating with prospective partners in joint ventures and with host governments. Altogether, then, steady acquisitions of market shares from rival foreign enterprises are facilitated.[40]

A third assortment of international firms is West European, principally German. Many of these enterprises have been losing shares of foreign markets and of the European Community market because of US and Japanese competition, and have been disadvantaged by the relatively small sizes of their home markets as well as the persistence of barriers to full market integration in the European Community. German firms, because of the dynamism of their home economy and its degree of integration, have been able to move into international operations more effectively than their French or British counterparts, but the strong location advantages of the home economy have tended to restrain outward direct investment. The volume of exports from the home economy has remained high in relation to overseas production by German firms. Within the home economy, moreover, German firms have had to maintain their market shares in the face of competition from US and Japanese enterprises producing in or exporting to that market, which has been especially attractive because of its high growth rate.[41]

The financial, managerial, technological, and market strengths of footloose US multinationals and of Japanese firms operating out of their home economy give them increasing advantages over European Community enterprises, whose growth has been hindered by the slackening of economic activity in the Community over the past two decades – in part a consequence of the degrees of market separation in the grouping. The strengths of the US and Japanese firms enable them to profit more from global rationalisation strategies, acquire and expand oligopoly power more rapidly, achieve faster technological progress, adapt more effectively to volatility in currency and product markets, develop more extensive linkages with each other and with smaller enterprises, and exert more leverage on governments. Over time, all these capacities are tending to become more substantial.

National economic structures are being changed in ways that reflect the relative strengths of the three main assortments of international firms. Industrial capacities under varying degrees of foreign ownership and control are being integrated into external hierarchies of economic power that include globally dispersed units, and can be expanded, contracted, reconstituted, and transferred at the discretion of the external corporate decision makers. Industrial capacities under local ownership and management are being deprived of customary shares in their own markets and, if sufficiently innovative, are being offered subordinate linkages with outside firms as these expand vertically, horizontally, and through diversification. Governments can seek to guide the evolution of the intrusive firms in accordance with plans for industrial development, but may be totally committed to *laissez faire* policies, or may focus on short term political gains expected from the entry of foreign firms on conditions negotiated in virtual competition against other potential host administrations.

The autonomy, mobility, and continuing expansion of international capital is changing markets and is affecting growth, employment, and inflation levels in many countries, but less so in the more integrated states. These, because of solidarity between national firms and links between those firms and their governments, can exercise greater control over inward direct investment. Their economies however are affected by the operations of international firms in their trading partners, and, of course, their own international firms are intrusive entities in those trading partners, capable of influencing and hampering the industrial policies of the host administrations as well as cooperating with those policies on a basis of shared interests and negotiated understandings.[42]

Competing and collaborating international firms produce increasingly sophisticated products and services for vast numbers of customers in globally linked markets. The complex and very extensive production and marketing processes could not be broken down into transactions between independent smaller firms without drastic losses of efficiency, high transaction costs and risks, and a slowing of technological progress as well as reductions in overall capacity to cope with volatility in financial markets and changes in business cycles. The oligopoly power gained, however, as markets become less contestable, tends to become a source of market failure, as the scope for collusive selling is used to drive up prices, and as restrictive business practices pose barriers to entry by potential competitors. International firms have very large resources to support the use of such practices. Labour markets, meanwhile, are affected, because they remain substantially national while capital is internationally mobile. Bargaining relationships between managements and unions become highly asymmetrical, as the demand for labour can in effect be moved out of the national market while the supply retains a fixed location and has utility only in that location. This has highly variable consequences for levels of consumer demand, since workers constitute large segments of each country's population. Those levels, moreover, are affected not only by the employment effects of corporate strategies but also by the distributional effects of high levels of reinvestment that are possible for large international firms.[43] Substantial profit retention for reinvestment is possible because of the financial flexibility and low tax exposure of major transnational enterprises, and is driven by competitive pressures for expansion in global markets.

Policy makers' concepts of optimum national industrial structures, operating in contestable and therefore efficient country markets, are becoming less meaningful in the less integrated national political economies, but retain significance in states where administrative–corporate links are strong, policy communities are broad social partnerships, and intrusive firms are subject to formal and informal regulation. In these more integrated nations growth remains largely dependent on the efficient operation of national firms engaged in foreign trade and production, and that benefit from the openness of the more pluralistic and *laissez faire* states.

Growth, to be achieved by increasing gains from trade specialisation made possible by market expansion, depends more and more on the collective management of markets that are being linked through commerce, transnational production, and, to a degree, by the reduction of tariff and nontariff barriers. These markets are being changed by independent and largely nonaccountable transnational corporations. Government efforts to promote balanced, diversified, and equitable national growth are encountering more and more serious problems, not only in the less integrated states but also in the more integrated ones, because of asymmetries in the structural interdependencies associated with international market linkages. Necessary increases in gains from trade have to be achieved in markets that are being in varying degrees internationalised. The operational consequences of the internationalisation of market forces – with marked asymmetries between managements and labour, and between administrations and managements, as well as between managements and consumers – are more evident to decision makers in transnational enterprises than to government leaders, officials, and legislators, especially in the more pluralistic states.[44]

2. Structural, Policy and Systemic Interdependencies

Questions of international economic cooperation have to be considered with an understanding of the dimensions and complexities of the interdependencies between the advanced states that will have to provide leadership for comprehensive collective management. These are firstly interdependencies between national political economies resulting from arm's length trade, intrafirm trade, and transnational production, and they involve relationships between firms, as well as relationships between firms and governments, especially with respect to regulatory functions and infrastructure development. At a second level there are policy interdependencies, because each administration's choices in determining its policy mix are conditioned by the decisions of other governments, and also by the consequences of those decisions on the evolution of structural interdependencies. Finally there are systemic interdependencies, because the management of each national political economy and the strategic planning of each corporation have to be related to the pervasive effects of trends in the international trading, monetary, and financial systems.

Trends in the evolution of the interrelated interdependencies have significance for problems of development in national political economies and in the international political economy. Such trends are shaped by firms and governments within an overall pattern of vertical and horizontal relationships. The coherence of this pattern is affected by problems of macromanagement in the largest state, the USA, and by the high degrees of autonomy enjoyed by the very numerous international firms which have emerged from its economy and which, as independent agents, are shaping national industry structures in many host countries.

In the structural, policy, and systemic interdependencies of the pattern complex processes of asymmetrically reciprocal causality operate, vertically and horizontally. Trends associated with the more prominent forms of causality become especially significant when these generate increasing asymmetries, reducing the strength of some causes and strengthening others. The competitiveness of countries, the competitiveness of firms, and entire macromanagement processes are affected. Shifting gains from trade associated with evolving structural interdependencies pose issues for governments and firms which are then reflected in the effects of policy mixes on the activities of firms and the effects of enterprise activities on the decisions of national administrations. The larger setting of systemic interdependencies offers opportunities for but also imposes constraints on administrative and corporate choices.

Structural Interdependencies

The growth and diversification of arm's length trade, intrafirm commerce, and international production are sources of structural interdependencies, between national economies, and between firms, as well as between firms and the countries in which they are operating. Because a very large and increasing volume of transactions are undertaken by transnational enterprises, intrafirm commerce and international production are becoming far more important than arm's length trade, which cannot offer comparable efficiency in the provision of technologically advanced goods and services on a large scale across great distances. Arm's length trade however is still a large part of Germany's foreign commerce, notably in the special context of the European Community. The volume of this trade reflects the cultural and institutional factors that incline German corporations to base their strategies on continued location within their home economy's system of cooperative capitalism.[1]

Interdependencies resulting from arm's length trade between the major industrialised democracies evolve according to differences in the comparative advantages of firms and countries, and in national policy mixes affecting trade flows. The contrasts are evident in much of the commerce between Japan and the USA, and Germany and the USA. Arm's length commercial interdependencies however become linked with those caused by transnational production and the intrafirm trade associated with foreign direct investment. Arm's length exports from Germany and other European Community states to the USA are roughly balanced by arm's length US exports across the Atlantic, but are overshadowed by the volume of US production in the Community, which is partially balanced by the production of Community firms in the USA. Financial flows add further dimensions to the Atlantic interdependencies, and, even more, to the arm's length and transnational production linkages between Japan and the USA.

The major causal patterns shaping the evolution of structural interdependencies indicate that these tend to become multidimensional. Vigorous arm's length exporting can prepare the way for overseas production in the markets which have been penetrated, and this is often stimulated by protective measures intended to promote balance in the arm's length commerce. Changes in that commerce through such measures reflect relative bargaining capacities, and these also affect the terms of direct investment flows. As those flows increase, however, transnational production affects the scope for arm's length exporting in host countries, through increasing market shares in those countries, while tending to reduce arm's length exporting from the home countries. The production and marketing capabilities of the international firms increasingly enhance their competitiveness in relation to national firms engaged in arm's length exporting. Yet those national firms may be greatly advantaged by strong positions in a large home market, as in the USA, or by a rather comprehensively supportive national policy mix, as in Japan.[2]

Imbalanced sectoral arm's length trade has characterised US–Japan commercial relations, and has evidenced the effects of Japan's acute resource deficiencies, and of the competitiveness of its exporting firms, as well as the greater openness of the US market. Because the trade has been sectoral, involving US imports of manufactured products in exchange for smaller volume Japanese imports of agricultural products and high technology items, the concerns of interest groups on each side have had only moderate compatibility. Greater compatibility has been possible in the relatively balanced intra-industry commerce between the USA and the European Community, which has resulted in more horizontal interdependencies. This Atlantic commerce however has included a large volume of intrafirm trade, managed principally by US international firms operating in the European Community. The flows of this intrafirm trade have been larger than those in other major commercial relationships because of the great volume of US direct investment in the European Community. Measurement however has been difficult because of the tendencies of international firms to understate the value of their consignments to branches of their own enterprises when this can reduce tax exposure.[3]

The growth of interdependencies related to arm's length trade can be related more directly and on a more stable basis to concepts of optimum national industry structures than the evolving interdependencies associated with transnational production and intrafirm trade. Transnational production is mobile, and its sourcing, processing, and marketing strategies are flexible; in addition it tends to accept local partners in joint ventures on a subordinate basis. The host economy thus tends to remain significantly dependent on the foreign corporate contribution to national growth, and the asymmetry can motivate concessions as well as toleration of foreign corporate discriminatory practices directed against local firms. Imbalanced transnational production interdependencies can thus become more imbalanced. The large uncertainties resulting from the flexibility of international firms, however, have the effect of making transnational production interdependencies much more difficult to manage than those resulting from arm's length trade. The cooperation of international corporate managements is needed, and so also is that of other governments, especially when the foreign firms are footloose.

Arm's length trade, expanding because of entrepreneurship and efforts by governments to reduce market separation, offers great possibilities for what may be called collective export led growth. These possibilities, however, tend to be overshadowed by the growth effects of transnational production undertaken by international firms, despite the greater uncertainties and asymmetries associated with their operations. The vulnerabilities entailed by transnational production interdependencies also tend to be greater than those resulting from arm's length trade interdependence. The volume of transnational production, it must be stressed, is large and is growing more rapidly than arm's length trade. The mobility of transnational capital, moreover, poses risks for local firms that become dependent on the multiplier effects of its operations in host countries, as well as for local firms against which the intrusive enterprises compete, or may compete later through the implementation of integration or diversification strategies.[4]

Financial linkages add to the significance of the growth effects and the vulnerabilities of the interdependencies resulting from arm's length trade and transnational production. Stock, bond and currency markets interact within and across national boundaries in ways that enhance or diminish the profitability of international production and arm's length commerce. Volatility in these markets can be managed more effectively by the larger transnational enterprises, and thus tends to strengthen trends toward the concentration of international market power that are driven by intensifying global competition. There is an overall efficiency problem, because the heavy demands of financial management divert energies from productive entrepreneurship and obligate low risk short term decision making. The importance of the linkages between the three types of markets, for confidence building and the transmission of stresses, has become very great in the USA, because of the interacting effects of high volume government borrowing, large balance of payments deficits, and alternations between expansionary and restrictive monetary policies. In this pattern the evolution of the high volume bilateral financial relationship between the USA and Japan has become a critical factor.[5]

The general evolution of structural interdependencies, because of all their asymmetries, results in problems of adjustment. These are normally thought of as requiring shifts of capital and labour to more productive operations in response to losses of comparative advantage. In the more integrated states the tasks of structural adjustment are less exacting, because of broad advances in productivity and the solidarity associated with cooperative capitalism. As a problem for country competitiveness, structural adjustment requires corporatist solutions, and is thus difficult in the pluralistic industrialised democracies. As a problem for the competitiveness of firms, structural adjustment is more demanding in the context of arm's length trade, for exporting enterprises, than in the contexts of intrafirm trade and transnational production, for international enterprises that can be highly adaptive in the use of their large resources.[6]

While structural adjustment by national political economies depends on their degrees of integration and their adaptive capacities, as well as on the magnitude of competitive challenges, it also depends on a country's situation in its pattern of influence relationships, especially in so far as these determine degrees of openness to commerce and direct investment. The current evolution of influence relationships between the major industrialised democracies, involving principally a decline of US leadership and bargaining power, the persistence of long social distances between the major European Community states and Japan, and a growth of pressures within the USA to externalise the adjustment costs of its deficits, is not conducive to the development of mutual responsiveness for the attainment of common benefits. Despite the constraints associated with the vulnerabilities of rising interdependence the USA is tending to exert greater leverage against Japan to overcome large imbalances in arm's length bilateral commerce. Problems of structural adjustment for US firms that are posed by this commerce remain difficult because of a general lack of capacity for broadly cooperative domestic solutions. Hence the use of pressure on the Japanese government for greater market access tends to become more important, but this, it must be stressed, can affect the asymmetric financial interdependence resulting from the US government's borrowing needs.[7]

All the forms of structural interdependence relate to the operation of markets that are in varying degrees open to each other and that accordingly have productive linkages but also others involving elements of market failure. These are affected by constructive government measures and also by government failures. The productive linkages, while enhancing gains from trade and international production, tend to become increasingly asymmetric, in the absence of comprehensive economic cooperation, because of differences in firm competitiveness and country competitiveness. Elements of market failure are present on account of the use of oligopoly power, and the absence of certain public goods necessary for general welfare and overall efficiency. The most important goods are stable functional balances between supply and demand, the lowering of transaction costs and risks, the curbing of restrictive business practices, and restraint on forms of speculation that can cause volatility. The problems of market failure invite constructive involvement by governments, and this is normally lacking because of policy orientations that are basically competitive rather than cooperative, but that in some cases are guided by liberal optimism about the effectiveness of market forces, notwithstanding the internalisation of markets by expanding transnational enterprises.

Policy Interdependencies

Because of the increasing magnitude of the structural interdependencies between the major industrialised democracies the macromanagement concerns of their governments, relating to employment, inflation, and overall growth, tend to obligate widening domestic economic involvement and efforts to control foreign economic relations, if only through protectionist measures. Capacities for such exercises of authority differ, as do perspectives on the appropriate objectives of the administrative measures, but the choices are conditioned by the options taken or expected to be taken by other governments. The domestic and external effects of their options determine in varying degrees what may be attained by any given national administration through its policy choices. A commonly identified example is the freedom to adopt expansionary macroeconomic measures: this is constrained by awareness that countries which avoid such measures can benefit from surges of exports into the expansionary country. An effect of policy interdependence, then, is that it can be a source of general deflationary bias.[8]

Policy interdependence is usually thought of with reference to issues in arm's length trade, but it has potentially greater significance relating to transnational production interdependencies. The dimensions of policy interdependence relate to the entire range of structural interdependencies, and are complex not only on that account but also because of national differences in policy mixes, as well as the familiar contrasts in bargaining capacities and influence relationships. Challenges to policy learning are implicit in policy interdependencies, but the options taken on the basis of interactions, constraints, and opportunities generally do not reflect common advances in policy learning. The consequences, however, can evidence significant differences in understanding the factors operating in the evolution of structural interdependencies under the influence of policies varying in autonomy and in adjustment to foreign choices.

Policy interdependencies operate within and across issue areas, and, in as much as this augments their complexity, it adds to requirements for high levels of integration within states, and indicates needs for discretionary cooperation. A prominent example of cross issue area policy interdependence is the US–Japan trading and financial relationship, in which US monetary choices and trade policy choices are influenced by Japanese financial and commercial measures, while a liberal US foreign direct investment policy is conditioned by those interactions and by a restrictive Japanese foreign direct investment policy. Further complexities result from the situation of the US–Japan relationship in the larger pattern of policy interdependencies within the group of five major industrialised democracies.[9]

Within the arm's length trade issue area, policy interdependencies – while not really separable from their linkages with foreign direct investment and financial questions – relate mainly to reciprocal and multilateral market access, viewed in liberal or neomercantilist perspectives, but influenced in some cases by felt affinities. The recent history of trade relations between the major industrialised democracies evidences strong restrictive trends, reflecting the assertiveness of interest groups activated by disruptive import surges. Liberal outlooks have been undermined, but with especially complex effects in the more pluralistic states, where relatively uncoordinated government agencies with trade responsibilities are involved in differing forms of policy interdependence, and assume different roles in domestic negotiations on interdependent cross issue area policy choices. Common impressions of the simplicity and clarity of arm's length trade policy issues however tend to dominate legislative attitudes, especially in the USA.[10]

Interdependence with respect to foreign direct investment policies and industrial policies related to such investment as well as to arm's length trade has very complex effects. Foreign direct investment flows can become more active in response to difficulties of market access, as well as on account of technological advances and productivity gains achieved by firms benefiting from industrial policies. Inward direct investment can be given official encouragement to serve industrial policy objectives, especially through technology transfers and multiplier effects. With high volumes of cross investment policy interdependence in that issue area imposes significant constraints on administrative options. Other important constraints are evident when high volume arm's length trade imbalanced in one direction is accompanied by high volume direct investment imbalanced in the other direction.

Overall, foreign direct investment policy interdependence is becoming more significant for national decision makers because of the growth of transnational production in the total pattern of economic activity and the increasing importance of the efficiencies of international firms for national growth, employment, and inflation control. Interdependence regarding industrial policies is also becoming more important, for the same reasons, as well as because of its implications for arm's length trade. If there is a commitment to a liberal or neutral foreign direct investment policy, as in the USA, it tends to be eroded by administrative concerns, responding to interest group pressures, about preserving the national character of vital parts of the country's industry structure, even though there may be only vague notions of a desirable pattern of national industrial capacities. Where foreign direct investment policy is interventionist the emphasis on administrative guidance of the incoming firms, in line with industrial policy, tends to become stronger as the overall significance of transnational production increases. Yet, with such increases, the capacities of firms to influence host country policies also become greater: their promises of expansion and their proposals to reduce local operations assume much significance for growth, employment, external trade, and inflation, as well as for technological progress or decline.[11]

The significance of a foreign direct investment policy depends not only on administrative technocratic capacity but on the breadth and mutual responsiveness of administrative relationships with firms, and on the quality of cooperation between firms. The asymmetries which all these factors can introduce into policy interdependence on foreign direct investment issues greatly complicate decision making. This need not strain the capacities of consensual policy communities engaged in holistically rational long term endeavours, but it does tend to strain the capacities of pluralistic policy communities operating cybernetically, through disjointedly incremental and experimental decision making, with differing centers of power diverging, conflicting, and producing awkward compromises.[12]

While the internationalisation of production and markets continues – with stresses related to multiple asymmetries – interdependence relating to foreign direct investment policies is a source of imperatives for increased integration within national political economies. Challenged to think in terms of optimum national industrial structures, policy makers are being obliged to recognise that these must be maintained and developed within national *communities*, whose internal cohesion can sustain the properties of systems, ensuring orderly operation and adaptation for common purposes. More than the simple regulation of foreign direct investment is thus required, and the interdependent management of foreign direct investment policies has to evolve in line with shared concepts of optimum national industrial structures and optimum linkages between those structures.

Policy interdependencies relating to financial links between national economies are inevitably connected with policy interdependencies on arm's length trade and foreign direct investment issues, but set more requirements for multilateral rather than bilateral cooperation. Thus far the most significant attempt to manage financial policy interdependencies has been the European Monetary System. This has been designed to provide a zone of monetary stability that can be defended against fluctuations in the value of the US dollar, and it has evolved very much under the influence of German monetary policy, which evidences tacit concern to prevent substantial appreciation of the Mark and to restrain the growth of consumer demand in the home economy. Further development of the system, in the direction of monetary union, is necessary to set up a central bank for the Community, and to introduce a common currency, so that the benefits of full market integration can be realised with greater monetary stability.[13] Financial policy interdependence involving much less solidarity is a basis for interactions between the USA, Japan, and Germany. In these interactions the USA seeks cooperation to maintain dollar stability in currency markets, through coordinated interventions. These have to be supported by large resources, but those are not substantial enough to cope with the effects of huge speculative flows in global capital markets. Trade objectives dominate US concerns, but there is a parallel interest in managing financial policy interactions to ensure that US government borrowing needs can be met to substantial degrees by outflows of funds from Japan and Germany. Hence there is pressure on these states to ensure that their capital markets remain substantially deregulated. Deregulation of Japan's financial markets began in the 1970s, mainly as a response to US leverage.[14]

The internationalised financial markets provide large funds to meet the requirements of international firms, and accordingly it is relatively easy for them to undertake expansion without having to cope with home or host country credit restraints, associated with inflation control, which do affect small and medium sized national firms. Policy interactions between major states that in effect perpetuate deregulation in international financial markets thus contribute indirectly to the continuing growth of disparities between the strengths of international firms and those of small and medium sized enterprises. Another effect is to allow the growth of inflationary pressures as credit is expanded in the unregulated global financial markets. Deflationary policies to counter such pressures then tend to slow growth, and have more negative consequences for small and medium sized firms than for transnational enterprises, which contribute to inflation themselves through the use of oligopoly power.

A further consequence of inaction that allows international financial markets to remain unregulated is that the ease of government borrowing reduces the concerns of US decision makers about the gravity of heavy US deficit financing. This tends to have extensive destabilising effects, and these tend to increase, while the policy interdependence related to financial matters retains bargaining asymmetries that enable the USA to continue its policy mix without external accountability.[15] US fiscal policy, shaped through executive–legislative interactions, is not significantly conditioned by the concerns of governments in other major industrialised democracies. US monetary policy, divided awkwardly between the Federal Reserve managing its domestic dimension and the Treasury managing its external dimension, is influenced by major foreign monetary choices, but does not have to contend with the bargaining power of any other large state.

Systemic Interdependencies

The structural and policy interdependencies of the major industrialised democracies are significant in a larger context of systemic interdependencies. Trade and transnational production interdependencies, for each of those large states, are multidimensional, and assume importance for national growth as they are identified in the more salient bilateral and multilateral relationships, but are components of the emerging multicountry world economy, whose overall and localised trends have diverse effects on virtually all nations. Policy interdependencies influence the decision making of governments in the major states within ranges of interactions related to structural interdependencies, but beyond those ranges the shaping of policy mixes is affected by trends and issues in regional and global patterns of interaction, especially those contributing to change or continuity in the international trading and monetary systems. Systemic interdependencies strain capacities for collective management, and adverse trends in these interdependencies, such as the weakening of the international trading system, can motivate attempts at bilateral or regional cooperation to overcome or acquire a degree of protection from the negative effects. The USA's interest in free trade with Canada and in the possibility of free trade with Japan can be understood as a reaction to general shifts toward managed trade that have reduced the significance of the General Agreement on Tariffs and Trade (GATT).[16]

Systemic interdependencies generally have secondary significance in policy processes. The influence of interest groups with specific concerns causes attention to focus on structural and policy interdependencies. These tend to be seen in broader perspectives by bureaucrats and executive figures, but their views of politically feasible options normally exclude issues of systemic interdependence. This has become more evident in the USA's policy processes as leadership functions in the international political economy have been relinquished. In the current pattern of relations between the major industrialised democracies there is a potential for collective leadership to engage with issues of systemic interdependence but consideration of those problems is severely restricted by the prominence of imbalances and strains in structural interdependencies and by the difficulties of achieving constructive interactions on policy interdependencies.

The issues of systemic interdependence concern the overall development of the international political economy, and, while they relate to opportunities for shared growth, they also relate to vulnerabilities. The expansion of trade, production, and financial links between national economies causes structural interdependencies within certain ranges, influenced by geography and the locations of resources, but the growth prospects inherent in those interdependencies are affected by changes in the entire international political economy. The consequences tend to be diffuse, and reflect a vast configuration of externalities associated with national policies as well as with corporate strategies.

The growth aspects and the vulnerabilities are evident in a rather hierarchical pattern, resulting from the status and influence of nations in the international political economy and their capacities to extract benefits from and cope with the vulnerabilities of systemic interdependence. The spread of a nation's structural interdependencies and the character of their asymmetries are major determining factors. The evolution of the international monetary and financial system has caused vulnerabilities more serious and less controllable than those associated with the expansion of trade and transnational production, and responses to these vulnerabilities have evidenced the different status rankings of the major industrialised democracies as well as their areas of influence. US initiatives have been principally responsible for the internationalisation of financial markets, but the USA has not had the will and the capacity to promote effective regulation of those markets. The systemic interdependence which it has since had to accept, moreover, has entailed a loss of capacity to intervene effectively in global money markets, while the markets themselves have become highly volatile, and accordingly are sources of vulnerability for the USA as well as for other states. Japan and Germany, although ranking next after the USA as major industrialised democracies, have not endeavoured to seek shares of leadership responsibilities for improvement of the international monetary and financial system, but have used their higher degrees of internal integration to manage their systemic interdependencies in line with neomercantilist policies. This has been done with more control over the vulnerabilities associated with those interdependencies.[17]

Systemic interdependencies associated with the global system of trade and transnational production are evolving under the influence of national policy mixes and the strategies of international firms, but are affected by the high volume speculation causing volatility in the international monetary and financial system. The main effect is to enhance the significance of the market power gained by multinational enterprises, and their capacities to cope with global financial volatility and with the attempts of national administrations to manage trade and direct investment policies. A secondary effect is increasing administrative involvement in managed trade and in endeavours to influence foreign direct investment. These effects, evident in the relatively hierarchical pattern of upper level relations in the international political economy, are increasing the contrasts between the more integrated advanced states that tend to retain the loyalties of their international firms and the less integrated states which fail in that respect.

Systemic interdependencies resulting from the diversification and expansion of linked product markets are being changed by the growth of oligopoly power as multinational firms become more active in shaping those interdependencies, through their competitive and cooperative strategies. Elements of market failure inviting collaborative action by governments thus result, but barriers to administrative intervention tend to be increased as the transnational enterprises acquire more and more substantial managerial, technological, financial, and production capacities that cannot be matched by state firms or brought under administrative regulatory control. Needs for higher degrees of internal integration are thus evident, especially in the more pluralistic industrialised democracies, in order to strengthen administrative technocratic capacities and secure greater social cooperation. These needs are more visible with respect to trade and direct investment issues than with regard to the systemic interdependencies relating to the international monetary and financial system. Greater prominence in national policy processes is a common result, because of the numbers of producer groups that are activated and the greater visibility of the growth, employment, and inflation problems related to the concerns of those groups.[18]

Because systemic interdependencies are diffuse and increasingly difficult to cope with, even for the more integrated states, and because the productive management of policy interdependencies is also becoming more difficult, while the political fortunes of governments depend more and more on growth achieved through the external as well as domestic gains from trade, stronger economic nationalism tends to be generated in policy communities. This trend derives impetus from awareness of competitive pressures in the internationalised product markets, and from reactions to discriminatory measures by trading partners. Since the economic nationalism is expressed mainly by states with major bargaining advantages, upper level relationships in the international political economy tend to become more hierarchical. Variations in the trend, however, result where the bargaining power of a larger state assumes less significance because of its macromanagement problems and because of its horizontal interdependence with a smaller state, as has been evident in the USA's relations with Japan.[19]

Perspectives

For administrations in the more integrated leading industrialised states, the growth opportunities of their structural interdependencies are clearly more significant than the related vulnerabilities, while the reverse appears to be true for administrations in the more pluralistic major states. For the latter, moreover, policy interdependencies tend to assume greater importance than for the former, because of felt needs to secure external cooperation on favourable terms. Decision makers in the more integrated states can expect continuing improvements in the positions of their nations in the international political economy because of the competitiveness of their firms.

Differing patterns of elite political psychology, however, affect perspectives derived from or suggested by fundamental national attributes. A conservative leadership in a more pluralistic state, although challenged by its problems of governance, may be more concerned with redistributing wealth for the benefit of the middle and upper classes than with overall macroeconomic performance and the consequent importance of managing interdependencies.[20] A degree of indifference to questions of international economic cooperation may be combined with beliefs that the main obligations of governments are to allow wide scope for international market forces. The variations in elite political psychology can be very wide, that is with respect to cognitive factors, including the influence of economic ideas and openness to policy learning; and with respect to motivational and operational factors, including values and methods of working toward objectives. The more prominent variations in a national pattern of elite political psychology factors evidence the effects of elite socialisation processes and are sources of continuity and change in policy communities. In general, however, in the more pluralistic advanced states policy elites tend to view interdependencies very much under the influence of representations by interest groups that have become sensitive to the vulnerabilities of market openness, especially where losses of competitiveness have been dramatised by extensive foreign market penetration. The socialising effects of protectionist interest groups interacting with policy makers tend to be intense and constant, because basic remedies to problems of competitiveness and restructuring are difficult in the less integrated industrialised democracies.[21]

In the more integrated advanced states leadership and elite political psychology patterns tend to be more uniform and more stable, and the socialising effects of interest group activity relate mainly to tasks of managing competitiveness in global markets from positions of economic strength. Interdependencies tend to be viewed from such positions, while the more pluralistic states are often seen as insufficiently reliable partners in any attempts at international economic cooperation. Instead of seeking greater policy interdependence, then, elites in the more integrated states tend to focus on methods of effecting further advantageous changes in structural interdependencies, through more active neomercantilism.

The perspectives of corporate managements engaged in global operations tend to be more patterned and stable than those of political elites, even in the more integrated industrialised democracies. Management cultures sustain operational styles focussing on competitive strategies which benefit from failures by governments to cooperate and from the pervasive roles of firms in shaping structural interdependencies while in effect limiting the capacities of governments for domestic and external economic involvement. In the perspectives associated with corporate expansion favourable influences have to be exercised on the policy mixes of individual governments, especially with respect to tax concessions and other measures that can add to location advantages. Where governments begin to cooperate for the management of interdependencies any limitations on the scope for corporate initiatives have to be overcome. Managements that retain strong home country ties, however, as has been noted in the cases of Japanese and German firms, tend to share some of the perspectives of their national administrations on commercial and investment linkages between their own and foreign economies.[22]

The *political sociology* of structural and policy interdependence has to be understood in terms of broad research concerns with the meaning and legitimacy of the emerging multicountry world economy, in which functions affecting that entire system are evolving without adequate governance structures and without the formation of communities of elites, except in the European Community. Other research concerns relate to attempts by national administrations to build up higher degrees of integration in their polities for the management of interdependencies, and to the ways in which such perceived imperatives are combined with leadership strategies for increased domestic support, which can entail the intensification and manipulation of social cleavages. The options taken reflect aspects of leadership political psychology but also the scope for leadership initiatives as determined by secondary elite and popular attitudes. The social psychology of beliefs and perceptions regarding basic questions of public policy becomes evident in the orientations and styles of policy communities, generally with more emphasis on felt imperatives for competitive rather than integrative approaches to problems of interdependent growth.

Cultural factors, which tend to be ignored in much political economy literature, are major determinants of the national structures and processes in which leadership and secondary elite views are shaped. Strong orientations toward community values in the more integrated states tend to foster economic nationalism, and facilitate the development of technocratic capacities and forms of social cooperation to further neomercantilist objectives. Individualistic cultures, such as those in the USA and Britain, are expressed in pluralistic policy communities that attract weaker loyalties but that can be more open to cooperation with foreign states and firms unless the vulnerabilities and costs of interdependence have become very prominent.[23]

Cultural affinities influence elite attitudes toward prospective partners in the management of interdependencies – but of course in conjunction with perceptions of status and policy. Cultural ties with Britain have effects on US elite views, but Germany is regarded as a more significant partner in the global economy, and Japan is considered higher ranking economically than Germany, but less accommodative on issues of cooperation. To the extent that the more prominent structural and policy interdependencies of a major state have developed with culturally very different nations, problems of understanding, trust, and cooperation tend to be seen, and the availability of leverage assumes greater importance. Prospects for the formation of international elite networks viewing interdependencies as matters requiring collective management can be considered much less significant than opportunities to further national interests through aggressive bargaining and through coalition strategies to exploit the weaker positions of less advantaged states.

Social changes in the advanced open states as they become postindustrial societies tend to make macromanagement more difficult, and thus can contribute to the development of less cooperative attitudes toward common problems of interdependence. These societies are aging, due to the effects of what can be called changing life styles, and, while their welfare burdens are increasing, the shrinking of their populations entails gradual reductions in consumer demand, with negative effects on growth. At the same time shifts in values associated with the changing life styles have effects on the behaviour of political elites: consummatory values are displaced, giving way to instrumental and manipulative approaches to issues of public welfare. This trend appears to be more pronounced in the pluralist advanced states than in those where cultures are less individualistic and more oriented toward community obligations.[24]

Political economy perspectives on interdependence are especially significant because of the influence of economic advice to governments. Differing concepts of state economic responsibilities and of the international economy guide the attitudes of national decision makers toward issues in foreign economic relations. Orientations derived from these concepts, of course, have been affected by experiences of severe stress in the international monetary and trading systems and of acute difficulties in macromanagement, especially since the oil price increases in the 1970s. The most important trend associated with these experiences has been a discrediting of Keynesian ideas regarding state capacities to promote growth through fiscal expansion, as rising interdependencies have tended to obligate fiscal discipline. Keynesian ideas, however, have in some cases encouraged hopes of collective growth achieved through concerted use of expansionary measures, or through expansion by trade surplus countries and contraction by trade deficit states.[25]

In the more integrated national political economies the emerging concept of the state is that of a governing structure engaged primarily in orchestrating growth through administrative promotion of nationally integrated corporate planning. Macromanagement in this sense provides the public good of co-ordinating the decisions of firms for implementation in markets that give signals for the adjustment of the macrocoordinating processes. Gains from trade are thus seen to be dependent on the continual improvement of market functions through the sponsorship of cooperative managerial planning. The significance of a supportive social structure is recognised, so that pervasive relational contracting, cooperative but also competitive, is matched by administrative-corporate partnership.

Such comprehensive macromanagement, it must be stressed, tends to result in aggressively competitive approaches to the management of interdependencies, and this is a basic problem affecting the development of the international political economy. Yet the concept is sound, because it is an effective response to malfunctions in highly diversified and highly advanced markets, in which information costs assume unmanageable proportions, and in which overall efficiency depends on large reductions of the uncertainties associated with unmanageable information costs. The concept can be seen as an extension of the logic of integration at the enterprise level. It sets requirements for dedicated macromanagement in the public interest, however, which may not be met because of shifts away from consummatory values that threaten abuses of administrative and economic power. The neocorporatist managerial state can become an oligopolistic state.[26]

In the more pluralistic advanced states the concept of administrative economic guidance has remained unacceptable, because of pervasive individualism and beliefs in the efficiency of free market forces. The discrediting of Keynesianism has been followed, mainly under conservative governments, by emphasis on reducing inflation, through monetary and fiscal restraint, to facilitate growth, that is by providing a more stable business environment and lowering the costs of government. The competitiveness of national firms, accordingly, has been expected to increase, so as to make structural interdependencies more manageable, while enhancing the leverage available in policy interdependencies. Justifications for such expectations have varied with pre-existing levels of vitality in national economies, the size of internal markets, the volume of foreign direct investment, and the overall costs of previous expansionary policies. The competitive gains of firms in the more integrated states, moreover, have been relevant. Optimism about gains in competitiveness by national firms has been difficult to maintain in Britain, but has had a credible basis in the USA. For firms that do make such gains, however, movement into transnational production has become increasingly necessary, and this has consequences for the competitiveness of each home economy, regardless of the hopes that national administrations have placed on monetary and fiscal discipline.[27]

The theoretical perspectives on interdependence evident in much economic advice to major governments are oriented toward emphasis on sound *domestic* management, and on the uncertainties of securing significant degrees of cooperation from other administrations, despite the potential for attaining large common benefits. Political judgements and economic reasoning enter into this advice, and it tends to be more persuasive in periods of slow growth and stagnation when macromanagement problems cause general increases in economic nationalism. The political judgements mostly downgrade the potential of international economic organizations to promote cooperation, while much of the economic reasoning avoids reference to the growth of multinational firms that are substituting transnational production and marketing for arm's length trade.[28] Liberal thinking about the effectiveness of market forces, however, it must be stressed, has to take into account the shaping of structural interdependencies by transnational enterprises that internalise what were market transactions. At the same time assumptions about the force of economic nationalism in each state's behaviour have to take account of the decreasing scope for such nationalism because of losses of economic sovereignty to international firms.

Policy Issues

The main policy issues commonly identified for interdependent states are to increase self reliance, seek international economic cooperation, or evolve new policy instruments that can regain elements of sovereignty lost through interdependence. These can be combined in various ways, depending not only on substantive choices but also on contextual factors in foreign economic relations that affect levels of understanding, trust, and cooperation between governments.

The most important choices, for each major state and for the international political economy, concern the scope and quality of cooperation, the principles, norms and rules on which it is to be based, the development of systems for assessing and guiding cooperative activities, and the institutionalising of cooperation, for equitable participation by governments and for the provision of interest aggregating and policy planning as well as administrative services through common structures. A model to consider, at an intermediate stage of development, is the European Community. This confederal structure is a relatively advanced institution for regional economic cooperation that has experienced most of the problems that can be expected in building institutions for the management of interdependencies at the global level.[29]

Recognition of the basic choices regarding international economic cooperation by national decision makers tends to be difficult because of absorption in complex issue specific processes of competitive cooperation and noncooperation in foreign economic relations and in domestic dealings with legislators, interest groups, and bureaucratic agencies. Opportunities to open discussions on fundamental questions of cooperation at the international level are generally felt to be lacking. If such questions are considered, moreover, they tend to be understood in the context of major influence relationships between the leading industrialised democracies, and any outcomes that might be visualised are expected to be determined by bargaining strengths rather than by integrative collaboration for common purposes. In the more pluralistic states experiencing macromanagement problems the activities of interest groups sensitive to the vulnerabilities of interdependence can raise the likely political costs of advocacy for international economic cooperation that might be attempted by government leaders, because of common expectations of losses of national autonomy, and suspicions that the terms of cooperation will be determined by available leverage and yet be manipulated by governments with strong interventionist capabilities.

Nevertheless, issue specific cooperation that may be managed quite competitively can be extended into other areas and assume a more integrative quality if there is a fairly balanced spread of benefits and if concepts of reciprocity are accepted by the main policy communities. An issue for each administration, then, is whether to strive for the expansion of ongoing processes of cooperation, for the realisation of larger shared benefits. Choices of that kind, of course, could lead to more active engagement with problems of interdependence. The recent history of the international trading system, however, with all its instances of noncooperation, discourages optimism about the activation of collaborative logic through initial cooperative ventures.[30]

The basic choices for states regarding international economic cooperation are matters affecting the development of the global political economy, although the concerns of decision makers tend to focus on opportunities and problems for each national political economy. The external choices are motivated for the most part by domestic political interests, but for the evolution of the global political economy much depends on whether internal political processes can be brought into line with needs for widening external collaboration. Degrees of guidance given to such processes by leaderships vary, as do leadership policy preferences and openness to policy learning. How all these factors affect policy orientations on questions of international cooperation is especially significant in the USA, as the largest industrialised democracy, and in Japan and Germany, as states ranking next in the upper level of the world economy.

The present pattern of relations between the major industrialised democracies does not encourage optimism about leadership willingness and capacities to promote concerns with the development of the global political economy in domestic policy communities. The gravity of the USA's fiscal and trade deficits, and debt burdens, gives a contrary thrust to its policy processes and thus restricts the scope for internationally oriented executive initiatives. Japanese and German decision makers see challenges to adapt defensively to perceived US attempts to impose costs of adjustment on their economies. It can be argued that the size of the US economy and the spread of its external economic interests can justify substantial identification of its interests with those of the international political economy, but for most US policy communities urgent adjustment issues in trade and fiscal policy marginalise the significance of global problems.[31] There is indeed an identity of developmental interests between the USA and the international political economy, but there is a similar identity between Japan and that global economy, as well as between Germany and the global economy. The German political economy, moreover, enables its leadership to provide more guidance for the evolution of internal consensus than is normally possible for a US or Japanese leadership. Economic nationalism is a potent factor in the dynamics of the German system, but its influence is mitigated by the effects of high levels of policy interdependence which Germany has to accept in the European Community.

Questions of international political economy development, entering on a limited scale into US policy debates, are conceptualised mainly with reference to global trade liberalisation. The positive significance of interdependence in a context of emerging world market integration however is overshadowed by the negative significance of foreign interventionist policies and of related gains in competitiveness by foreign firms. The current US endeavour to promote wide ranging trade liberalisation through GATT negotiations is thus being matched by administrative interest in special bilateral trading arrangements such as the Free Trade Agreement with Canada. An issue of increasing importance is whether to devote more effort to the negotiation of similar pacts with other major trading partners. Such an option could be seen as a means of gaining stronger direct and indirect leverage against interventionist and more competitive states, and, in a larger context, of offsetting bargaining advantages gained by the European Community through expansion and the deepening of its integration process.[32]

German policy choices, restricted to the West European context by relational factors dating from the Second World War but expanded substantially by political liberalisation in Eastern Europe and the USSR, tend to be seen in perspectives which exclude global concerns. Deepening integration in the European Community entails higher levels of policy interdependence, but utilisation of the opportunities to build strong economic and political ties with East European states and the USSR requires much autonomy. Within the European Community context Germany stands to gain more than any other member state from full market integration, but with further institutional integration may encounter redistributive pressures from the less competitive member countries.

Because of all the factors that virtually obligate regional perspectives on German policy options, Japan has special significance for the evolution of the global political economy, as a state with more extensive international interests, and a larger and more dynamic economy, as well as higher levels of structural and policy interdependence with the USA. Japan's policy options at the global level however are considered in policy communities less sensitive to external influences than Germany's, and leadership orientation functions are usually weak. Because of vulnerabilities in the interdependence with the USA and a lack of international status, moreover, policy choices tend to be viewed very much on the basis of concerns to defer to US preferences on global economic issues. But to the extent that the USA is seen to be encountering problems in its efforts to promote global trade liberalisation, and is felt to be giving more attention to the assertion of its own commercial interests, Japanese perceptions of interdependence problems for the world economy tend to be peripheral to the routine decision processes driving the nation's macro oligopoly policy mix.[33]

Corporate Planning Issues

The various kinds of governmental indecision on issues of international economic cooperation and the strains and stresses between national political economies, which continue because of differences in competitiveness and macromanagement, allow wide scope for expansion by transnational enterprises. While the primary force of this expansion is rivalry for global market shares, it derives thrust from imperatives to spread risks, in view of uncertainties about overall performance by economies burdened with macromanagement problems. In addition there are imperatives to disperse operations widely for reduced exposure to forms of governmental regulation.

The development of linkages with other multinationals is commonly a high priority operating principle, as it adds to the benefits of corporate expansion by further reducing risks, increasing assured market access, and enhancing capacities to deal with governments, as well as by facilitating technology sharing. Increased capacities to influence government industrial, infrastructure, trade, taxation, and monetary policies can result, mainly in interactions with the more pluralistic states. These states, while giving their own firms motivations to move operations abroad, especially because of the costs of macromanagement failures, endeavour to attract foreign direct investment, in order to enhance growth and increase employment.

Utilisation of the location advantages offered by less competitive states holding out incentive packages is a commonly identified option, but has to be considered in relation to the benefits of location in the dynamic centers of innovation within the more integrated and more advanced states with administrative capacities to regulate foreign direct investment and support the competitiveness of national firms.[34] These two major choices evidently tend to be evaluated, increasingly, in the light of global strategies which require adjusting the differing combinations of benefits to calculations about shares attainable in principal markets. Complicating factors can include the attractions of competitive opportunities in states such as France with few dynamic centers of innovation but potent regulative capacities, and the incentives to operate in an economy such as Britain's, with a very liberal policy environment but bad management–labour relations and a recent history of industrial decline.[35]

For optimum combinations of location advantages on which to base corporate strategies the linkages which can be developed with other multinationals clearly become more and more important. The utility of such linkages is determined by relative market shares, financial resources, managerial capacities, and technological levels, as well as political ties with home and host governments. The most prominent trend is a growth of linkages between West European firms and US multinationals expanding their operations within the integrating European Community market. A further trend is the general expansion of Japanese transnational enterprises that have superior capacities for adaptation to locational problems and opportunities because of the cultural ties which facilitate cooperation between these enterprises, even while they compete, and which ensure informal support from their home government. With the expansion of a Japanese corporate presence, host governments in less advanced states are given incentives to offer taxation, infrastructure, and other inducements that will draw further investment.[36]

Issues for nonJapanese multinationals, operating individually and mostly out of the USA, concern the basic options of expanding linkages with each other and with Japanese firms, and securing host government favours, similar to those sought by the Japanese. The expansion of local operations, at the possible cost of reducing the global spread of risks and limiting involvement elsewhere, is the principal means of obtaining favours on taxation, infrastructure, and trade questions, and of ensuring that those favours can become exclusive and discriminatory. In the absence of cooperation between governments on industrial and direct investment issues, the increasing bargaining strengths of transnational enterprises enhances the significance of their options, and, therefore, the importance of strategic orientations in their management cultures. The distinctive cultures of Japanese managerial elites, which tend to be stable because of the continuity of advantages derived from communal intra-industry ties and home government links, are tending to be reflected in a relatively integrated pattern of responses to the general expansion of structural interdependencies.[37]

For US international firms there are extraordinary opportunities to join political campaigning in support of protectionist demands in the home economy. Pressure can thus be exerted to induce trade concessions by other states, and to limit penetration of the US market by competing foreign firms. Maintaining large shares of that home market then becomes a more secure means of generating resources for the support of overseas operations. Since those market shares can also be threatened by foreign direct investment in the USA, there are advantages to be gained through political agitation for the restriction of such investment, and for its toleration only on a basis of reciprocity by other states that impede the entry of US firms.

The domestic political options for US international firms have special significance for their strategies toward the European Community. Trade, industrial, and foreign direct investment measures adopted by that grouping or any of its members that tend to favour Community enterprises can become targets of campaigns within the USA for pressures to secure European accommodation. While the USA's trade deficits remain high, causing the growth of strong legislative pressures for protection, and without disturbing general ignorance about the scale of overseas production by US firms, the opportunities for corporate involvement in campaigning for trade reciprocity and direct investment reciprocity will be especially prominent in corporate planning.

Altogether, then, the significance of global increases in structural and policy interdependence for the transnational enterprises that are most active in establishing linkages between national political economies has considerable adverse implications for the development of the international political economy. Increasing strains and asymmetries have to be expected, with shifts of economic power to firms rather than governments and growing macromanagement problems for governments, as well as widening disparities between the more integrated and competitive and the less integrated and competitive countries. The main effects on national policy communities are tending to make constructive approaches to the management of interdependencies more difficult to promote, notably in the USA, despite the status which it has enjoyed as the main advocate of global economic cooperation. Systemic imperatives for extensive international economic cooperation however are becoming stronger, in functional and moral terms.

3. The Logic of International Economic Cooperation

Policy makers in the major industrialised democracies, because of their own failures in collective management, and because of the vast extent to which national economies are being linked by the mostly independent activities of firms, are being obliged to respond to multiple challenges. Actual and impending disruptions of large industrial sectors, incidental to unregulated competition in internationalised markets, are posing immediate adjustment issues. These raise questions about the overall growth potential of enterprise activities in substantially open markets where the absence of collective market governance opens the way for severe conflicts of interest. The entire context of trade relations and the pattern of international production moreover are overshadowed by acute strains in the international monetary and financial systems, for which the United States has to bear much responsibility, and which cannot be overcome without extensive collaboration between the leading industrialised states as well as drastic improvements in US domestic management.

The developmental problems of asymmetrically interdependent states, and of the global political economy, set requirements for international economic cooperation. When the rationale for this is sufficiently elaborated, imperatives for *comprehensive* and *institutionalised* collaboration become evident, that is full and sustained engagement with the tasks of collective management. A further imperative can also be recognised: a need for *integrative* cooperation, conducive to the growth of understanding, trust, and goodwill, and, therefore, to community formation. Cooperation resulting from aggressively competitive bargaining is of course subject to change with shifts in available leverage and the emergence of alternative opportunities. The resultant uncertainties obligate defensive precautions and encourage betrayals of whatever principles may have been affirmed.

Degrees of governmental openness to policy learning in the international interest vary with national configurations of problems of advanced political development. Such problems, for the present, are exceptionally burdensome for the United States, and the magnitude of its difficulties is tending to motivate attempts to impose its costs of adjustment on other countries, rather than to improve macromanagement through policy learning. At the same time, long standing reluctance to accept any losses of independence through collective decision making endeavours has become a stronger factor in US foreign economic policy. Many current proposals for US initiatives to promote economic cooperation between the large industrialised democracies advocate informal collaboration, under nonbinding arrangements.

Policy learning that has reflected the logic of economic cooperation has been evolving in the European Community, in line with perceived imperatives for regional market integration under collaborative market governance. Member governments have begun to recognise a need for further advances in regional economic integration. Collective regional management for improved growth however is being promoted with a sense of vulnerability to US and Japanese competition and penetration, and this reflects failures in Atlantic and Pacific cooperation which affect prospects for collective management at the global level. Nevertheless, important lessons can be drawn from the European experience for a theory of international economic cooperation.

Theory

In conditions of high asymmetric interdependence and increasing unregulated international oligopoly power, holistically rational domestic macromanagement, based on concepts of optimum national economic structures with appropriate external linkages, becomes an ideal, but must be extended into global economic cooperation. This can be sought in a spirit of economic nationalism, but the resultant aggressive leverage will make the collaboration limited, unstable, and unresponsive to opportunities for policy learning. If the cooperation is sought on a liberal basis the restraints on interventionist policies which governments are urged to accept are not likely to be honoured, domestic pressures for the expansion of administrative economic involvement are likely to remain strong, and the liberal orientation will not provide a sufficient foundation for rapport and the development of goodwill. The spread of gains from commerce in the liberalised setting, moreover, will be uneven and will thus be a source of pressures for change and redistribution.

Pragmatic combinations of economic nationalism and liberalism, adapted according to relative bargaining capacities, can result in shifting processes of expedient international economic cooperation. These need not preclude policy learning in the general interest, but of course may be affected by pervasive increases in the expression of economic nationalism because of imbalances in the distribution of benefits, to which the activities of firms as well as the measures adopted by governments may contribute. In this respect the recent history of protectionism in the global trading system is instructive.[1]

The international economic cooperation required by developmental imperatives, at the national and global levels, has to be oriented toward the provision of what may be called high public goods. Some low level public goods for the international economy are produced through collaborative management of market infrastructure services, including communications, but, while these forms of cooperation continue, much more must be attempted, and with integrative motivations. The high public goods which are increasingly needed relate to market governance, industrial complementarity, the spread of gains from transnational production, the operation of the international monetary and financial systems, and the harmonising of national policy mixes. The requisite public goods, while international, depend on but also contribute to the realisation of domestic public goods.

Since economic growth is made possible by increasing gains from trade, national markets have to become open to each other. Governments have to cooperate by reducing barriers to commerce, but they also have to cooperate to prevent failures in the integrating markets. Collective market governance is needed to restrict the development of monopoly and oligopoly power as large firms expand to provide – through technological advances and economies of scale – the growth expected from market integration. At present the high order public good of trade liberalisation is given much recognition in policy literature, but there is little understanding that it has to be complemented by the international public function of collaborative market governance. The main reason for this omission is that the requirements for such governance would be much more demanding than those for large scale trade liberalisation. Yet the rationale for what would be in effect a common competition policy is becoming more persuasive as numerous major firms expand the global reach of their production and marketing strategies. At the regional level the need for a common competition policy has gained acceptance in the European Community, but it has not been recognised at the transregional level, in Atlantic relations.[2]

National and regional competition policies of course in effect encourage firms to undertake abroad integration and linkage strategies that are restricted at home, and thus give impetus to the development of operations on a global scale. On this account the need for broadly cooperative international market governance is becoming greater. The effective implementation of an international competition policy however would require a strong common structure, operating at a high level of institutional development, and sufficiently insulated against the pressures of interest groups. Because of this difficult requirement one can argue that the tasks of restraining monopoly and oligopoly power should be left to national administrations, but this would not be in the general interest. Global multinationals are increasing their capacities for leverage against governments, especially in small countries, and even in several large states can exert strong influence by threatening to relocate. In view of these problems it would be possible to argue that perhaps competition in the internationalised markets will prevent the growth of monopoly and oligopoly power, but this claim is not sustainable. Without governance, markets do tend to be destroyed by the growth of concentrations of economic power as competition forces weaker firms into decline.[3]

With restraints on concentrations of power, internationalised markets need collaboration for the provision of extensive infrastructure services that can hold down transaction costs and risks, especially for the benefit of small and medium sized firms which would otherwise be disadvantaged more than the large established multinationals. The provision of such services, for improved market efficiency, is a high order public good, as important as an international competition policy. The necessary infrastructure services include advanced communications, banking, legal assistance, transportation, and insurance. Failures by governments to provide or sponsor the provision of these at adequate levels of efficiency, and in full cooperation, constitute hindrances to commerce, and thus have dampening effects on entrepreneurship aiming at new productive ventures for trade.

The list of public goods necessary for international market efficiency also includes industrial cooperation. Competitive ventures by firms, aimed at increasing market shares in conditions of uncertainty, result in problems of excess capacity and can contribute to imbalances within and between national industrial structures. Industrial restructuring, meanwhile, becomes necessary with shifts of competitive advantages, between as well as within countries. The public policy issues posed by excess capacity, industrial imbalances, and restructuring requirements are very difficult for governments acting individually. The most distinctive achievements have been in Japan, where they have been made possible by a high level of integration in the political economy, but even in that setting they may well diminish because of problems in foreign trade expansion. The Japanese experience however is internationally significant because it indicates how administrative–corporate cooperation can ensure balanced industrial development and adjustment. Further, the Japanese experience suggests that much can be achieved by governments cooperating with each other while engaged in collaboration with firms operating in their economies. The international public good to be visualised is collective administrative guidance for the development of more harmonious and more dynamic patterns of industrial complementarity. Many of the disruptions effected by the pressures of market forces, including the activities of noncooperating firms, would be avoided.[4]

Liberal perspectives influencing policy in the more pluralistic states tend to prevent recognition of industrial policy cooperation as an international public good, but such perspectives can be maintained only by refusing to concede that, in the absence of such cooperation, the evolution of national economic structures, and of growth rates, employment, and inflation, is being shaped more and more decisively by the competitive strategies of firms unresponsive to public policy concerns. Pragmatic liberalism can be given persuasive expression in claims that the propensities of many governments to cheat on commitments make the benefits of industrial policy cooperation very doubtful, but this argument does not invalidate assertions that such cooperation is an international public good, and the danger of failures in cooperation calls for the building of strong global economic organizations.

Industrial policy cooperation, to realise its potential as an international public good, would have to be supported by collaboration in foreign direct investment policies. Such a requirement is clearly becoming more and more necessary because of the continuing expansion of operations by transnational enterprises. At present, many industrialised democracies compete against each other in offering inducements to international firms, and these firms tend to acquire widening scope for choice regarding the expansion and contraction of their activities at given locations. The interests of these enterprises and their plans have to be made compatible with those of national firms if governments are to foster the growth of optimum national economic structures that are appropriately linked with the global pattern of trade and production. The public goods character of foreign direct investment cooperation of course can be obscured if this amounts to bilateral or group collusion directed against less competitive states. What has to be asserted is the need for broad cooperation in the general interest, and this raises questions about structuring collective management which must be investigated in the context of discussions of policy learning and policy interactions.

All the gains from market efficiency improved through trade, industrial, and investment cooperation are inevitably predicated on the high international public good of monetary and financial collaboration. The need for this is especially evident because of the persistence of grave threats to the stability of the international monetary and financial systems. Because of high American fiscal deficits, the health of the world economy now depends to a considerable extent on US borrowing from the rest of the world, and on the declining capacity of the USA to manage an unstable dollar in highly volatile international currency markets in which there is no collective control on vast flows of speculative funds.[5] The US problem of financial governance, moreover, has become politically intractable. The international public good required in this situation is not hard to recognise, but it has not caused any significant policy learning, and the magnitude of the problem demonstrates the need for strong external accountability as a corrective and harmonising force on the macroeconomic policies of major states. At the basis of the difficulty is the well entrenched position of the Democratic Party as a vast distributional coalition dominating the US Congress.

Fiscal cooperation has to be linked with international monetary and financial collaboration. Fiscal expansion and contraction affects consumer demand, and, therefore, trade and investment flows, depending on the management of monetary policy, although there may be expansionary or contractionary effects from large increases or decreases in trade and direct investment flows. Commonly identified features of the international political economy are fiscal restraint in Japan and Germany, and fiscal expansion in the USA. The contrasts are reflected in Japanese and German trade surpluses and US trade deficits. Market forces are not causing appreciations of the German and Japanese currencies and depreciations of the US dollar sufficient to reduce the trade imbalances, but many factors are operating in these trade relationships, and they do not invalidate the basic principle that fiscal cooperation is a high order international public good. An objection frequently made is that fiscal cooperation can be on an unsound basis, resulting in concerted expansion or concerted deflation or a faulty mix of expansionary and deflationary measures, but this possibility does not negate the proposition that collaborative fiscal management, directed toward collective noninflationary growth, is in the common interest.[6] The danger of seriously flawed collaboration, reflecting perhaps the compatibility of expedient political concerns, is significant mainly because it strengthens the case for surveillance by a strong international economic organisation.

Theory and Policy

Economic advice to governments, especially in more pluralistic states, often reflects low assessments of their capacities for rational choice, because of their preoccupations with multiple constituency concerns which necessitate cybernetic decision making, in conditions of uncertainty, information overload, demand overload, and rampant or confined pluralism. Most of the advice offered, however, is based on sophisticated understandings of major causal relationships operating domestically and transnationally in national political economies, with sensitivities to the dangers of stresses and shocks generated by conflicting processes in markets under imperfect governance.[7] At a very fundamental level two basic choices are indicated: an administration can devote much energy and large resources to the analysis of relevant trends in global trade and finance, in order to make predictions for the guidance of contingent adjustment measures, to be implemented with aggressive competitiveness, while coping with the cost externalising strategies of other states; alternatively, recognising the uncertainties of that option, an administration can seek broad integrative cooperation with the states to which its economy is linked by large structural interdependencies. Efforts can be made to combine the two choices, under the influence of liberal or neomercantilist ideas, which may be represented in different ways within any administration.

Economic advice that attaches little importance to international economic cooperation mostly reflects serious doubts about the political capacities of governments to undertake such collaboration and stresses that administrations have to be urged to undertake sound domestic policies and will be more likely to follow such advice if under the discipline of international market forces. Other sources of guidance on economic policy show some optimism about the prospects for policy learning by governments and stress the potential benefits of international economic cooperation, especially in conditions of severe strain in the global trade and monetary systems. The significance of the differing currents of advice varies with the policy communities to which it is addressed, and in this respect the main comparisons concern trade and monetary relations.

Large streams of economic advice, especially in the USA, endorse the principle of cooperation for trade liberalisation, and are directed at most sections of the national economic bureaucracies, legislators, and leaders of major business organisations. General trade liberalisation as a public good to be realised through genuine cooperation however tends to be considered unattainable, because of pervasive economic nationalism and the weaknesses of GATT. This appears to have become the prevailing view in US economic policy communities, while in Japanese and West German policy communities the benefits of market openness in trading partners are understood in neo-mercantilist terms. The feasibility of substantial reductions of the barriers to commerce between the main trading states, and therefore in the global economy as a whole, can thus be considered low. Because of the ranges of politically active interests that are directly affected, production of the international public good (trade liberalisation) would have to be a very broadly collaborative process, especially in conditions of economic strain. Policy advice urging monetary cooperation however is directed at small policy communities operating at high levels of sophistication and with more scope for independent choice. Collaboration in this area of policy thus becomes more feasible than collaboration for trade liberalisation, and can be initiated at short notice, while negotiations to lower barriers to commerce tend to be protracted. Yet economic advice addressed to monetary decision makers can also fail to evoke choices in the general interest. The responsible officials are usually experts in their own right but operate under political pressures, domestic and external.[8]

Economic advice on fiscal policies tends to be even less effective than it is on the thinking of trade policy communities. Fiscal choices have more direct significance for the political fortunes of governments and involve very large numbers of participants. Executive level figures are generally less open to guidance on budget matters than on trade issues, because of vital constituency interests. Fiscal cooperation between governments, accordingly, is very difficult, and, if attempted, is likely to be implemented with a readiness to make unilateral changes. Credible promises of fiscal cooperation moreover can be made only by administrations presiding over well integrated political economies – not by executives unable to command stable legislative support.

Because of the difficulties of trade and fiscal cooperation, ventures in monetary cooperation assume special significance for stabilisation and adjustment in the current pattern of global economic relations. This is straining capacities for monetary management and the capabilities of economic decision makers, and is being hampered by general losses of exchange rate sovereignty in the volatile internationalised financial markets. An extraordinary difficulty for policy oriented economic analysis is the unprecedented mix of upward and downward pressures on the US dollar, related to the enormous volume of deficit financing in the USA, the dimensions of its trade imbalances, the vast scale of speculative activity in global currency markets, and potentially destabilising trends in US stock markets. Differing estimates and predictions by economists pose large uncertainties for monetary authorities in the USA and other leading industrialised democracies, including those with strong currencies, notably Japan and Germany.[9]

The undue dependence on monetary cooperation, and on unilateral monetary measures in the absence of monetary cooperation, in the strained conditions caused by trade imbalances and financial uncertainties, tends to lead to increasing assertions of economic nationalism as objectives sought through monetary policy become less attainable. On present indications, limitations on what can be achieved for stability and adjustment are increasing, and the frustrations tend to be expressed in discriminatory trade policies. Vicious cycles then result, as escalating trade problems increase pressures for more effective uses of monetary policy while increasing the magnitude of the intended tasks. The dynamics of interaction between monetary and trade policies are especially prominent in the USA's policy mix, which has to cope with substantially unsatisfied trade expectations based on the engineered depreciation of the dollar. The most powerful trend in that policy mix is the growth of legislative protectionist pressure, especially in response to trade deficits felt to be insufficiently adjustable through monetary policy.

Political Designing

The logic of international economic cooperation thus has to be formulated with reference to the dynamics of diverging and conflicting measures in the trade and macroeconomic relations of the large industrialised democracies. The political feasibility of substantial collaboration for the provision of high order international public goods has to be considered if this concept is to become sufficiently relevant for policy. An initial focus, then, has to be on policy inputs, and there a key requirement, clearly, is transnational interest aggregation.

Expressions of economic nationalism in national policies reflect exclusive administrative concerns with aggregations of domestic interests. The main partial exception is the European Community, in which the European Commission has a significant regional interest aggregating function, and, therefore, a basis for regional policy advocacy in interactions with representatives of member governments. These interactions involve policy learning and forms of external accountability not available for national administrations outside the Community. New kinds of neofunctional logic can thus be activated, that is for consensus on deepening the processes of regional integration, in the common interest.[10]

Transnational interest aggregation is needed to to support and contribute to processes of international economic cooperation: it has to enter into the activities of national policy communities and the interactions of governments engaged in collective management. To the extent that this can become possible it can strengthen the logic of collaboration by increasing its legitimacy and enhancing its results. Difficulties to consider are that transnational interest aggregation in the context of regional or global cooperation endeavours could well be dominated by large international firms, using their superior resources for policy advocacy as well as for leverage on governments, and that the actual reconciling and harmonising of interests on a transnational scale could encounter vast problems because of national differences and the strong influence of national attachments. To meet all these difficulties, structural arrangements would be necessary, as the European experience suggests: the high order international public good of economic cooperation would have to be made possible through structures at advanced levels of institutional development as well as on the basis of transnational interest aggregation. Informal *ad hoc* cooperation, managed by governments at their discretion and with emphasis on preserving independence in decision making, could not be expected to be sufficiently extensive, stable, and responsive to common interests, or, indeed, sufficiently professional, since some government leaders would remain as free to express their subjective preferences as they would be in their own states. This type of problem has been evident in the recent history of attempts at economic cooperation at summit meetings of leading industrialised states.[11]

Institutionalised cooperation entails substantially increased policy interdependence and some losses of economic sovereignty, depending on the emphasis given to collective decision making and to the surveillance and advocacy roles of common structures such as secretariats or commissions, and representative bodies, such as the European Parliament. The logic of international economic cooperation thus has to be expressed with reference to leadership functions, the building of elite networks, the promotion of broad consensus, and the development of intergovernmental links, as well as the formation of regional and global associations of interest groups. These requirements are lessons to be drawn from the European experience. They are more difficult to meet in settings where cultural affinities like those in Western Europe are absent, and where long distances limit communications, but in such settings they are all the more important. The most basic need is leadership, and, for potential contributors to policy learning, this is a fundamental challenge.

At the national level, leadership is of vital importance for the provision of public goods, and especially for sound macromanagement, because the public interest tends to be insufficiently represented. This is quite evident in the more pluralistic industrialised democracies, but it is also apparent in the neocorporatist states, despite their relatively high levels of integration. At the international level, in the interactions between governments, there is very little representation of public interests shared across national boundaries, except, it must be stressed, in the European Community. The need for international leadership, then, for the provision of regional or global public goods, is very great.

Much of the current literature on problems of the international political economy refers to the decline of American leadership and the possibilities for a transition to collective leadership by the five large industrialised democracies. The attention of most US decision makers is considered to have shifted from maintaining a liberal international economic order (in which it had formerly benefitted because of the competitiveness of its firms) to the assertion of its commercial interests in dealing with competitive trading partners. Renewed efforts to provide American leadership on a liberal basis are not expected, because of a continued weakening of the US role in the global economy, and this view is given some support from literature on problems of governance in the US political system. Little optimism, however, is expressed about the possibility of collective leadership, and this is generally considered with reference to problems of strengthening the still relatively liberal international trading system.[12] The higher order public goods of comprehensive collective management are given little consideration.

The prospects for collective leadership are not favourable because little consensus has developed in Group of Five elite networks on problems of reducing strains in the world trading system. Suggestions for group endeavours that would be much more ambitious can thus be considered inappropriate. The building of a transnational network of mixed elites however is clearly feasible, and could begin under the sponsorship of leaders of business and political organisations in the Group of Five, and especially in Japan, Germany, and the USA. The modest efforts of the Trilateral Commission indicate how initial ventures could be planned, but they could develop with a potentially very significant innovation: the fostering of Trilateral conferences on direct investment planning. These would draw in numerous representatives from transnational enterprises, and, among these, efforts to promote consensus on the high order public good of comprehensive international economic cooperation could be rather effective. Although international managements concentrate on acquiring larger shares of global markets, and have interests in avoiding administrative regulation, especially where major political uncertainties are involved, their relative security can be conducive to long term planning with wide ranging perspectives. Political activists sensitive to the imperatives for comprehensive collective management may well be able to build a strong international corporate network which, with legislative and bureaucratic co-operators, would have a potent influence on policy communities in Japan,

Germany, and the USA. Of course business concerns could overwhelm political commitments in such a transnational grouping, but, if the political entrepreneurship aimed at collective management were sufficiently vigorous, that danger could be avoided.

Structural Issues

For comprehensive collective management, existing organisations for economic cooperation may be restructured, or new ones may be built. As institutions, the major existing organisations have serious deficiencies which are consequences of failures in cooperation, attributable in varying degrees to economic nationalism and to inadequacies in domestic management. While the production of public goods by these institutions has been failing, governments whose political economies have been affected have not contributed sufficiently to the operation and development of those institutions.

The rationale for comprehensive engagement with tasks of collective management has to specify a need to institutionalise that cooperation. The public goods intended to result from collaboration will have to be provided on a continuing basis, with adjustments in the common interest, but this will not be possible if the cooperation is *ad hoc*, informal, and subject to change at the discretion of participating governments. Binding commitments by governments to collective decision making arrangements will be necessary. The collaboration to produce public goods moreover will have to be internationally responsive, and for this the institutional arrangements will have to include a common structure, like the European Commission, capable of giving professional representation to the shared interests of the participating states and assuming advocacy functions on behalf of those interests. Such representation would pose a necesary challenge to the cooperating administrations, and, as the European experience indicates, governments could be inclined to bypass and weaken this type of common service if it were not established as a potent factor in the collective decision making system. The European endeavour to attain full market integration by 1992 could have been undertaken much earlier if the European Commission had not been restricted in its advocacy role by short sighted governments and had been able to accelerate policy learning processes necessitated by the adverse effects of community nontariff barriers operating in previous decades.[13]

Institutional arrangements for an independent review function will also be necessary for comprehensive collective management, that is in addition to the integrative thrust provided by the advocacy role of the proposed common structure. A representative body of specialists, possibly a Council of Economic Advisors, could fulfill the necessary review function. Governmental reluctance to give this body a strong role could be a problem, but the political entrepreneurship of promotional groups working for international economic cooperation could engage vigorously with this difficulty. In the European Community the independent review function is assumed by the European Parliament, but this body comprises politicians who lack expertise and whose degrees of task orientation are affected by the restriction of their organisation to a modest advisory role.

Organisations set up for collective management will have to function on the basis of a doctrine of comprehensive cooperation accepted by participating governments, and, with ongoing collaboration to provide high order international public goods, these organisations will tend to have positive effects on the political psychology of leaders and officials in the member governments. Of course the influence of economic nationalism may well cause failures in cooperation which will lead to more assertive economic nationalism, and vicious sequences of this kind may be likely if the spread of benefits from collaboration is seen to be very uneven. The intended institutions, because of this danger, will have to have redistributive capabilities, and the rationale for their use will have to be made explicit in the doctrine of collective management. Use of these capabilities could be vital for the development of the collective management structures, and the strengthening of their international legitimacy.

The inadequacies of the present global economic institutions have several implications for the structuring of collective management. These institutions were set up in the immediate post War period to facilitate the development of a liberal international economic order, under US leadership, and their framers were not able to anticipate the magnitude of the interdependencies that would evolve or the weakening of the US role that was to obligate collective management of those interdependencies. The primary US objective, an open global trading system served increasingly by the most efficient firms, was promoted with care to favour Cold War allies, including Japan, but the international monetary system, which had to ensure stable financial arrangements for the service of trade, was later undermined by a very loose US monetary policy. The International Monetary Fund, in which the USA had the largest voting share, failed to respond to the challenge, and, after confidence in the US dollar had been seriously weakened, its convertibility was unilaterally ended by the Nixon administration. The system of floating exchange rates which emerged proved to be much more volatile than was initially expected, especially because of a rapid internationalisation of financial markets, driven in part by technological advances.

The volatility of currency markets has imposed caution on trading and longer term production decisions by firms. Meanwhile the global trading system, liberalised by successive tariff reductions but restricted by introductions of nontariff barriers, has functioned under the disadvantages of extreme weaknesses in the General Agreement on Tariffs and Trade. As a bargaining forum this institution has been vulnerable to the unilateral and joint violations of its principles and norms by the major trading nations. These have led to a large volume of managed trade, reflecting extensive use of bargaining leverage in the service of economic nationalism.[14] Contributing factors have been the slowing of growth and the widening of differences in competitiveness between several of the large industrialised democracies since the sharp oil price increases of the 1970s, and the changes in trade patterns resulting from the spread of transnational production by international firms.

Streams of advice to governments in the policy literature have had little effect on the deteriorating trend in the world trading system, and for the West

European states and Japan its future is overshadowed by the USA's need to earn surpluses for high volume debt service. Resistance to US demands for trade liberalisation thus tends to take priority over general concerns with the state of the global trading system. In this setting it must be stressed, the US administration places much reliance on monetary measures as instruments of trade policy, but has to act under constraints set by its own borrowing needs, its tasks of preventing inflation and maintaining business confidence, and its relative losses of exchange rate sovereignty in the internationalised currency markets.

The recent history of the trading and monetary systems thus indicates that structures for international economic cooperation on a scale larger than that planned for a liberal world economic order should not be under the domination of one large industrialised democracy. Collective leadership is clearly necessary, and has to be combined with the aggregating and policy advocacy roles of strong common institutions functioning with substantial autonomy, like the European Commission. A further conclusion to be drawn is that, because of high levels of structural interdependence, national administrations have to be made significantly accountable to collective management structures, so that the direct and indirect effects of their policy mixes will be kept within limits set by common interests. The importance of this kind of imperative can be seen in the current evolution of the European Community. When that Community's experience is considered, moreover, it can assist appreciation of an additional conclusion to be drawn from the history of contemporary attempts at global cooperation: comprehensive collective management will have to be structured at the regional level as well as globally. Strong regional economic communities, in concert with the European Community, could have prevented the deterioration of the international trading and monetary systems. In the structures now needed at the global level the performance requirements for comprehensive collective management will be less demanding if successful drives for regional integration are undertaken in Latin America, the Pacific, and Africa.

Functional Issues

New or restructured institutions for international economic cooperation will have to be activated by leaders of the participating governments. Unanimous decision making would seem to be appropriate, at least initially, because of the importance of building a sense of community, even though some governments might exploit the system by demanding large concessions in return for cooperation. Decision making by a majority rule, it can be argued, would not command sufficient initial support to make the institutions viable. The European Community's experience suggests that the expansion of structural interdependencies after modest cooperation on a unanimous basis can lead to widening understanding that large common interests must be managed, and that the importance of this imperative can persuade governments to accept a shift to majority decision making.[15]

The need to reconcile solidarity building with functional requirements however obligates careful examination of decision making models, and of these the most instructive at the national level is Japan's. The Japanese emphasis on intensive commitment to problem solving consultations in the common interest will clearly be needed for effective international economic cooperation, in which the bureaucratic structure giving professional representation to the needs of participating countries will hopefully play a vital role. Value orientations in the Japanese culture of course cannot be transplanted easily, but Japanese approaches to industrial management have been introduced successfuly into Western enterprises, and the results provide some ground for optimism about what could be achieved in international economic organisations if efforts were made to set up Japanese style decision processes.

Progress in community formation through the utilisation of Japanese methods would depend on the development of a common political will, for which much leadership would probably have to come from the European Community, after it reaches a higher level of integration.[16] The solidarity building however could be aided greatly by substantial achievements in collaboration if the bureaucracy serving under the collective decision making authority were infused with motivations like those responsible for strong task orientations in the Japanese economic ministries. International bureaucracies, particularly those with contributed staffs rather than independently recruited officials constituting permanent staffs, tend to be inefficient, and thus discourage the growth of trust and goodwill between participating governments. The need for strong task orientations in structures for comprehensive collective management will be very great, since failures in such management would have very serious effects. To ensure that the need will be met, demanding functions for the provision of international public goods can be specified.

The main concern of the collective management structures will have to be orderly growth with equity. A vital function, then, will be concerting national policies to cope with potentially destabilising strains in the trading, transnational production, and monetary systems. Such strains tend to result from the competitive quests of individual firms for global market shares and the attempts of governments to provide supportive policies as well as to meet general constituency demands in political competition against opposition parties. The managements of firms learn within the limits of rationality about factors relating directly to their market interests but generally not about the overall health of the world economy. Governments do learn about that larger matter, but under the pressure of constituency demands tend to respond with little concern for the developmental problems of the international economy. The responses, motivated by perceived national needs, can aggravate the destabilising effects of large trade imbalances, market disruptions, and volatility in financial markets. The adaptive capacity of the global economy can thus be weakened, and, over time, there can be a continuing decline in that capacity.

The stabilising and growth promoting functions of the collective management structures will have to be substantial, and accordingly some significant transfers of power to those structures will be necessary, after they have become established through successful performance on a virtually confederal basis. This can be concluded in view of the European Community's experience of modest confederal cooperation, at an elementary stage of economic integration, which opened the way for policy learning on the need for advancement to a higher stage. The European experience moreover can be viewed as confirmation of the need for a *unified* process of collective management, rather than one in which trade and monetary issues are kept entirely separate. In the present relatively liberal world economy the weak surveillance function and the Third World debt lending of the International Monetary Fund are not linked in any way with the interactions of the major industrialised democracies on trade issues in GATT. The US administration's preferences, moreover, are opposed to any attempts at linkage, especially because of an interest in preserving autonomy in the management of monetary policy, and a reluctance to allow monetary issues to become negotiable in the context of bargaining over trade issues.[17]

Affirmation of the need for unified collective management can raise questions about the desirability of checks and balances for the operation of international economic institutions. If it is to be comprehensive, however, the process of collective management must be unified, for example by coordinating the operations of monetary and trade organisations under a global authority, perhaps a strengthened and more representative Organisation for Economic Cooperation and Development (OECD). The necessity for an effective accountability function could be met through the processes of transnational interest aggregation that have been identified as essential features of the structures needed for collective management. At another level, accountability could also develop as regional economic communities emerged to complement the structures for collective management at the global level. The activities of the regional economic communities would have to become compatible with those of the global structures, through agreed divisions of functions. The danger of conflicts between regional authorities and the global structures would have to be recognised, but the principle of dividing functions between the two levels would have to be maintained, especially in view of the achievements of the European Community. At the national level, a model to consider in dividing functions between the global and regional levels is the system of cooperative federalism in Germany. Although the main elements of the German political culture cannot be reproduced in an emerging multicultural setting at the global level, the values of that German culture can be given strong affirmation in a doctrine of collective management.

Normative Issues

The moral imperatives for comprehensive collective management become stronger as levels of interdependence continue to rise, and as the costs of failures in international economic cooperation affect larger and larger numbers of people, especially through disruptions of established industries and instability in financial markets. Recognition of these moral imperatives tends to be hindered by the influence of some strands of economic theory which assume that individuals act solely as rational utility maximisers, and which accordingly interpret government behaviour as a series of disjointed outcomes from the competition and cooperation of such maximisers, or as coherent striving after national power and wealth by coalitions of those maximisers. Questions about the legitimacy of government activity tend to be marginalised by either interpretation, but reasoning based on methodological individualism cannot escape the problem that an industrialised economy has to function in a context in which certain public goods, including regulatory activity and contract enforcement, are provided by government leaders and officials acting in the public interest, that is not as rational personal utility maximisers.

The need for public spirited government activity can be accepted in domestic settings without acknowledgement that the principle has an external application. Recognition of this application tends to be restricted because of the strength of national attachments, which remain strong despite rises in interdependence because social integration lags behind processes of economic integration. The development, in transnational elite networks, of intense awareness of responsibilities to the international community will be necessary for the building of international structures designed for collective management. This will require more than enlightened political entrepreneurship, and with respect to that need high tribute must be paid to the moral leadership of Pope John Paul II.

The moral imperatives for comprehensive collective management obligate *integrative* cooperation, based on goodwill and on recognition of the uncertain magnitude of future needs for adjustment in the global economy, as well as of the fundamental requirement to provide the public goods necessary for orderly global development with equity. Integrative cooperation has to be based on strong moral commitments, but it has to be inspired in part by experiences of its functional utility, and the commitments at its basis must be expressed in vigorous concerted efforts to make it fully productive.[18] The danger of cheating by participating governments seeking to exploit the goodwill of others has to be recognised, but it is not necessary to concede that this danger justifies pragmatic reciprocity, in the sense of extending cooperation only to the degree that favourable behaviour is received. Game theoretic reasoning can provide a rationale for emphasis on demonstrations of goodwill only in response to expressions of goodwill, and resorts to pressure in order to counter attempts at leverage, but the type of cooperation which would result would be much less productive than integrative cooperation.

Comprehensive collective management will have to be a consensual process guided by a common aggregating structure, and will not provide the intended high order international public goods if governments cooperate only on the basis of bargained understandings and in response to receiving satisfactory behaviour. Integrative cooperation can certainly be exploited, but where cheaters and free riders operate the principal international economic organisation sponsoring collective management has to become responsible for enforcement of its rules. Integrative collaboration of course will be needed for the building of strong collective management institutions – a process which should not be limited or delayed by governments seeking maximum benefits in return for given degrees of cooperation. If such institutions can be built, vital forms of reciprocal causality will operate. The socialising effects of the institutions on national elites will help to sustain governmental orientations toward integrative cooperation, while that cooperation will in turn help to sustain the international institutions.

The development of transnational elite networks dedicated to the promotion of integrative cooperation is a task for reform minded politicians, economists, and corporate leaders. Opposition is to be expected from elites intent on advancing their own and group interests in the routine competitive processes of the industrialised democracies. Political journalism related to that competition will also make the task difficult, as has become especially evident because of the effects of anti-Japanese journalism on public attitudes in the USA since the early 1980s. The endeavour to promote strong commitments to integrative cooperation will thus be arduous. When its requirements are understood, however, the need for integrative cooperation *within* industrialised democracies, between their economic groups, communities, political parties, and administrations, will also become evident. Because of vital links between political development at the national level and at the international level, integrative management of internal interdependencies will have to complement integrative management of each major nation's external interdependencies. This is a theme of developmental issue linkage which has to surface in discussions of institutionalised international economic cooperation.

4. International Organisations

The logic of international economic cooperation has been given only limited application in the global trade and monetary organisations, and these have been weakening. Their decline, however, does not reflect on that logic, but on the quality of macromanagement and policy learning in the major industrialised states. The effects of the decline, moreover, are making institutionalised economic cooperation all the more necessary, although the requirement for stronger global organisations tends to be obscured by much of the current policy literature. This literature focuses on problems in the interactions of major states outside the International Monetary Fund and GATT, the General Agreement on Tariffs and Trade. Little optimism is shown that these mechanisms can assume more effective roles through renewals of commitments to work through them for the provision of international public goods, or indeed for the exclusive club goods which were formerly sought by the larger industrialised states through those mechanisms.

Policy elites are more aware of GATT's problems than of those affecting the IMF. International trade issues have greater prominence than monetary questions in the politics of each major state, because of very active constituency interests. Monetary policy, viewed as a specialist preserve because of its technicalities, tends to be considered politically less significant. Shifts by trading partners to discriminatory commercial measures are usually given considerable publicity, with commentaries in the policy literature implying that GATT can promise no remedies. In the USA's policy communities and business groups active concerns about trade deficits attributed to discriminatory foreign practices understandably reinforce negative views of GATT.

The less prominent defects of the International Monetary Fund are recognised to be serious, in the small concerned policy communities, mainly because the Fund is unable to impose significant accountability on US macroeconomic policies that have potentially very destabilising effects. Despite the magnitude of the problems that have already resulted, remedial action tends to be viewed, by European and Japanese as well as US monetary elites, as an American responsibility. The global trading system is affected by problems in the international monetary system, because of volatility in capital markets which necessitates complex forms of risk management by exporters and importers, but pressures from interest groups activated by trade issues contribute little to the dynamics of monetary policies in the USA, Japan, and the larger European Community states.

The decline of the main global economic organisations has been accompanied by a strengthening of the European Community, and its current advances toward a higher stage of integration are positive expressions of the logic of international economic cooperation. Through advances toward economic union the Community members are enhancing their capacities to attain public policy goals collectively. This process may not go far enough to enable the members to strengthen sufficiently policy instruments weakened by the expansion of their own, US, and Japanese transnational enterprises operating in the Community, but a common industrial policy and a common foreign direct investment policy may well be attainable.

The contrasts between the weakening of global economic organisations and the deepening of the European integration process, it must be stressed, have very significant theoretical and policy implications. European policy learning regarding the attainability of public goods through full market integration has led to further policy learning about monetary cooperation as a public good that facilitates market activity. In the global economic institutions however cooperation conducive to policy learning that would motivate further cooperation has not been the general trend. Policy learning associated with involvement in those institutions has led mostly to increasing emphasis on assertions of perceived national interests. Cooperation at the global level has been promoted, under US leadership, on a more hierarchical and less integrative basis than in the European Community. The benefits have been less substantial and spread more unevenly, and have not constituted strong incentives for further cooperation.

Developmental Problems

The cooperation which can develop between members of an international economic organisation, although it is likely to be in varying degrees hierarchical and conflicted, tends to facilitate the growth of structural linkages between national economies. Advances toward elementary levels of economic integration result, but with asymmetric costs and benefits, and the prospect of further asymmetric costs and benefits, because of differences in the competitiveness and bargaining leverage of states, and in the competitiveness of firms. Distributional issues, especially evident where the cooperation has dealt with trade, tend to assume much significance in the policy processes of the less competitive states. Advancement to more stable and more productive forms of international economic cooperation thus becomes necessary in the common interest. This public good however becomes difficult to attain because relations between the participating countries deteriorate. The distributional issues are difficult to resolve and indeed tend to become worse because of the cumulative effects of differences in the degrees of national and enterprise competitiveness.

Distinctions of policy and theoretical significance can be made between international economic organisations with reference to their structures, functions, elite cultural patterns, contested issues, and developmental issues. The structures may be broadly inclusive or quite selective in membership; hierarchical or egalitarian in the arrangements for participation and decision making; institutionally developed or underdeveloped; and oriented in different degrees toward functional achievements in the provision of public goods or toward political exchange processes based on bargaining leverage. In the activities of the organisations, functional and political exchange elements tend to be linked with functional and political exchange processes in the politics of member states. Principles, norms and rules, to the extent that they are internalised by elites in member countries, assume practical significance in the contexts of national political cultures, and the divisive effects are moderated only if elite networks aid the emergence of a common elite political culture. The contested issues concern the frequent mix of national and club goods with public goods, and the likely evolution of the mix. The developmental issues relate principally to national and collective choices that have to be made for the ordering of national and club goods toward public goods, and the provision of more substantial public goods.

The principal economic organisations at the global level have evolved as hierarchies, on the basis of influence relationship shaped by affinities, interests, and leverage. In the International Monetary Fund hierarchical principles have been institutionalised through weighed voting, with the USA having the largest share, and Japan and Germany underrepresented, while outside the organisation the hierarchical pattern of relations has been maintained by US separate dealings, from a position of relative economic strength, with Japan and Germany. These two states have done little to develop joint bargaining strength, despite sharing concerns about their needs for improved leverage against the USA. In the GATT system the hierarchical features of the triangular configuration formed by the three major trading states have become less pronounced, because of a weakening of US bargaining strength. In the monetary system the USA has remained a very strong power because of its importance as the top currency state, and because Germany and Japan have been reluctant to allow wide international use of their currencies in the unregulated and volatile international capital markets. In the trading system the USA has leverage because of the size and relative openness of its domestic market, but the US share of world trade has been greatly reduced by the growth of the European Community and by the rapid increases in Japan's foreign commerce.[1]

The main effect of the changes in the trading system has been increased policy interdependence between the USA and the European Community in the domination of GATT processes and of trade interactions outside GATT. Reflecting Atlantic affinities and compatible perceptions of interest, this has served to keep Japan isolated, while diverting Community attention from the rational choice of strengthening economic ties with Japan. The recognised identities of Atlantic interests however have been changing, as the American corporate presence in the Community becomes more active, in effect limiting opportunities for European firms to realise the benefits anticipated from full market integration – including increased competitiveness in external markets. Lacking a common industrial policy and a common foreign direct investment policy, the Community's main option is to place greater reliance on managed trade, while introducing a discriminatory thrust into its competition policy.[2]

While the changes in the trading system have been under way, the system itself has become more closely linked with the international monetary system, with generally negative results. Yet the formal separation of functions between the IMF and GATT has continued, with the US role in the IMF in effect hindering Fund responses to the destabilising consequences of US macroeconomic policies. The increased links between the trading and monetary systems have been due to the internationalisation of financial markets, the growth of speculation in those markets, and the growing importance of financial risk management for traders, as well as to an extensive use of monetary measures for trade purposes, especially by the USA since 1985.

Issues concerning the interaction of the trading and monetary systems and indeed the overall development of the world economy have of necessity been taken up by the Organisation for Economic Cooperation and Development, as a consultative club of industrialised states. This organisation's research capabilities have a broader scope than those of the IMF, or of the small GATT Secretariat, but serve only consultative functions. These, moreover, are undertaken principally by an inner group comprising the major industrialised democracies whose hierarchical pattern of relations is prominent in the trading and monetary systems. Most of the smaller industrialised democracies in OECD are members of the European Community, and thus are basically aligned with Germany and France, its leading members. If the exclusive inner group of large states were to accept a more inclusive system of consultations the USA, and Japan also, would have to interact with informal accountability to the larger number of effective participants.

The emergence of grave problems of stability and growth in the international economy has challenged OECD as a whole to evolve an active role in the promotion of cooperation between the industrialised states. That however has been precluded by US and European Community preferences. Emphasis on independence in the shaping of policy, it must be reiterated, has become stronger in US political processes, due to Congressional assertiveness and the administration's commonly perceived need for wide ranges of options in coping with domestic-international macromanagement issues in the face of Congressional obstruction. For most European Community members the preservation of individual and organisational independence has also become more important, due especially to defensive considerations related to the dangers of competition from both the USA and Japan.[3]

The European Community's advances toward higher stages of integration while the global economic organisations have exhibited failures in collective governance suggest that it should assume an active role in strengthening and reconstructing OECD, the IMF, and GATT. The present regional focus of most Community concerns does not encourage optimism that such a global role will be undertaken, but the rationale for assuming such a responsibility is strong and will become stronger as the Community moves further toward economic union and as the potentially destabilising effects of American macroeconomic difficulties become more serious. Emphasis can be placed on the European Community's capacity for evolving a strong global role because, despite deficiencies in its confederal processes, its processes of collective governance under German-French leadership exhibit degrees of stability and rationality that contrast with the protracted macromanagement failures of the United States.[4]

Social Foundations

Institutionalised processes of international interaction can acquire broad acceptance among elites in participating countries and elicit commitments to principles, norms and rules felt to be guiding their operations in line with shared interests. Understanding, trust and goodwill can thus be fostered, and ongoing cooperation can be maintained and expanded without the strains of successive rounds of tenacious bargaining. Problems of adjustment posed by asymmetries in costs and benefits can then be manageable, and their resolution can aid the formation of an international community by each group of participating states. Community formation of this kind has begun in the European Community, and is helping to strengthen the legitimacy of its structures while inducing national elites to recognise obligations to the welfare of the entire Community. All this has been made possible by advances in social integration within the community, and by its significant, although slow, achievements in collective management.

The main global economic organisations, however, have weak social foundations. Their ostensible purposes have not assumed much significance for macromanagement processes in the major industrialised democracies which dominate their activities, and they do not produce, and do not promise to produce, substantial benefits for the club of large industrialised states or for the international community. OECD's consultative functions have not been sufficiently oriented toward the promotion of economic cooperation to foster broad support in transnational elite networks. Those consultative activities have long been routine middle level affairs, and have been marginalised by the degrees to which most of the major industrialised democracies, especially the USA, have emphasised bilateral and multilateral exchanges outside the OECD context, and with little regard for the interests of other OECD members or for analytical contributions to policy debates which might be made by OECD staffs. Support for GATT principles within elite networks in the large industrialised democracies is low, it must be stressed, because the interactions on commercial issues within the GATT framework have relativised those principles and are not regarded as processes of collective management but as interplays of expedient bargaining that have only contractual significance.[5] Support for the IMF, in the same elite networks, relates mainly to its convenience as a mechanism for aiding the resolution of Third World debt problems. Its incapacity to engage with problems of international monetary and financial disorder is recognised, and for the present there is no question of concerted action by any group of members to force the adoption of a meaningful role in global monetary management.[6]

Major participating governments have not sought to build up the status of OECD, GATT, and the IMF as structures deserving broad elite commitments to their nominal functions. Attitudes to these organisations have been manifestly instrumental, and there have been common tendencies to show that no elements of policy independence have been sacrificed by involvement in their activities. Interest groups in the member countries, moreover, have been remote from those activities, in part because of the preferences of their national administrations. In elite and public perspectives, then, the global economic organisations have been seen mainly as arenas for interactions in which interests can be asserted only in modest degrees, and at the risk of involvement in potentially counterproductive multilateral processes.

Commitments made by a government to an agreement under the auspices of a global economic organisation may to a degree be made acceptable to domestic groups because of their understanding of international obligations, but that will depend on the status of the global organisation and the perspectives of the domestic groups. In the USA congressional assertiveness on foreign trade issues has severely limited the executive's capacity to secure legislative and business group acceptance of agreements on trade matters that might be reached under the GATT system, and this has virtually obligated administrative acceptance of the need to have Congressional members in direct contact with trade negotiating processes. Questions about the domestic acceptability of commitments to the IMF do not arise for the major industrialised democracies, because of the virtual ending of the organisation's exchange rate surveillance functions. If those functions were revived and made stronger however commitments that might be entered into with the IMF by the US administration could lead to difficulties within the small US monetary policy community, especially because of the low status accorded to the IMF and the domestic orientation of the Federal Reserve's operating principles.

Institutional Development

The main global economic organisations have lacked the social foundations necessary for institutional development, and that deficiency has impeded their functions. Needs for institutional development are not being met principally because of general emphasis on managing foreign economic relations independently, in order to cope with the stresses of asymmetric interdependencies and with uncertainties about the goodwill of trading partners. Leadership for the strengthening of the global economic institutions is not being provided, as the weakening of the dominant American role has not led to collective acceptance, by the major industrialised democracies, of responsibilities for structuring trade and monetary cooperation.

The most vital dimension of institutional development in an organisation for collective management is the establishment of principles, norms, and procedures for collaborative decision making in the area of organisational responsibility. If the principles bind the participating states to collective decisions requiring coordinated national measures on a continuing basis, with collective surveillance, and with guidance from a common secretariat for policy analysis and planning, a relatively high level of institutional development will be attainable. The quality of that development will have a normative aspect in so far as the decision processes and the common secretariat's guidance are oriented toward sound collective management with equity, rather than toward the interests of a dominant coalition. Institutional development can thus be seen to depend on appropriate patterns of elite political psychology. Initially, the distinctly national processes shaping the political psychology of elites for engagement in the tasks of international economic cooperation have to overcome parochial and nationalist restraints in order to be supportive of collective management ventures. If this becomes possible, however, the institutions given support will develop capacities to mould the psychology of elites involved in their activities.

The common service functions of a secretariat can develop without institutional development at the decision making level. This has happened at the International Monetary Fund, with respect to the now purely nominal tasks of reviewing exchange rate policies. Balance of payments lending to Third World countries is facilitated by institutional development at the decision making level as well as the common service level. At both levels however there is bias affecting the welfare of Third World states and a tendency to demand their acceptance of demographic advice. Conditions for lending to Third World governments struggling with the consequences of usurous interest rates and dollar appreciation during the 1980s are burdensome, and include demands for trade liberalisation despite the Fund's incapacity to promise reciprocation by the industrialised countries.[7] In GATT at the common service level institutional development has been quite modest, as the contracting parties have not wished to cope with a secretariat capable of expressing forcefully its independent assessments of trade issues. The bargaining on such issues at what was originally intended to be the decision level benefits from little institutional development, and for the most part results in expedient exchanges of trade concessions between the USA and the European Community.

Levels of institutional development in member states affect prospects for institutional development in the global economic organisations. A neo-mercantilist ethos can pervade highly advanced national political institutions, but if an orientation toward integrative cooperation is to aid the building of effective global economic organisations it will have to be activated through appropriately developed national political institutions. This will be necessary for stable, coherent, and functional affirmations of the values to be endorsed by governments as a basis for institutionalised cooperation. The provision of high order international public goods through collective management, it must be reiterated, will have to be institutionalised, and the degree of institutional development in the necessary global structures will have to be quite advanced, especially at the decision making level.

Problems of advanced political development in the major industrialised democracies can thus be seen to have adverse implications for the structuring of international economic cooperation. Difficulties of institutional development in the USA are especially serious. The shifting dispersals of responsibilities in executives subject to frequent restructuring contributes to administrative pluralism, hinders consensus, and typically overloads the president with information processing and directive tasks. Decision making thus tends to be cybernetic rather than rational, and this would tend to persist even without the complications resulting from legislative assertiveness. The more integrated, more functional, and more stable executive structures in Japan and Germany present different problems because they operate in the service of neomercantilist policies and constitute major potentials for the manipulation of international economic relations.

The planning of ventures in economic cooperation, within a strategy for building collective management structures, can promise solutions to the difficulties caused by institutional factors at the national level. Of course the ventures could fail because of disruptions attributable to pluralistic governance in the USA and neomercantilist manipulations by Japan and Germany. Reforming entrepreneurship for cooperation, however, could help to make the cooperative ventures productive, so that the building of collective management structures would indeed make progress. This theme often reappears in policy literature on international economic cooperation, and it can be stressed because problems of advanced political development can generate vicious circles of decline, while gains from trade can reinforce neomercantilist orientations in states with institutionally advanced administrations.

Interactions

The large advanced market economy states interact bilaterally and as a group, outside and within the global trading and monetary organisations. A relatively stable pattern of influence relationships, perceived interests, and policy orientations continues to limit the significance of GATT and the IMF, as well as the consultative functions of OECD. Strains in the international political economy, interacting with strains in the national political economies, are tending to cause more active assertions of economic nationalism in external relations, while inequalities in the spread of bargaining power are providing incentives for the formation of coalitions. Some impetus is also given to the development of regional economic groups, while the basic logic of establishing these reflects awareness that engagement with many problems of collective management can be more feasible regionally than at the global level.

The interactions have to be considered in the totality of each state's international economic involvement, with its direct and indirect effects on trade and investment processes shaping national economic structures and their external linkages. Differing policy mixes implemented in the course of the interactions have effects on several levels, influencing the coherence and utility of the resulting processes of conflict and cooperation. The liberal expansionary policy mix of the USA allows wide scope for independent trading and transnational production activity by firms, while contributing to adjustment problems on that account and because of the investment and growth effects of deficit financing. West German and Japanese interventionist, contractionary, neomercantilist policies produce trade surpluses, enlist much cooperation from national firms, and cause adjustment problems for the USA as well as other industrialised democracies.

The USA, as the principal initiator of interactions, outside and within the global economic organisations, shows a preference for bilateral dealings. This, it must be stressed, is understandable in view of the losses of economic power that have been experienced and the opportunities to take advantage of the social distances that tend to preclude collaboration between Germany and Japan, thus enabling the USA to deal separately with both of them. The bilateral interactions do not exclude consideration of concerns about the operations of global institutions, but these tend to be peripheral, because of practical concerns with exploiting the advantages of superior bargaining power and focussing US negotiating strategy on the extraction of benefits from German or Japanese dependence on the US market. US interest in the utility of bilateral dealings tends to increase because of the growing costs of fiscal and trade deficits and awareness of the weaknesses of the IMF and GATT.[8]

States effectively excluded from the USA's bilateral dealings with its two main trading partners lack opportunities for intervention. Such involvement by other parties is not sought by Japan, since West European attitudes are not encouraging and could be expected to favour the USA over Japan on many issues. Germany, meanwhile, does not seek third party involvement, since the principal candidate would have to be France, and the main effect would be to allow France to align with US demands for more expansionary German policies. For Germany, the relationship with France continues to be managed best within the European Community context, while French opportunities for global involvement remain restricted outside the US–German and US–Japan interactions.

The high level pattern of *interactive* policy interdependencies thus retains an exclusive character, within a larger pattern of mainly *noninteractive* policy interdependencies. Germany and the USA and Japan and the USA significantly influence each other's policies through their interactions, while the policies of each of these states influence those of France, Britain, and the smaller industrialised democracies, mostly in the absence of significant interactions. Germany's role in the two patterns is being substantially strengthened by domination of the increasingly integrated European Community, and a large expansion of its functions as the principal supplier of technology to the USSR and the East European states. Japan's role, while restricted because of European discrimination, is being strengthened more than Germany's at the transnational level, on a global scale, through continuing commercial expansion and international production, and through US dependence on Japanese financing of fiscal deficits.

Within GATT, in the context of trade liberalisation discussions that exclude monetary issues, the USA's drive for the reduction of mostly nontariff barriers encounters a somewhat passive Japanese response and a reactive German response that is a large factor in European Community negotiating strategy. The principal European interest, it must be stressed, is protection against American and Japanese exploitation of the integrated European market. An important feature of the US drive is a demand for the liberalisation of trade in services, and from the European point of view this threatens the interests of Community firms within their own market and portends unfavourable shifts in the terms of competition against US enterprises in other markets.[9] US competitive advantages in services are at the basis of European concerns, and also present problems for Japan. For Japanese business groups the personalised bonds between their firms, based on relational contracting, assume special significance as informal protections against the intrusion of foreign firms into the national market for services, and also into the markets for services in other countries.

In the GATT setting Japan appears to benefit indirectly from the European Community's moderate if not low level of interest in the US drive for trade liberalisation. The European Community, meanwhile, appears to benefit indirectly from Japan's degree of passive resistance to the trade liberalisation campaign, which tends to increase the US need for European cooperation. US negotiating strategy has to take into account the political and economic costs of alienating the twelve members of the Community through aggressive trade bargaining. Those likely costs have considerable prominence in the calculations of US decision makers and their policy communities, because of the size of the US corporate presence in Western Europe and the growth potential of the Community market, as well as because of the domestic situations of friendly governments in the Community.[10] Negotiating strategy toward Japan however is affected by weaker political constraints, because of Japan's degree of isolation in the international political economy and intense resentments over the USA's trade deficits, and also because the US dependence on Japanese purchases of American debt, although heavy, is not given prominence in the more public US policy processes.[11]

In the IMF context US policy is mainly resistant to change. This contrast with the activist role assumed in GATT evidences the importance given to preserving autonomy in the management of US monetary policy while urging Germany and Japan, outside the IMF setting, to adopt expansionary policies. While the adoption of a strong IMF supervisory role on exchange rate matters is thus prevented, however, the IMF's balance of payments lending to Third World states continues, with the use of influence to protect the interests of US banks heavily exposed in Latin America, and to assist recoveries by major debt burdened Latin American trading partners. Interactions on the question of exchange rate supervision do not occur because of the US reluctance to accept an IMF role in that area, and because German and most European Community attention focuses on the development of the European Monetary System, especially as a defence against US policies with monetary consequences that are not accountable within the IMF and are not open to negotiation.[12]

Outcomes

The policies of the industrialised states and trends in the global economy are reviewed by OECD in highly professional studies designed mainly for forecasting. Policy prescriptions have to be left implicit in the forecasting, because the common secretariat is not given an advocacy role. Any recommendations for action by member governments have to be made in negotiated documents, and the leading industrialised states are reluctant to commit themselves to interactions that would produce more than generalised statements about shared concerns and objectives. Failures to resolve major trade and monetary issues in the high level interactions outside the global economic organisations, it must be stressed, tend to sustain if not increase reservations about the desirability of attempting to reach consensus on a common policy document in a multilateral context, except at a high level of generality.

OECD professional studies provide inputs into the policy processes of member states, but in generally unequal competition against assessments by national bureaux, commissions, and institutes. These come in greater volume, are usually more timely and more attuned to domestic political concerns, and are amplified through informal channels. The processing of OECD material moreover tends to be very much a working level matter. The high level decision makers, under pressure, rely on simplified politically crafted drafts from domestic sources that can be adapted quickly in the course of external dealings and of cabinet deliberations. The development of an OECD advisory role, which would be feasible in view of the organisation's research capabilities, is thus not encouraged.

As a consultative institution, OECD has a potential to foster trade and monetary cooperation. Through independent assessments of economic trends and policy alternatives, and critical reviews of national proposals for collaboration, a very effective role could be assumed.[13] Ranking and reconciling such proposals could, so to speak, reduce the transaction costs of effective bargaining between member governments, while providing each and all with a kind of international administrative guidance, thus enhancing prospects for the harmonisation and coordination of policies implemented by the participating states. If this were to result, expectations of further successes would strengthen the transnational social foundations of the organisation and it would acquire greater international legitimacy.

OECD's potential deserves special consideration because of the weaknesses of GATT, the virtual restriction of the IMF to Third World balance of payments lending, and the manifest requirements to link these two institutions, if they are to be restructured, under a coordinating organisation with capabilities for comprehensive surveillance of the world economy. The outcomes of GATT interactions are unevenly bargained and relatively unstable forms of trade liberalisation, unsupported by arrangements for adaptation to changes in competitiveness and in the spread of benefits from freer commerce.[14] The IMF's performance, a matter of failure in collective monetary governance and of limited achievements in Third World adjustment financing, is in effect allowing dangers of monetary instability to become more serious, threatening the already strained pattern of trade relations.

GATT interactions are tending to become less productive because the principal trading states relate to each other as economic powers resorting to managed commerce and bargaining mainly over restrictions or expansions of that commerce, with little regard for GATT principles. Concessions, in the form of reductions in managed trade, are exchanged mostly between principal suppliers, and ways are found to ensure that they are not generalised, so that GATT norms are negated. The United States, as the contracting party with the most potent leverage, has been gradually losing its capacity to dominate GATT interchanges since the Tokyo Round in the 1970s, and has been losing status as an advocate of GATT principles because of its use of nontariff barriers and the unilateral thrust of legislated retaliatory measures mandated as a basis for its trade policy.[15] The European Community, favoured by the shift in bargaining power caused by its Southern enlargement and deepening integration, has been given increased incentives to protect its internal market, not only for the benefit of its firms but also for a general strengthening of its internal cohesion. Japan, coping with US and European grievances over trade deficits and the difficulties of entry into its home market, has very strong incentives to preserve the high level of integration in its political economy by resisting pressures for increased openness.

The significance of interactions within GATT is being affected by the growth of protectionist pressures in the US Congress. These pressures are tending to strengthen legislated retaliatory requirements which the administration must implement under the 1988 Omnibus Trade and Competitiveness Act against trading partners accused of 'unfair' commercial practices. The determination of fairness, under that Act, is in effect a US administrative responsibility, and Congressional as well as executive interpretations of this reflect disinterest in GATT's dispute settlement arrangements. These are weak, but the US administration, coping with legislative and business pressures over the nation's continuing trade deficits, shows little inclination to work for improvement of the GATT dispute settlement function.[16] For other GATT members the US drive within the institution to liberalise trade is an expression of strong forces in the US policy process that threaten leverage against trading partners regardless of any agreements that might be reached in GATT. The unilateral US determinations of fairness in trading practices, while thus far related to trade deficits, may at some stage be directed against states with which the USA has favourable trade balances.

Non-cooperation with US trade liberalisation proposals can therefore be a pragmatic choice for other industrialised democracies in GATT negotiations. With this option, the USA is in effect challenged to concentrate its leverage against a vulnerable state that can offer large concessions, although general reactions to the use of that leverage can aid the formation of coalitions to resist any redirected US pressures. For the European Community such a coalition option could be superior to the possible alternative of cooperating moderately with the USA in Atlantic trade liberalisation and discrimination against Japan. Utilisation of the growth potential of the fully integrated Community market clearly requires considerable protection for Community firms. Denying the USA support in discrimination against Japan would oblige the United States to rely very much on its own bargaining capabilities, with indirect benefits for the Community when responding to pressures in the Atlantic relationship.

Because the USA's economic difficulties are tending to accumulate, European Community members can expect their organisation's bargaining leverage in Atlantic relations to increase, that is as their gains from fully liberalised intrazonal commerce become larger. Over time, then, the advantages of limiting cooperation with the USA's trade liberalisation drive could well become more significant, while Atlantic trade develops within its present pattern, as set by GATT Rounds and resorts by each side to managed trade. Of the large Community members, those which benefit substantially from the Common Agricultural Policy, especially France, are normally major sources of opposition to US trade liberalisation proposals, because these give priority to commerce in farm products. Virtually all Community members, meanwhile, are reluctant to endorse global service trade liberalisation proposals, which are high in the US agenda on Atlantic issues.[17]

Relative inactivity in GATT is clearly Japan's preferred choice. Since any successful trade liberalisation arrangement would have to be settled between the USA and the European Community, and European reluctance is evident, Japan remains the main target of the American drive in GATT. Like the European Community, Japan benefits over time from the accumulation of US debt and trade problems, and, more than Germany, from the USA's growing need to finance a substantial part of its fiscal deficit with the help of Japanese investors. Inactivity in GATT, meanwhile, accords with Japan's status as a trading nation that maintains large surpluses in the present system of global commerce.[18]

The USA's activist role in GATT is not significantly aided by the smaller nonEuropean industrialised democracies or by Third World states. Canadian and Australian support is of little utility in dealing with the European Community and Japan. The larger and more advanced Latin American countries have considerable significance in European Community and Japanese commerce, but are resentful of US neglect of their debt problems and discrimination against their exports of primary products and manufactured goods. The United States can exert stronger pressures than the European Community or Japan on most Third World states, but cannot expect to extract substantial support for its trade liberalisation endeavour. Their cooperation has not been sufficiently encouraged in the recent past, and they mostly see the US interest in liberalised services trade as a threat to their own weak industries.

Interactions within the IMF, focussing on Third World balance of payments lending, leave unresolved the larger problems of the international monetary system. This state of affairs entails more risks for the European Community and Japan than for the USA, as they are more seriously affected by the instability of the US dollar but remain dependent on its extensive international use. Non-cooperation between the European Community and Japan on fundamental issues of monetary reform however leaves the USA in a position to ensure the IMF's continued inaction on questions of exchange rate supervision. The potential for external pressure to overcome deficits that contribute to dollar instability is thus not utilised, despite the adverse implications for the USA's trading partners. US policy, while concerned with maintaining monetary independence, recognises needs for macroeconomic cooperation, especially by Germany and Japan, that will aid reduction of the trade deficit, but seeks this collaboration through bilateral dealings outside the IMF.[19] A basic problem, it must be stressed, is that on the US side the only credible offers of cooperation that can be made are in the monetary area, due to Congressional intransigence on the issue of fiscal restraint.

Issues

The provision of international public goods has suffered because OECD has not provided motive force for substantial cooperation between the major industrialised democracies; because GATT has been weakened by shifts to unequal and discriminatory managed trade; and because supervisory functions necessary for order in the world monetary system have not been undertaken by the IMF. Structural, policy, and systemic interdependencies have continued to grow in dimensions, complexities, and asymmetries, and firms have increased their capacities to shape national economic structures and external linkages, but the effects of policies and interactions on global economic organisations have been generally negative. Unilateral expressions of economic nationalism, modifying liberal elements in policy orientations, have shifted meaningful interactions out of the weakened international economic institutions, but without productive outcomes that might have helped to restructure those organisations or build new ones. Policy learning in line with requirements for high order public goods has not occurred. Political change in the less effectively managed states has made such learning difficult, while political continuity in the higher performing states has sustained neomercantilist orientations.

Issues concerning the evolution of international economic organisations as institutions with potentials for the provision of public goods are matters contested between states, mainly in the dominant patterns of interaction. These issues have developmental aspects, related to public goods requirements, and are contested in terms of perceived national interests, club interests, and public goods. Invocations of club interests and public goods give elements of legitimacy to different forms of advocacy in the interactions between states. Hence different balances result between uses of leverage to advance national purposes and the affirmations of club or public values that can give legitimacy to negotiated solutions and to the status asserted by participating governments. Where interactions are almost entirely struggles to assert decisive leverage the status of the organisation and its developmental prospects are negatively affected. The scope for advocacy in terms of club and even more of public goods moreover is lessened, and understanding, trust, and goodwill diminish. The developmental needs of the organisation and of the international political economy thus become larger and more urgent.

The reactions of markets may not generate pressures for the resolution of contested issues in the global trading and monetary systems, but do have effects which make the resolution of those issues more necessary in the public interest. Product markets and financial markets in the USA have been profoundly affected by the strains in the trading and monetary systems, but business demands have not been aggregated and harmonised to force comprehensive executive action, and administrative leadership for aggregating functions in the highly pluralistic US system has been lacking. The various business demands that have been asserted have caused increased protectionism, but not more constructive involvement in GATT. In Japan and Germany business demands have been incorporated more functionally into policy decisions, but these have mainly served neomercantilist purposes. Managements in most international firms, whether based in the USA, the European Community, or Japan, have been given incentives to spread their global operations widely, for risk reduction and the development of a presence in all important markets. The expansion of managed trade, as well as the volatility in financial markets, encourages the global expansion by transnational enterprises. Reductions in arm's length trade and increases in intrafirm trade then affect the commercial flows controlled through managed trade and those governed by negotiated liberalisation arrangements.

The increasing substitution of transnational production for arm's length commerce affects trade balances and payments balances, and, therefore, financial markets. What can be achieved through managed trade, then, depends on direct investment decisions by international firms which may or may not respond to administrative concerns. If they do not, a government's efforts to liberalise trade in areas where its exporting firms have advantages may not yield the anticipated export increases, since those firms and others will still have incentives to move operations abroad. Differences between the larger industrialised democracies, not only in terms of industrial competitiveness but also in terms of foreign direct investment policies and degrees of enterprise cooperation, contribute in diverse ways to the practical consequences of expansions and contractions in the areas of liberalised trade. The management of GATT interactions, then, responds to affected business interests as these are expressed in national policy processes.

Market responses to problems in GATT and the global trading system thus exhibit complexities with which the methods of a trade bargaining forum cannot adequately engage. Yet these are relatively more manageable than the problems of monetary order. The operation of financial markets, having grown enormously through speculative flows unrelated to the settlement of trade accounts, constitute very difficult problems for national monetary authorities. The speculative flows are market responses to opportunities to cause and exploit volatility, but produce a new kind of market failure which contributes to elements of failure in product markets and threatens them with very serious disruption.[20] This danger is commonly identified in the policy literature's frequent warnings about the effects of a general loss of confidence in the US dollar.

5. Trilateral Relations

The weaknesses of the major international economic organisations reflect the preferences of several of the large industrialised democracies – especially the USA – for interactions outside institutional frameworks which can be managed with maximum flexibility, in settings in which available bargaining power can be used as effectively as possible, and in which agreements to cooperate can be implemented with discretion as circumstances change. Responsiveness to shifting patterns of domestic political demands and pressures is facilitated by the informal methods of interchange in bilateral, trilateral, and multilateral contexts. These methods, moreover, tend to persist because of the effects of social distances that limit understanding, trust, and goodwill, notably between the larger West European states and Japan. Yet the persistence of such noninstitutionalised interactions also evidences limited achievements. The modest forms of cooperation that result are offset by failures to collaborate, and do not lead to steady expansion of stable and productive dealings. There are few achievements in joint or collective management that can increase in a self sustaining fashion through the effects of common benefits on mutual accountability, policy learning, and elite socialisation processes.

Within what may be called the Trilateral pattern however the European Community members constitute exceptions, because of their achivements in economic cooperation with each other, which have activated neofunctional logic in ways that are resulting in progress toward economic union. The deepening of the European integration process has great significance for the future of the Trilateral pattern, as it constitutes a model for the development of an effective system of Trilateral collective management. For the present however little is being done to promote cooperation in this larger setting. The consultations between the Five major industrialised democracies within and outside OECD result in quite limited collaboration. Outside that context the main interactions, which overshadow it, are the bilateral interchanges between the USA and Germany, and the USA and Japan. These are mostly initiated by the USA, on the basis of national concerns, and generally do not relate to Trilateral interests. The United States does not seek to bring the two interactive processes together, and this is evidently not sought by either Japan or Germany, although both could benefit from the development of triangular interactions in which they could press shared interests instead of being individually vulnerable to US pressures. France is the only member of the Group of Five closely associated with Germany, but this association is based on partnership with the Germans in leadership of the drive for deepening integration in the European Community. Britain, under its Conservative administration, is in a somewhat peripheral position, showing reluctance to support Community advances toward economic union, and endeavouring to maintain a traditionally special relationship with the USA.

For the USA, interactions with Germany have assumed greater significance since the changes in Eastern Europe in 1989 and the subsequent progress toward German reunification. Germany's dominant economic role in the European Community has been strengthened, and on this basis there is an entitlement to a stronger role in world affairs. The USA now has to accept a less unequal relationship with the Federal Republic. Japan, however, remains in an inferior bargaining position when dealing with the USA, despite substantial increases in global economic status because of the appreciation of the Yen and the retention of world market shares through increases in competitiveness which followed that appreciation. There may be a serious deterioration of the US–Japan relationship, because of negotiation failures deriving from sharp contrasts in policy styles, and because of the large vulnerabilities on each side that are associated with asymmetries in structural interdependence.

Severe economic strains between the USA and Japan would have adverse effects on the European Community, and on the entire global trading and monetary systems. The accumulated problems of macromanagement in the USA could be made very much worse if Japanese investors lost confidence in US business conditions. The danger of serious failures of joint management in the US–Japan relationship raises questions about the potential for constructive involvement by the European Community. Meanwhile, at a more fundamental level, the continuing growth of asymmetric structural and policy interdependencies in the Trilateral pattern obligates recognition of imperatives for collective management. To meet those imperatives, it is clear, the European Community will have to play a vital role.

Trilateral Affinities

Ethnic, cultural and political affinities that can facilitate the growth of understanding, trust, and cooperation, are spread unevenly in the pattern of Trilateral relations. They do not correspond with contrasts in the configuration of structural interdependencies, which has been shaped mainly by the activities of firms. They are not altogether matched, moreover, by converging policy orientations. The evolution of affinities in the Trilateral pattern has been shaped by economic and political rivalries, which have accompanied shifts in power and status, but a basic contrast has persisted between the Western and Asian segments of the pattern. Racial, cultural, and political ties have remained fundamental features of the Western segment, comprising the USA and the European Community, although the evolution of the Community has been influenced very much by the problems of managing economic rivalry with the USA from an inferior position. Japan, with an economy larger than Germany's, is the sole component of the Asian segment of the Trilateral pattern. The marked ethnic and cultural dissimilarities which limit communication potentials between Japan and the Western Trilateral states have added significance because of geographic distances, and in recent years have assumed greater importance because of conflicts over trade issues.

In the Western segment the main ethnic and cultural affinities are between the USA and Britain. These are strong, and have facilitated large scale cross investment, but their economic and political significance has been diminishing because of Britain's decline as an industrial power and failure, thus far, to assume a leadership role in the European Community's advances toward economic union. With this change in relative power and status the cultural basis for rapport has weakened, giving some prominence to cultural differences, evident in British disdain for the lack of intellectual depth in American culture, and American disdain for the deficiencies of British firms and of the British system of government. There have been degrees of policy convergence while conservative measures have been implemented over the past decade and a half in Britain and the USA, as in each case there has been emphasis on freeing market forces and limiting the economic functions of government. In Britain however the results have been much more socially polarising than in the USA, and thus have raised great uncertainties by causing shifts of electoral support to the left wing opposition Labour Party. In the USA there has been less subordination of welfare to growth, but the quality of macromanagement has been severely affected by heavy deficit financing. Neither state has been able to project itself as a model of advanced political economy development, and there has been no question of evolving a common *laissez faire* conservative doctrine for adoption by other industrialised democracies.[1]

Secondary ethnic and cultural affinities link the USA with Germany, France, and the other members of the European Community. Associated with these affinities are weaker political ties, reflecting the effects of linguistic differences and the stronger influence of ideological factors, notably in French and Italian politics, as well as the influence of nationalism, particularly in France and Germany. On the American side the organisational weaknesses of the major political parties and their lack of coherent political doctrines, as well as the localised character of most of their activities, have largely precluded the development of interest in developing ties with political forces in the major European Community members, including Britain.

The principal political parties in the Community members have had distinctly national characteristics which have also restricted interest in foreign ties. Most of the Socialist parties are linked in a loose association, but it is virtually confined to Western Europe, and its potential for supporting the development of transnational political ties in the Community is modest. The institutionally rather well developed German Social Democratic Party is further to the right than the factionalised and organisationally weaker French Socialist Party, and has a tradition of cooperation with the ruling coalition, comprising the Christian Democratic and Free Democratic Parties. The Socialist groups in the Community are associated with each other in the European Parliament, but the growth of cohesion within the party clusters of that organisation is discouraged by the unwillingness of the member governments to allow it to assume significant powers. The conservative parties in the Community members relate to each other very distantly, and the most extreme social distances affecting what could be significant potentials for transnational elite interactions are those between the British Conservative Party and the two main French conservative groups, which are very loose organisations still influenced by the Gaullist tradition.[2]

All Community political parties are being challenged to develop ties with their counterparts in other member states for effective interest representation as progress continues in the direction of economic union. Such ties are evolving slowly, however, despite impetus that is being given by the formation of regionalised interest groups seeking opportunities to influence the European Commission. Corporate networks interacting with the Commission in support of the drive for deepening integration have links with the regionalised interest groups but appear to concentrate, as do those interest groups, on dealings with national bureaucracies. These dealings can continue, on a Community wide basis, while differing political parties come into office in member states. Managements however have incentives to build strong links with affinitive parties in their home economies, not only for consideration of their interests in those economies but also for the advancement of their interests in other member states.

At governmental levels in the Community, despite differences between parties in office, political affinities are developing through productive interactions related to full market integration and advances toward monetary union. The most important of these affinities are those between the French and German administrations, and they evidence mutual awareness of complementary interests in guiding the Community's advances toward a higher level of integration. While the Franco-German ties remain active the smaller Community members are in effect encouraged to develop their links with the French and German administrations. For these smaller states there are no feasible alternatives, in view of the distribution of bargaining power in the Community. The governmental collaboration that is fostering political affinities however may be weakened if there are large disparities in gains from fully liberalised intraCommunity commerce. Enthusiasm for full market integration has been encouraging expectations that benefits will be widely spread, but it must be stressed that the Community lacks a common industrial policy. A common foreign direct investment policy is also lacking, and this, together with the absence of a common industrial policy, leaves the way open for a large expansion of the American corporate presence in Western Europe. Weaker national firms in the less advanced member states could encounter severe competition from US enterprises expanding their operations in the integrated market.[3]

Outside the complex Western segment of the Trilateral pattern Japan is in a rather isolated position and has to relate to the other members across very large social distances. Japanese remoteness from the Western configuration of affinities, moreover, is tending to become more significant because of German reunification, and because East European states are drawn toward membership of the European Community. The Western part of the Trilateral pattern would be balanced to a degree by the evolution of a Japan centered East Asian grouping, comprising South Korea, Taiwan, and the ASEAN states, but the development of economic links which could foster political affinities in such a grouping is not yet being aided by Japanese diplomacy.

Trilateral Interdependencies

The evolution of structural interdependencies in the Atlantic pattern has evidenced the influence of cultural and political affinities: these have facilitated the growth of trade, cross investment, and financial links between the European Community and the USA. In the Pacific part of the Trilateral pattern however cultural and political contrasts have had to be overcome, mainly through Japanese entrepreneurship, for the development of structural interdependencies between Japan and the USA. These interdependencies, while large like those in the Atlantic context, have greater asymmetries, and yet are growing more rapidly. They are more difficult to manage, of course, because of cultural and political dissimilarities, as well as because of their imbalances.

In both the Atlantic and Pacific settings the evolution of Trilateral interdependencies has been shaped by the effects of more efficient macromanagement in the more integrated states, notably Japan and Germany, and of less efficient macromanagement in the less integrated states – the USA, Britain, and France. The competitiveness resulting from superior macromanagement has caused asymmetries in structural interdependence, notably between Japan and the USA, but also between Germany and the USA. Differing contextual factors have been operating, however, because of the process of regional community formation in the West European setting and the much less favourable immediate environment in which Japan has had to function. In the Japanese case the challenge to achieve international competitiveness through superior macromanagement has been much more intense than it has been for Germany. Associated with the contextual factors and also with the contrasts in levels of political integration have been the trends at the transnational level – the large scale movement of US firms into international production, the strong German reliance on exporting, and the contemporary Japanese combination of aggressive exporting and international production.

The dimensions of Trilateral policy interdependencies have been mainly the results of balances and imbalances in structural interdependencies, although differences in bargaining power related to the size of each national economy have also been important, as have contrasts in political capabilities for the management of structural interdependence. Problems of governance in the USA have tended to weaken the bargaining power derived from the size of the national market, and have hindered engagement with the issues posed by large scale outward direct investment that has substituted overseas production for US exports. In the Atlantic context structural interdependencies have less severe asymmetries than those in the US–Japan relationship, and this has also been true of the Atlantic policy interdependencies. Relative equalities in bargaining power have imposed restraint on each side in US relations with Germany and with the entire European Community, while in the relationship with Japan the USA has tended to utilise its superior capacity for leverage.[4] In that relationship however both the USA and Japan have been challenged to develop greater capacities for the management of structural interdependencies, and these challenges have been more demanding, as well as potentially more rewarding, than those in the less stressful Atlantic relationships.

Policy interdependence involves interdependent policy learning, depending on the approaches taken to management of that interdependence, and on cultural and institutional factors that may or may not be conducive to meaningful exchanges that can help to clarify identities of interest and shared obligations to provide public goods. The high levels of policy interdependence within the European Community have been managed in ways much more conducive to interdependent policy learning than the policy interactions in the Atlantic setting, and even more than those between the USA and Japan. Policy learning in the Community is beginning to engage with issues of *comprehensive* collective management that receive only limited recognition in the US–Japan relationship and Atlantic relations.[5]

Policy interdependencies, it must be stressed, have transnational dimensions, and these differ in the Trilateral setting. In addition to the interdependence which obliges governments to avoid divergence from common trends in their major trading partners, for example on monetary issues, there is interdependence with respect to mixes of policies that directly or indirectly influence the activities of national and international firms. Such mixes can affect infrastructure development, market regulation, the promotion of technological progress, and the fostering of entrepreneurship. Policy interdependence in the Atlantic context exhibits interplays between the transnational dimension and what has been called the strategic interaction between governments in which there is often little awareness of transnational processes. The Japanese policy mix engages rather comprehensively with the transnational dimension, on a unilateral basis, through the collaboration of industry groups, banks, and general trading companies with the Ministry of International Trade and Industry. Management of the external political component of that policy mix in interactions with governments is difficult, however, because of cultural differences and what is widely regarded as the neomercantilist thrust of the policy mix.[6] The US policy mix includes a more effective external political component, which is aided by the cultural affinities in the Atlantic context, but tends to be aloof from the transnational dimension, in accord with liberal commitments to allow free play for market forces.

In the European Community high levels of policy interdependence and varied efforts to engage with its transnational dimensions are evident because of the drive for deepening integration. Policy communities are being drawn into convergence by general elite consensus on the imperative to advance toward economic union, as well as by intensive intergovernmental exchanges and the advocacy role of the European Commission. At present however there is no common endeavour to extend outwards the processes of cooperation that are developing within the Community, and, if such an endeavour begins, it will probably be directed at the new democratic states in Eastern Europe. American policy communities remain quite apart from the collaborative European pattern, and, under the strong influence of domestic political exchange demands, intensified by macromanagement problems, are not generating initiatives for substantial Atlantic cooperation. Japanese policy communities operate with greater remoteness, both from the USA and the Community, but, it must be stressed, with the advantages of effective engagement at the transnational level, where structural interdependencies are shaped through trade and direct investment.

Interactions

In the Trilateral pattern the evolution of interactions has been influenced by changes in national growth rates and competitiveness, and by related increases and decreases in relative levels of structural and policy interdependence. The principal sequence has been an initial phase of American leadership for the development of an Atlantic dominated liberal international economic order, followed by the current phase of modified US commitment to such an order, in a new context in which Japan and Germany have risen to prominence. In this second phase, which began after the ending of the fixed exchange rate system early in the 1970s, there have been numerous shifts toward managed trade by the leading industrialised democracies, and trade flows have been altered also by the increasing substitution of transnational production for exports. Imperatives for collective management have become stronger and more urgent, but as leadership for such management has been lacking, because of the focus on adjustment problems in the USA's policies, and the European Community's absorption in its integration process, Trilateral interactions have been insufficiently productive. These indeed have severely limited opportunities for the activation of neofunctional logic like that which has been operating within the European Community. The spread of constructively oriented elite networks in the Trilateral setting is thin, intergovernmental exchanges are rather restricted, and there are few international business associations working for transnational interest aggregation to which Trilateral administrations could respond.

The principal changes in levels of national economic power and interdependence, together with shifts in the priorities of the USA as the main initiator of Trilateral interactions, have led to the emergence of the US–German and US–Japanese interactions as the central interchanges in the Trilateral context. These interchanges result from US efforts to develop forms of bilateral cooperation that will aid American macromanagement, especially by increasing German and Japanese domestic demand for imports and by keeping the dollar's role in international money markets at levels preferred by the United States. For effective use of US bargaining power separate rather than combined dealings with these two states have been desirable. The long social distances between Germany and Japan it must be repeated, have thus far precluded coalition behaviour that could challenge the USA. Of the European Community members with interests in the US–German interactions France has remained apart from those dealings not only because of the US preference for bilateralism, and because of inferior economic status, but also because the scope for American rapport with the French Socialist administration has been quite limited, and because the German negotiating position has not been in need of French support. This has become more evident as German reunification has continued. On the Pacific side the US–Japan interchanges remain bilateral because of Japan's lack of regional coalition partners that might help to develop a more balanced bargaining relationship.

The USA's bargaining strength, based on the size of its internal market, adds credibility to threats of trade discrimination, but more against Japan than

Germany, and subject to important constraints in each case. Dependence on Japanese private financing of US government debt is quite heavy, and Japanese as well as German cooperation is needed to restrain fluctuations of the US dollar in world currency markets. These fluctuations, is must be stressed, are related in complex ways to trends in US stock and bond markets, and to the effects of the domestic as well as external management of US monetary policy. The use or threat of trade restrictions by the US administration, moreover, to the extent that is feasible because of the major financial and monetary interdependencies, can be less effective than expected because of the ranges of options for national and foreign firms involved in the rather open US economy.[7] Where there are shifts to managed trade there can be domestic political benefits for the US administration, but there can also be politically encumbering effects because of the encouragement given to protectionist lobbies.

Japan implements a strategy of incremental accommodation with US demands, and this evidences the slow pace of consensual decision making in the very large Japanese policy communities, as well as perceptions that the complex business and administrative networks in the highly integrated domestic economy are threatened by foreign economic penetration. There is also awareness that long standing US requests for fiscal expansion by Japan would increase government debt and have inflationary effects. Germany is more assertive than Japan, because of the strength of the leadership position gained in the European Community, a lower degree of dependence on the US market, and a political culture that generates expectations of decisive responses to external challenges by the Chancellor. Germany, moreover, can become more actively associated with European Community efforts to enhance opportunities for Community firms in their integrating market through commercial and foreign direct investment measures aimed against US and other outside enterprises.

Political and security cooperation has aided US Atlantic and Pacific diplomacy for several decades, until recently, and has in some respects motivated US acceptance of trade deficits, especially in the relationship with Japan. The decreasing prominence of security issues since 1989 however has contributed to the development of a more forceful US trade diplomacy, while reducing German and Japanese concerns about the possible security implications of weaker US roles in the global and regional strategic balances. US attempts to use leverage based on European needs for defence support now have little significance in dealings with Germany on trade issues, and any attempts to pressure Germany for greater economic cooperation risk provoking indirect retaliation in the form of support for Community trade and industrial measures directed against US firms penetrating the Community market.

The US interactions with Germany are of course in some degrees merged with US–European Community relations. These have restricted scope because the Community's external competence is limited to the management of a Common External Tariff and the protectionist aspects of its Common Agricultural Policy. The member states, while endeavouring to concert their foreign policies through the informal system of Political Cooperation, remain independent in the implementation of those policies.[8] Cohesion in the grouping however has been sufficient to resist US demands for reduced agricultural protectionism, and Community assertiveness on trade and trade related issues has been a potent challenge for the USA's efforts to promote general liberalisation in the current GATT round on terms in line with its own special interests, notably regarding trade in services. The US bargaining position is indirectly aided by the degrees to which British policy under the Thatcher administration has hindered the development of unity within the Community, but as consensus for deepening integration has continued to grow in the organisation the USA has been obliged to show increased consideration for Community interests. The reunification of Germany, moreover, and the prospect of Eastern enlargements of the Community, have made it all the more important for the United States to base its policy on identities and complementarities of interest with the Community. In this regard the US administration can act with greater freedom than is possible in the relationship with Japan, as there is less parochial Congressional assertiveness on Atlantic economic issues.

The elementary logic of working for broader cooperation with the European Community as it advances toward economic union is recognised in current American policy literature, but US management of the relationship tends to focus on immediate trade and investment issues of concern to domestic business groups. On the Community side the complex tasks of full market integration are very absorbing, as are the further tasks of achieving monetary union and building a system of fiscal coordination. Capacities for political entrepreneurship related to larger external issues are lacking. A new phase of policy learning, more ambitious than the one which launched the current drive for complete market integration, is clearly needed, but this will undoubtedly require initiatives from within the complex internal structure of the European Commission.

Japan's interests are involved in the Atlantic interactions, but there is little scope for Japanese diplomacy to seek the development of Trilateral interchanges. Japan has to reckon with the prospect of pressures over trade issues from both the European Community and the USA. A more cooperative US–Community relationship could well be based in part on tacit discrimination against Japan. Alternatively, if there were a more conflicted US–Community relationship both sides could seek advantages at Japan's expense. Either or both could also seek Japanese cooperation, while managing their conflicted interactions, but on present indications it would be difficult for Japan to influence their choices. The recent history of these relationships suggests that European and US inclinations would be to discriminate against Japan, but if a new phase of policy learning begins in the European Community the potential advantages of wide ranging cooperation with Japan could become more evident.[9] European utilisation of these opportunities, which could help raise technological levels and general efficiency in Community firms, could have beneficial effects on the strained US–Japan relationship.

Issues

Questions of combining the main Atlantic and Pacific interactions for Trilateral collective management can be raised because the pattern of structural inter-dependencies underlying those interactions is not sharply divided into two regional segments. The pattern is continuous, even though the most dynamic political economy – Japan – stands apart from the system of Atlantic relations in which most of the less effectively managed Trilateral states are active. Japanese economic vigor can be seen as a threat to the less competitive European Community members, but it can also be viewed as a potential source of managerial, technological and financial support for European firms in unequal competition against the numerous American enterprises operating in the Community. Expanding Japanese business involvement in the Community is possible without substantially increased interchanges at the governmental level, but would certainly be aided by such interchanges. For the Community an incidental benefit would be the challenge presented by the degree of integration to be expected in the Japanese corporate presence. Recognition of this challenge could give impetus to efforts to evolve a common industrial policy.

While Trilateral policy interdependencies constitute a system impaired by a serious participation problem, to Japan's disadvantage, but also to the European Community's disadvantage, the US–German relationship is evolving with only limited cooperation because of the difficult issues posed by US fiscal and monetary requests. There is strong German elite opposition to fiscal expansion that would reverse the current decline in government debt.[10] Linked with this attitude are beliefs that fiscal restraint is necessary for growth, that is to reduce costs of government and diversions of resources from productive use. There is also recognition that the burdens of aiding the reconstruction of the East German economy may be heavy. On the question of monetary cooperation to keep the exchange value of the dollar in line with US preferences the main perspective influencing German policy is based on concepts of fiscal responsibility that are seen to have been neglected by US decision makers. Fundamental US measures are felt to be necessary to remedy this neglect and to eliminate the need for monetary interventions in the service of US trade policy. Conditional and graduated monetary cooperation with the USA however is maintained, and this accords with German interests in access to the American market. On the US side appreciation of the Mark somewhat above German preferences is desired, so that US exports will be more competitive, but there is some ambivalence because the German fiscal and monetary expansion which is also desired, to increase consumer demand, would tend to cause depreciation of the Mark.

Over time, German bargaining strength is tending to increase. While Germany benefits from national unification and from deepening integration in the European Community, as well as from continuing export successes, the United States has to cope with the accumulating effects of heavy deficit financing, and with the domestic consequences of vast disparities between overseas production by its international firms and the exports of those and other firms from the home economy. These disparities affect the entire US involvement in the global trading system, and in the relationship with

Germany they are especially significant, as German firms serve Community and foreign markets much more through exporting than through transnational production.[11]

In the US–Japan relationship the main contested issues are designated and managed more assertively by the USA than those in its somewhat restrained dealings with Germany. Representations to Japan by the US administration have to respond to pressures from the well entrenched Democratic Party members whose numbers dominate Congressional proceedings. These pressures, related to the Democratic Party's role as a large distributional coalition, are influenced by political journalism which mostly ignores the extent to which American firms are serving foreign markets through overseas production that substitutes for exports. This journalism, moreover, reflects naive assumptions about the importance of bilateral rather than overall trade balances. Antipathies on each side have been roused by this journalism, as well as by abrasive public US attempts at leverage that have had provocative effects in Japan. These antipathies tend to hinder perceptions of complementary interests and cause each side to focus on ways of gaining added leverage. Over time, however, as in the relationship with Germany, the USA's bargaining position is tending to weaken, because of the multiple effects of its large fiscal deficits and the virtual detachment of its large corporations from their home economy.

US demands for greater market access are intended to achieve more balanced bilateral trade. This objective has assumed urgency because deficits in commerce with Japan are the largest single items in the USA's overall trade deficits and the leverage available to press trade demands against the European Community is weaker and is declining more than that which can be utilised against Japan. Surpluses in trade with Europe which offset deficits with Japan before the appreciation of the US dollar in the late 1970s are no longer being generated. That state of affairs however is largely a consequence of the vast extent to which US firms are serving the European Community market through overseas production rather than through exports from the United States. If Japan becomes more open to US direct investment a similar trend will have to be expected, on a scale which could balance and then become greater than the volume of Japanese production in the USA for the American market.

For Japan, US pressures for market access and related demands for wider direct investment opportunities represent threats to the pervasive social bonds within the national business community and between it and the national administration. These bonds facilitate high levels of entrepreneurial and technological achievement, while providing a very supportive environment for risk taking. The level of political economy integration, moreover, has begun to assume greater significance for the achievement of increased competitiveness in trade rivalry with richly endowed states, and for coping with stresses in the global economy. Concessions to the USA on trade and direct investment issues are necessary to retain substantial access to the US market, but indirect advantages are derived from the US administration's dependence on Japanese private investors to finance roughly 30 per cent of the Federal deficit. Increases and decreases in the purchases of US debt tend to heighten the sensitivities of American decision makers to this financial dependence, as it increases over time. Reduced Japanese lending, it must be stressed, would obligate higher

US interest rates, causing upward pressure on the dollar. This would make US exports less competitive, while increasing the incentives for US firms to produce abroad for foreign markets, including the Japanese market, and straining the capacity of the United States to influence financial markets through monetary interventions. A further effect would be to slow growth in the USA because of the higher cost of credit.[12]

The utility of interactions in the US–Japan relationship is affected not only by cultural contrasts and differences in policy styles, and by the asymmetries of structural interdependence, but also by the absence of third party accountability. This is a consequence of the inadequate development of the Trilateral pattern of relations. The US–German interactions have to be managed by each side with informal accountability to France and to other members of the European Community, but the US–Japan relationship, despite its higher levels of strain, is managed in relative isolation. This, it must be reiterated, could be changed by the development of a fully Trilateral pattern of interactions, or by the evolution of a regional economic community in the Pacific. For the present, however, frictions in the relationship are serious hindrances to Pacific regional collaboration.

Japanese monetary cooperation is sought by the USA to keep the Yen–dollar exchange rate within limits appropriate for US trade purposes, and in this respect the interactions are similar to those in the US–German relationship. On the Japanese side there is appreciation that the USA has to devise its own methods of coping with the fiscal deficits that require substantial foreign borrowing at interest rates that contribute to dollar appreciation and that have to rise if business confidence in the US economy falters. There is also appreciation that expansionary fiscal measures requested by the USA, to increase Japanese consumer demand, will tend to cause Yen depreciation. Japanese willingness to intervene in currency markets in order to lower the value of the US dollar can thus be affected, especially because of judgements about the feasibility of going against market trends. On the US side a looser monetary policy could produce further dollar depreciation without Japanese cooperation, but at the risks of inflation, increased imports due to stronger consumer demand, and serious difficulties in meeting government borrowing requirements. The domestic monetary concerns of the Federal Reserve, it must be stressed, tend to preclude adoption of a looser monetary policy because of imperatives to counter the inflationary effects of heavy deficit spending.[13]

Transnational Problems

The issues of structural interdependence which occasion interactions in the Trilateral system involve activities by firms that affect the growth and employment objectives of governments. The configuration of these activities by enterprises is dominated by the large scale operations of US international firms that supply world markets and the home economy from numerous overseas production bases. This is done with high levels of efficiency, because of managerial, technological, and financial resources, and capacities to initiate linkages with other transnational enterprises. National administrations seek to influence the production and marketing activities of these and other firms by enhancing location advantages and adopting industrial measures, but firms increase their bargaining power by expanding in line with global strategies, thus gaining advantages, especially in dealings with the more pluralistic states.

The most extensive effects on the evolution of structural interdependencies are caused by the operation of US international firms that become footloose multinationals. The operations of these firms are sources of problems for the US economy and for its involvement in the global economy. International operations by Japanese international firms are on a much smaller scale, and those by West German enterprises are of modest significance. The overall contrasts are quite marked, and are becoming more severe because of the large scale expansion of transnational production by US enterprises, especially in response to the opportunities of the European Community's integrating market.

The substitution of overseas production for exporting by US firms, which became quite extensive in the 1950s, with a concentration on Western Europe, has been based mainly on market power gained in the large home economy, and has been responding to strong incentives. These include overseas location advantages such as lower production costs, closer access to markets, and concessions from host governments, but there are also tax benefits provided by the US government. Profits are not taxed by the US administration unless they are repatriated, and if they are reinvested abroad they are virtually free of US tax. Tax liabilities with respect to repatriated profits moreover can be reduced by complex intrafirm transactions, involving the use of transfer pricing. A somewhat obscured issue, then, is the volume of lost US tax revenue. This might be computed in various ways, but it is clear that large reductions of the US fiscal deficit would be possible if there were more effective taxation of these firms.[14] It is also clear that there are additional tax losses to be considered, as national firms, confined to the home economy because of modest size, are adversely affected by the reductions of growth and employment resulting from the movement of production processes to foreign locations. These are firms that bear relatively higher tax burdens, and are more affected by the monetary restraint necessary for inflation control in the USA. Operations in the USA by foreign firms also occasion substantial losses of tax revenues, mainly through the use of transfer pricing, and are not sufficiently extensive to offset the negative growth effects of outward US investment.

For the present the issue of tax losses through export substitution is politically inactive, and it could become intractable because of lobbying activity if it were taken up. Large questions of equity regarding tax burdens are posed, however, and meanwhile the continuation of large fiscal deficits affects growth, employment, and inflation in the home economy, and its external trade. At the same time disparities between the large US firms prospering through overseas operations and the smaller firms in effect confined to the home economy and bearing higher tax burdens tend to increase.

Linked with the tax problem are the effects of export substitution through overseas production on the trade balance. The volume of export substitution, together with imports into the USA from overseas production bases, increases the US trade deficit, and this is also affected by the administrative pricing of intrafirm exports from the USA that are related to overseas production. The current effects on the trade deficit are offset to a degree by increases in exports made possible by dollar depreciation since 1985, but the export capabilities of many US firms are still recovering from the consequences of losses in foreign markets caused by dollar appreciation during the first Reagan administration. The trade deficit is a very large factor in the US balance of payments, as there is only modest repatriation of profits from the overseas operations of US firms. The general effect is downward pressure on the dollar, but often not sufficient to counter the upward pressure resulting from the high interest rates associated with the fiscal deficits. This upward pressure however could decline if a looser monetary policy were adopted to cope with the beginnings of a recession. The trade deficit of course can be reduced by protectionist measures, to the extent that these do not trigger matching retaliation. Such measures could increase foreign production in the USA for the US market, causing further declines in imports, and could reduce dependence on monetary interventions to serve trade policy objectives. The retaliation that could be provoked, however, could seriously reduce US exports, and could restrict opportunities for US international firms producing in foreign markets.[15]

The trade and transnational production issues, while related to the USA's twin deficits, have longer term significance regarding the efficiency of internationalised markets. US international firms, gaining strength in world markets, can strengthen their positions in their home market. Their global operations tend to be aided by linkages with other transnational enterprises which can be managed more freely and with larger rewards than forms of business cooperation in the home economy. Increasing oligopoly power in that economy and in other markets can result. This form of market failure, it must be reiterated, has adverse implications for small and medium sized firms in the USA. The interests of these firms are much less secure than those of their counterparts in Japan, which are respected by the larger Japanese industry groups and general trading companies.

Japanese enterprises are sources of transnational issues ranking next in importance after those attributable to US firms. Japanese overseas production substitutes for exports on a much smaller scale, and for the present causes only modest reductions of the nation's trade surpluses. Tax losses associated with the operations of these firms, it is clear, are much smaller, although possibly rising, and reductions of growth and employment in the home economy do not appear to be significant. National firms that have moved into overseas operations retain strong home country ties, and with administrative encouragement seek to maintain their technologically most advanced activities at their main domestic plants. Enterprises still engaged primarily in exporting operate with high levels of efficiency, because of restructuring that has to a considerable extent overcome the disadvantages of Yen appreciation.

For the present, then, a functional balance between overseas production and exporting is being maintained. Japan's unique general trading companies are helping to preserve this balance by continuing to market internationally products from the nation's small and medium sized firms while also assisting outward direct investment by such firms.[16] The balance however may well be changed by large shifts to transnational production over the next decade, and with those shifts the managements of firms engaged in large scale overseas activities may become less responsive to their home government's administrative guidance. Trade deficits and major losses of tax revenues could follow, with a slowing of growth in the national economy.[17] Yen appreciation and foreign protectionism are the major factors inducing export substitution, and they are not likely to change, but the high level of cohesion in the Japanese business community and the degree to which its interests are aggregated by its peak association, Keidanren, will tend to prevent strains in the relationship between transnational production and export oriented domestic activity.

For other states and firms, Japanese enterprises are potent challenges, threatening relentless market penetration. Because of their collectively enhanced firm specific advantages these enterprises have superior competitiveness. Indications that they are collaborating with their government to implement a macro oligopoly strategy can be considered justifications for protective reactions. The enlightened responses that can be advocated however include the utilisation of opportunities for joint ventures with Japanese companies and the development of national industry groups that can work together cooperatively, generating superior organisational efficiencies. In the Trilateral setting German firms are especially well qualified to collaborate with Japanese enterprises, because of levels of managerial and technological capabilities already attained.

For Germany, issues at the transnational level are of relatively smaller dimensions and are more manageable. The main reason for this is that German firms are moving much more slowly into international production. Operating in a political economy that approaches Japan's level of integration, but with access to the vast market of the European Community, German firms retain strong domestic ties and rely very much on exporting for the service of Community and foreign markets. There are no major losses of tax revenues and there is only modest export substitution to reduce trade surpluses. Industrial restructuring, aided by the supportive functions of the banking system, ensures continued competitiveness in external markets. The large concentrations of industrial power which are principally responsible for the nation's export successes however do benefit from oligopolistic domination of the internal market. Small and medium sized firms do not enjoy the consideration and support that is customary for their counterparts in Japan, and lack comparable opportunities for involvement in foreign trade.

For effective involvement in world markets, in rivalry with Japanese and American firms, German enterprises have incentives to undertake transnational production on a large scale outside the European Community. The active participation of German banks in the operations of these firms, however, and the influence of their unions, continue to act as restraints on outward direct investment. To the extent that such investment is undertaken, moreover, it evidently tends to respond to opportunities in Eastern Europe rather than the USA. There is a rationale for seizing these opportunities before they can be exploited by US and Japanese firms, and for taking advantage of the larger presence which is being acquired in the area as East Germany is absorbed into the Federal Republic.

Volatility in financial markets, as a transnational issue with systemic proportions, affects the USA more seriously than the other two major industrialised democracies. The internationalisation of these markets was promoted by the

USA to increase opportunities for its financial institutions, and has assisted its large scale borrowing for deficit financing. Vast speculative activity in these markets, however, has occasioned losses of exchange rate sovereignty by limiting the effectiveness of monetry interventions, while complicating the effects of monetary expansion or contraction.[18] Economic structures in the USA meanwhile are gradually altered because US multinationals can utilise international financial markets more effectively than the small and medium sized firms virtually confined to the home economy. These firms, it must be stressed, have to accept higher tax burdens and have less scope to spread their risks, but must cope with the market power gained domestically by the enterprises that have moved into international operations.

The most serious aspect of the volatility in international financial markets is that it could lead to drastic losses of confidence in the dollar. Upheavals in these markets could push the dollar to very low levels. Adverse trends disturbing these markets could be initiated by severe stock market declines in the USA, and by a loosening of US monetary policy intended to revitalise domestic markets. The USA's continuing balance of payments problems are major sources of the uncertainties which encourage speculation in the global financial markets, but improvements in the balance of payments are difficult to achieve. The factors causing upward pressure on the dollar remain strong, and for the present tend to be augmented by speculation, while the incentives for firms to engage in overseas production remain potent, and tend to become more significant when there are indications of strain in the home economy.

Financial market volatility is a more manageable problem for Japan, but one which requires preparations to cope with uncertainties regarding the dollar. Informal as well as formal administrative discipline in the internationalised Japanese financial markets is still considerable, and is backed by large reserves. Very active links with US financial markets however are sources of vulnerability, and are not sufficiently balanced by operational bonds with West European financial centers. The vulnerability resulting from financial interdependence with the USA is increasing, because of the large flows of investment into the USA and the accumulation of dollar reserves through trade surpluses.[19] Diversification of the nation's foreign economic relations, with an emphasis on Western Europe, is thus becoming all the more desirable. At the same time reductions of informal trade barriers to facilitate increases in imports from the USA is becoming a more logical choice.

Germany is in a more secure position, because of leadership of the European Monetary System, supported by the operation of a national financial system almost as disciplined as Japan's and less dependent on links with the USA. The European Monetary System provides a zone of monetary stability for its participants, and, as it is being strengthened with the transition to a form of monetary union, Germany will be better protected against swings in the value of the dollar.[20] For increased security, Germany is being challenged to provide leadership that will ensure increasing international use of a European currency unit, after the attainment of monetary union in the European Community, because on present indications the US dollar may well become more unstable, due to fiscal inaction and continuing balance of payments problems. With the development of an international role for a European currency unit a further contribution to international monetary stability could be made by establishing a strong mechanism for monetary cooperation with Japan.

Policy Learning

The differing policy styles of the states that dominate the Trilateral pattern reflect contrasts in capacities for cooperative policy learning that could prepare the way for collective management, i.e. to realise high order international public goods. The differences in aptitudes for policy learning affect prospects for productive experiences of reciprocity, and more significantly for activating neofunctional logic of the kind that has acquired new significance in the European Community over the past half decade. Processes of political continuity and change affect these differing capacities for learning, especially because of the influence of elite preferences on policy orientations. Continuity associated with successful neomercantilism can be a source of indifference to the potential benefits of integrative cooperation. Another kind of indifference to those possible benefits can develop among elites in liberal states confronting intense domestic political competition because of macromanagement problems.

In the USA a reactive policy style, responding incrementally and disjointedly as well as experimentally to the conflicting pressures of strongly pluralistic interest representation, tends to be burdened by overload that results partly because of elite aggregating failures. Concentration on the demanding tasks of political exchange and brokerage relativises considerations about the interests of other states, especially because of the magnitude of growth, employment, and inflation issues accumulating on account of multilevel pluralism. While compatibilities of interests are obscured in foreign economic relations there are tendencies to rely on leverage in order to secure cooperation on terms that will help externalise the costs of overcoming macromanagement problems. Leadership for Trilateral policy learning becomes a more remote possibility, despite the USA's prominence in the global economy, and failures to secure sufficient levered collaboration increase strains with other major industrialised democracies. Political change, moreover, associated with shifting balances and preferences at elite levels, and with phases in the political business cycle, limits the significance of incidental advances by high level decision makers toward understandings with their foreign counterparts.[21]

The more rational and consensual Japanese and German policy styles are receptive to policy learning, but in line with their established orientations. Possibilities for realising shared benefits through cooperation are open, but with expectations of superior competitiveness in the pursuit of those benefits. Such expectations of course could be changed if appropriate interactions widened the scope for policy learning, that is of a kind less influenced by neomercantilism. For the present such interactions are not in prospect, despite the domestic problems and pressures affecting American policy, and little is being done to promote rapport and trust in the Japanese–German relationship. But in this relationship the basic similarities in policy styles could be conducive to broadly cooperative policy learning. This could develop on the basis of compatible neomercantilist interests, and shared concerns about the American role in the world economy.

The scope for policy learning with a cooperative potential is likely to remain very restricted on each side of the US–Japan relationship. The contrasts in policy styles will tend to remain severe, the social distances will remain long, and the structural interdependencies will probably become more imbalanced. Strains in the relationship, it must be reiterated, may well become more severe while stresses in Atlantic relations remain manageable, because of the influence of more asymmetrical structural interdependencies. Opportunities for policy learning that would assist increases in cooperation between the USA and Japan however could be provided if the relationship were brought into a new pattern of wide ranging institutionalised Trilateral interchanges. The new dimensions of accountability, the socialisation factors, and the enhanced awareness of potential common benefits could help to overcome barriers to collaborative policy learning. On the Japanese side the process would tend to be aided by the rather high degree of elite stability and consensus, the breadth of the established consultative activities under administrative sponsorship, and awareness of the urgency of developing a more harmonious relationship with the USA. Economic nationalism roused in the trade disputes and suspicions of European–American collusion would be the main difficulties.

On the US side, it must be stressed, there would be reluctance to lose the advantages of superior leverage in the mutual relationship, but if substantial interchanges involving the European Community developed several factors could aid collaborative Trilateral policy learning. The USA has been losing influence in European affairs because of the ways in which German unification has proceeded while the European Community has advanced toward economic union and strengthened its links with prospective members in the new East European states. German and European Community initiatives therefore demand increasing attention, especially because the main concentration of overseas activities by American firms is in the Community, and can be expected to further expand as the Community enlarges after attaining full market integration. The beginnings of an industrial policy in the Community could lead to some restraints on the expansion of the American corporate presence, to improve prospects for presently less competitive European firms. With those restraints there could be endeavours to encourage increases in US arm's length exports to rather than production in the Community, for more balanced structural interdependence. In US policy communities, meanwhile, openness to Trilateral solutions to the problems of asymmetric interdependence with Japan could develop because of appreciation that the imbalances to be expected in relations with Germany and the European Community are making a more cooperative relationship with Japan more desirable.

Political Cooperation

Strains in economic relations between the major Trilateral states can hinder but can also be moderated by their processes of political cooperation. There is a relatively long history of such cooperation, more in the Atlantic than in the Pacific dimension, and much of it has been based on shared international security concerns, with the USA as the principal initiator. The use of pressures over trade issues has been restrained by the influence of concerns about continuing political cooperation, especially in the Atlantic context. Security motivated commitments to political cooperation, however, have been weakened throughout the Trilateral pattern over the past few years because of changes in Eastern Europe and the USSR. Perceived political interests have tended to diverge, and recognition of these interests has been influenced by conflicts over trade and monetary issues. These issues, meanwhile, have assumed greater prominence because of the accumulating effects of failures in economic cooperation and the general increases in structural imbalances caused by the activities of firms and by uncoordinated and conflicting policy mixes.

The modest coordination of foreign policies by the European Community members, through consultations in their informal system of political cooperation, is at an elementary level, without commitments to integrate these external policies, but the Community's advances toward economic union entail an increasing need to evolve a common European foreign policy.[22] This will be necessary for effective representation of Community interests across a wide range of issue areas as intrazonal structural interdependencies rise to higher levels. The European Commission will have to assume large responsibilities for promoting convergence in the external relations of the member states and then providing guidance for collective management of those relations.

Questions about the Eastern enlargement of the Community, about European security, and about restructuring the global trading and monetary organisations, will have to be taken up in the European process of political cooperation, and how these will be dealt with will depend very much on the progress made toward economic union. Cooperation will have to be sought principally from the USA, and this obvious requirement raises questions about structuring the anticipated interactions as well as adapting whatever arrangements will be in place for evolving a common European foreign policy.

Atlantic political cooperation has thus far been mainly a fairly restricted informal consultative process in which Germany, France, and Britain relate individually to the USA, while communicating with each other in the European political cooperation system. There is an overlap with Atlantic security interactions in NATO, in which France is only partially involved, but as NATO's significance declines its utility as a forum for political exchanges is also tending to decrease. The USA's continuing bilateral dealings with each of the major Community members are likely to be altered not only on that account but also by the gradual development of more active informal foreign policy cooperation between the Community members, keyed to their shared interests in full market integration and advancement toward economic union. Growing efforts to concert their policies toward the USA are likely to have significant effects on the European political cooperation process. For the USA this will mean reduced scope for diplomacy that could have divisive effects in the Community, and the change in relative bargaining strengths will be a challenge to establish a firmer basis for Atlantic political cooperation. The political economy dimension of such a basis will clearly have to be very extensive.

For the present there is no endeavour to enlarge the restricted processes of Atlantic political cooperation by drawing in Japan. The USA has been urging Japan to play a larger role in world affairs, because of its prominence in the global economy, but it must be stressed that the USA has an established preference for maintaining the virtual separation between its interactions with Japan and its Atlantic relations. Losses of influence in European affairs evidently tend to reinforce this preference, and it may also be sustained by perceptions of Japanese unwillingness to be involved in what would become a large pattern of Trilateral interchanges. Perceptions of European reluctance may also be involved, especially in view of the recent history of European discrimination against Japan.

Political and economic change in the USSR, however, is opening up possibilities for substantial Japanese as well as German foreign policy initiatives, related especially to opportunities for technology exports, notably for the development of the rich resources in the Soviet Far East.[23] Soviet decision makers, moreover, may begin to see ways of taking the Japanese system of guided capitalism as a superior model for reconstruction of their economy. At the same time, European Community views of Japan as a predatory trading power may change as questions of technological upgrading for Community firms become more significant, because of losses of shares of foreign markets and increasingly evident dangers of similar losses in the Community market. Reasons for US and European initiatives to widen dialogues with Japan can thus be anticipated. Apart from the motivations derived from current and expected interests, however, there may well be increasing awareness that the tasks of extended constructive engagement with Eastern Europe and the USSR may not be adequately managed just by Atlantic cooperation.

Questions of developing an extensive pattern of Trilateral political cooperation have to be considered in conjunction with questions of moving above the level of foreign policy coordination to a level at which community formation and the building of institutions for collective management will become possible. At that level solidarity can be striven for through affirmations of shared values, principles, and norms. Common structures can be set up for collaborative endeavours to produce high order international public goods. Imperatives to realise such benefits are evident in the entire pattern of Trilateral inter-dependencies and in the present state of the international monetary and trading systems. The conditions of these systems reflect Trilateral failures, but it must be reiterated that the logic of cooperation, based on the magnitude of the major structural interdependencies, obligates careful examination of the problems of collaboration, firstly at the macroeconomic level.

6. Fiscal, Monetary and Financial Cooperation

The development of the entire international political economy, through more and more diverse forms of advanced specialisation that increase the benefits of all forms of trade, depends on national administrative functions. Economic infrastructures have to be continually built up, markets for goods and services have to be regulated, and stable currencies have to be provided. As structural interdependencies rise higher these administrative functions have to be co-ordinated, for the efficient operation of international market forces. Substantially integrative coordination would be a high international public good. For the present, however, the collaboration achieved is very limited, and results from uses of unequal leverage, with some convergence in responses to international market processes: it is uneven and episodic, and does not activate neofunctional logic that would result in improved and more extensive collaboration.

Questions of fiscal cooperation are treated in the policy literature mainly as issues of growth promotion through the expansion or contraction of government spending, but of course the productive significance of different types of spending has to be considered, and in certain cases fiscal contraction can facilitate overall growth by reducing diversions of resources from highly productive to less productive functions and lowering the costs of government. Increased Federal spending under the Reagan administrations was expansionary in the accepted sense, but a substantial part of the resulting growth was accounted for by military production, while the costs of government were greatly increased. The extraordinary effects on the global economy indicated acute needs for fiscal cooperation between the major industrialised democracies.

Fiscal policies, because of their overall effects on growth and trade, affect and are affected by the practical consequences of monetary policies. Increases in government spending may have inflationary effects which restrictive monetary measures do not overcome. Alternatively the growth intended to result from fiscal expansion may be greatly limited by drastic monetary restraints that increase the cost of productive investment and exert upward pressure on the exchange rate, thus increasing imports while making exports less competitive, and adding to the incentives for firms to move operations to overseas locations. Restraint on inflation is often a high priority objective of monetary policy, but this has to be related to trade policy concerns to prevent currency appreciation. The use of monetary measures to serve trade objectives tends to be competitive, depending on capacities to maximise benefits while limiting risk and costs, and on bargaining resources. Difficulties result for these reasons and because of the diminishing effectiveness of interventions in money markets, due to high volume speculation.

The weakening of capacities for monetary interventions, and the dependence of the international trading system on stable exchange rates reflecting the strength of national economies, set demanding requirements for monetary cooperation. These requirements are exceptionally demanding because of the US role in the international monetary system as the top currency state coping with extraordinary debt burdens and seeking to manage its monetary affairs very independently, in support of its trade policy. The US dollar remains the principal international currency, despite its instability, because of the long standing reluctance of the Japanese and German administrations to allow very extensive foreign use of their currencies.

Cooperation for the regulation of financial markets has become necessary for the support of monetary collaboration. The internationalisation of those markets has facilitated trade, but their volatility has increased its risks. International cooperation to stabilise those markets is becoming more and more necessary, but collective engagement with this problem is lacking. The current strengthening of the European Monetary System and the advances toward European monetary union are positive developments, but are not sufficiently offsetting the danger of severe stress in financial markets resulting from general losses of confidence in the dollar.

Fiscal Cooperation

In the major industrialised democracies fiscal policies are very closely related to the distributional concerns of groups seeking to remain in office. Hence there is reluctance to be bound by commitments to international fiscal cooperation.[1] There is also appreciation that the potential benefits of such cooperation would depend on its qualitative as well as its quantitative dimensions, since the productive significance of differing national allocations can vary. Allocations to enhance transportation and communication services have growth effects superior to those for military hardware and the subsidising of inefficient state enterprises. Further, allocations that enhance location advantages for international firms have greater significance for growth than spending for drug or disease control.[2]

In addition to the difficulties of judging equivalence in the qualitative dimension of fiscal policy the question of international fiscal cooperation is overshadowed by problems resulting from the USA's heavy deficit spending. Possibilities for working toward convergence in growth rates and the reduction of trade imbalances have to be considered not only with reference to questions of equivalence between US deficit reductions and fiscal restraint or expansion by other major states, but also with reference to the feasibility of US fiscal restraint and the dangers which its absence poses for the international economy. These dangers may be seen as justifications for extraordinary measures to impose international fiscal accountability on the United States, rather than to negotiate US fiscal remedies in return for fiscal expansion, however evaluated, in the other major industrialised states.

Policy and structural interdependencies between the major industrialised democracies influence fiscal policies, especially through the more evident trends in market forces. These interdependencies discourage substantial spending increases that would raise levels of internal demand, draw in larger flows of imports, and add to national debt burdens. In the European Community the restraints of interdependence have become more significant because of discipline imposed through the European Monetary system, under German leadership. Fiscal restraint in Japan can be considered to complement that in Europe, leaving the USA as an exception that raises very grave questions about the growth effects of fiscal expansion that has large nonproductive elements, including military spending and the rescuing of bankrupt financial institutions, as well as excess production of bureaucratic services.[3]

Fiscal cooperation can help to promote more balanced and more harmonious structural and policy interdependencies between the larger advanced market economy states, especially by reducing trade surpluses and deficits and thus making exchange rates more stable. The cooperation required however is often conceptualised as a general levelling process, to lower domestic consumer demand in states with trade deficits while raising demand in surplus countries. There are assumptions that some overall equivalence is desirable between the respective fiscal reductions and increases, and there are also expectations that growth, employment, and inflation rates will be levelled, although it is clear that the quantitative fiscal comparisons will mask qualitative contrasts. Large national differences in macromanagement capacities and methods will remain significant, and substantial proportions of the increased government spending in the surplus countries may not appreciably raise demand, especially for foreign products, but may indirectly enhance national competitiveness, to the disadvantage of states with trade deficits. Increases in spending, it must be stressed, may be productive, for example through infrastructure development, or unproductive, and of course may add to government debt, and to the costs of government. The results, moreover, will have positive or negative effects on a nation's location advantages for foreign firms, and on strategies of its own firms. Trade flows may or may not become more balanced, and the continuing competitive substitution of overseas production for exports, in patterns that are not likely to be symmetrical, will tend to have differing growth effects, more significant than those caused by trade.

The more broadly balanced growth hoped for in the major industrialised democracies could be promoted through fiscal cooperation between governments operating at similar levels of macromanagement efficiency, and with substantial collaboration from transnational enterprises as well as their own national firms. Monetary, financial, and other forms of cooperation between the national administrations however would also be necessary. The importance of macromanagement efficiency is stressed in policy literature emphasising that fundamental problems of fiscal responsibility have to be resolved at the national level. The principal concern is the common tendency to resort to fiscal expansion in political business cycles, because of opportunistic short term considerations. Such expansion, because of the dominance of political exchange factors, tends to be insufficiently productive, or nonproductive, and obligates later deflationary measures.[4] Both effects contribute to losses of national competitiveness, the outward movement of production processes, and shifts to protectionism, as well as to the growth disparities and trade imbalances that motivate requests for cooperation from surplus states.

International cooperation with an emphasis on improving macromanagement efficiency could prepare the way for fiscal collaboration aimed at the promotion of generally even growth. The efficiency cooperation could develop as an OECD initiative, with most of the drive coming from the European Community. Within the Community, potentials for a relatively level regional growth rate and an even spread of gains from fully liberalised intrazonal commerce depend to a large extent on degrees of macromanagement efficiency. There may well be growing recognition of the need for a European Commission endeavour to foster administrative improvements in member states, for evenness in the national growth processes after 1992, so that the danger of disunity resulting from disparities will be reduced.

The most urgent task for an OECD endeavour would be the encouragement of improved fiscal management in the United States. The systemic effects of the USA's fiscal deficits are so serious that constructive external involvement in American policy processes will be necessary to overcome its political barriers to deficit reduction. These political barriers derive from the effects of constituency interests on legislators and from executive concerns with national popularity. For the present the barriers remain strong, making the deficits politically intractable, despite their increasing dangers for the USA and for the international community. As these dangers grow the rationale invoked for US requests to secure German and Japanese fiscal expansion is all the more seriously weakened, and for the Europeans and the Japanese it becomes increasingly important to adopt risk reduction measures that will reduce vulnerabilities to shocks resulting from deterioration in the US economy.

The rising levels of structural interdependence make external accountability in the management of fiscal policies more and more obligatory for the major industrialised democracies. This principle, however, tends to be violated by uses of leverage to secure fiscal cooperation on advantageous terms, so as to impose costs on other states. The scope to exert such leverage can be extensive if the disparities in bargaining power are large and the principle of external accountability is not generally accepted. Fiscal compliance by a state under leverage can in effect aid fiscal negligence by the more powerful state. The negative growth effects of that negligence however may not be significantly mitigated by the fiscal compliance which is imposed on the other state. That state's increased spending, moreover, may be productive, enhancing its competitiveness, and may entail greater consumption of domestic rather than foreign products.[5]

Multilateral bargaining on issues of fiscal cooperation would be an advance on the present pattern of bilateral dealings in which the USA endeavours to impose compliance on Japan, and, to a lesser extent, on Germany. The multilateralism would provide opportunities for coalition formation, based on shared interests in avoiding submission to undue leverage, and would entail much informal accountability that could have positive effects on US decision makers. The multilateral setting, moreover, could open the way for strong representations of European and Japanese interests in the US fiscal process. That involvement could develop through the formation of Trilateral legislative committees, which could function under an OECD advisory role. To the extent that improvements in macromanagement efficiency then became possible questions of concerting fiscal policies could be taken up. Greater certainty in judgements about matching qualitative as well as quantitative factors would be feasible, and there could be complementarity between national areas of emphasis in fiscal policies.

If the European Community does not assume an active role for the development of broadly Trilateral interactions on fiscal issues, and problems of fiscal reform remain politically intractable in the USA, the defensive options for the Europeans and Japan may be taken up resolutely. These could include reducing assets denominated in dollars, increasing international use of a European currency and the Yen, the development of wide ranging cooperation between the Community and Japan, and joint pressures on trade and investment issues to counteract US leverage. The retaliatory sequences that could follow could become seriously conflicted because of the difficulties of managing adversarial multilateral economic interactions. Serious damage could be done to the US economy and to the global monetary system before learning processes could motivate constructive US responses. The importance of European capacities for leadership in international economic cooperation can thus be given great emphasis.

Monetary Cooperation

Because of the present difficulties of fiscal cooperation policy makers have tended to focus on the potential benefits of concerting monetary measures, to influence trade flows, through exchange rates and levels of internal demand, and according in various degrees with criteria for economic rationality. In most domestic contexts, if there is no highly visible external leverage, the adoption of such measures can be more feasible than fiscal changes. The monetary decision processes are elitist, knowledge intensive, and somewhat insulated against pressures from interest groups and legislators. National monetary authorities, however, can be in varying degrees independent of or subordinate to their governments, they can differ in competence, institutional development, and orientation, and their close or distant associations with foreign monetary decision makers can influence their responsiveness to proposals for cooperation. Monetary decision making in Germany is a highly independent central bank function, and follows the national policy style of problem solving in the public interest, ensuring integration into a functional policy mix. In the USA however only the domestic aspects of monetary policy are managed independently of the administration, and these and the external aspects tend to be more politicised, because of macromanagement problems; in the US context, moreover, shifting elite idiosyncratic factors have more significance than in Germany.[6]

High levels of structural interdependence make monetary cooperation desirable. The management of interest rates, the money supply, and of interventions in currency markets, can be more effective if major trading partners collaborate. Growth, trade, employment, and inflation control objectives can be better served. The most significant results can be achieved through integrative cooperation, but for the present the terms on which collaboration develops are often bargained outcomes, determined mainly by the leverage of states with superior negotiating strengths. The terms may accord with economic logic, as can be claimed with respect to the German role in the European Monetary System, or they may be at variance with that logic, as can be suggested regarding the US administration's endeavours to maintain dollar exchange rates in line with trade objectives.[7]

The results of monetary cooperation, while depending on the influence of integrative, competitive, or demanding attitudes, are inevitably affected by the consequences of entire policy mixes. A large state with strong bargaining power implementing a seriously flawed policy mix may demand monetary cooperation from a more efficiently managed smaller state. Securing compliance may yield benefits, through increased exports, but not to a degree that would compensate for the overall negative effects of inefficient macromanagement – effects which may activate greater efforts by national firms to substitute overseas production for exports. Efficient macromanagement in a large state of course may enable it to extract greater benefits from a smaller state that is accommodating on monetary issues, but upward pressures on the large state's currency will tend to hinder achievement of the trade objectives that will have motivated its demands for cooperation.[8]

Market forces, influenced by diverse interacting policies, obligate degrees of convergence in monetary policies. Tendencies to loosen such policies, even for important political gains, are normally restrained by awareness that unless similar decisions are made by other states the rises in consumer demand will increase imports and the costs of producing for export, and will add to the incentives for firms to move operations abroad. Monetary tightening, to reduce inflation, has to be moderate to avoid currency appreciation that will reduce exports and open the way for gains in world markets by firms in states less committed to deflation. Currency markets however are affected by high volume speculation, which tends to intensify the effects of shifts in monetary and fiscal policies, and in balances of payments. Interventions in currency markets by national monetary authorities, to change exchange rates for trade purposes and to enhance business confidence, have to cope with speculative activities that may be triggered by the interventions and by reactions to current and impending events, including rises or falls in the inflation and growth levels of major states. The difficulties encountered tend to be greater when the interventions are attempted by a state burdened with the effects of inefficient macromanagement. Large funds may have to be used for interventions that may have disproportionately small trade effects through the shifts in exchange rates.[9] The losses of exchange rate sovereignty, that is of elements of market control, will of course be greater over time for a state with a flawed policy mix than for a state under efficient macromanagement.

The forces making for market induced convergence in monetary policies are not sufficiently effective because of the vast problem of speculation and the special problem of inefficient macromanagement in the USA, the largest advanced market economy state which provides the main currency for global trade and the holding of reserves. Convergence, it must be reiterated, is necessary for order in the international monetary system, but speculative agents have incentives to produce and exploit volatility. The volatility offering the greatest gains is that which can affect the US dollar, because of its global use and the conflicting pressures that frequently alter its role in financial markets.[10]

While US interventions in currency markets tend to have decreasing utility, supporting interventions by other states have to be requested, but the influence of a wide range of factors affecting business confidence in the USA and abroad becomes more significant. Cooperation is discouraged by the American emphasis on maintaining monetary autonomy, which is related to refusals to accept external fiscal accountability. Monetary cooperation is also discouraged by US efforts to secure compliance from trading partners on fiscal and trade as well as monetary issues. In the absence of international monetary cooperation, then, unintended, unexpected, and uncontrolled events influencing foreign and national assessments of the US economy affect stability in world financial markets. Such assessments are reflected in the production, location, and marketing activities of firms, which can intensify the negative growth effects of uncertainties and phases of volatility.

Coordinated management of interest rates, money supplies, and interventions, on a basis of goodwill and trust, is necessary to lower the transaction costs and risks of monetary disorder that reduce the efficiency of international product markets.[11] This systemic imperative can be stressed with emphasis on the disproportionately negative effects of those costs and risks for small and medium sized firms in all those markets, and the relative benefits indirectly gained by large transnational enterprises, whose interests in risk reducing oligopolistic collaboration are increased. Representation of the systemic imperative in the policy processes of the major market economy states however is weak. The basic public goods requirement of monetary order, with exchange rate stability at levels undisturbed by speculation and uninfluenced by bargaining leverage, is not attained.

The immediate prospect is more serious monetary disorder. While extensive international use of the unstable dollar continues, the USA's capacities to cope with the conflicting forces in currency markets and to enlist Trilateral cooperation will tend to diminish, especially because of the multiple effects of its heavy fiscal deficits. Gradually increasing international use of the Japanese Yen and a European currency is needed but may not provide a sufficiently extensive zone of monetary stability that could restrict the damage liable to result from more serious dollar volatility. This prospect, it must be reiterated, makes rapid attainment of monetary union by the European Community a matter of great urgency. Whether that will be attained is very uncertain, but if it can be attained a strong European role in the reform of the international monetary system will be possible.

While overshadowed by the danger of more serious monetary disorder the Europeans and the Japanese have strong incentives to cooperate with each other. If through determined efforts the present obstacles to such collaboration are overcome the large zone of monetary stability that could be established could provide a basis for a vast efficient Euro–Japanese product market, into which the high growth East Asian developing states could be drawn. Euro–Japanese monetary cooperation could become powerfully motivated by this positive consideration as well as by the negative concern with protection against the volatility of the dollar. Much of the literature that could contribute to policy learning on those imperatives for cooperation however reflects assumptions that national monetary policies will continue to be dominated by narrowly conceived short term interests, despite a general lack of optimism about potentials for fiscal reform and more effective monetary management in the USA.

The context for the national concerns about monetary issues in Europe and the USA has been set by decades of unequal bargaining about exchange rates, viewed primarily in the light of trade interests. Concerns about those interests are still valid, because of the growth potential of commerce between advanced markets. That commerce however is being altered by increases in the large volumes of transnational production and intrafirm trade, managed by powerful international enterprises. The scale and flexibility of their operations enables them to cope with volatility in financial markets. Their interests are affected by increases and decreases in consumer demand associated with phases of monetary loosening and tightening, but these shifts and the changes in financial markets tend to be manageable problems. Indirectly, moreover, it must be stressed, such problems can assist the acquisition of larger market shares. Weaker firms, virtually confined to national markets, experience difficult adjustment problems. Financing expansion and restructuring can be costly for those firms when national monetary policy is restrictive, but the large international enterprises can operate with few financial constraints, as well as with the advantages of linkages with each other that facilitate market sharing.

Financial Cooperation

Vast problems of financial cooperation are being posed because financial markets have been internationalised without adequate regulatory arrangements. The internationalisation has been promoted mainly by the USA, to enhance global opportunities for its financial institutions, and has been aided by advanced communications technology. The scope for efficient allocations of investment has become very wide, with great advantages in the spreading of risks. Trade expansion and the growth of transnational production have benefitted. The competitive pressures channeling global investment flows toward profit maximisation however have operated mainly on a short term basis, especially because of instability caused by speculation.[12] Improvident government borrowing, especially by the USA, has been facilitated, large scale expansion by transnational enterprises has been aided more than the development of small and medium sized firms, and the financing of long term productive ventures has lagged. The heavy US government borrowing from the rest of the world has induced complacency among American decision makers who would otherwise be forced to cut the large deficits that obligate the borrowing. While that borrowing continues it diverts investment from productive use in the USA and abroad; and since it is becoming unsustainable, it tends to reduce domestic and foreign confidence in the US economy, and poses a threat of severe instability in the global financial system. The high interest rates associated with the borrowing constitute a drag on the growth which the internationalisation of financial markets has assisted. Recovery for the debt burdened Third World countries that were severely affected by dollar appreciation and exorbitant US interest rates during the first Reagan administration, moreover, remains very difficult.

National differences in the regulation of financial markets and in the quality of macromanagement have resulted in significant contrasts that are affecting the evolution of the international financial system. The highly integrated and efficiently managed German financial system has to a considerable extent protected itself and the national economy from the effects of volatility in global financial markets. Utilisation of financing available in those markets by German firms, in support of export expansion, has been mainly a function for German banks, because of their close links with the nation's industrial establishments. Low savings levels in the USA's less integrated and insufficiently regulated national financial system, together with the high level of domestic government borrowing, make international financing especially advantageous for US firms, particularly for the support of overseas operations. Japan's very high savings level has sustained a well integrated financial system, benefitting from high quality macromanagement, but less protected than Germany's against external shocks. Portfolio and direct investment in the USA has resulted in a high degree of financial interdependence. Japanese international firms, moreover, extending their transnational production activities, have been raising large funds in the Euromarket, indirectly giving impetus to vast increases in overseas activities by Japanese banks. These have assumed great influence in world financial markets since the appreciation of the Yen in the mid 1980s, but the danger of instability in those markets has continued to grow, primarily because of the USA's macromanagement problems.[13]

The efficiency of the internationalised financial markets, driven by global competitive forces, entails dangers despite the spreading of risks on a large scale through collaboration between multinational banks. Risks for the system as a whole are caused by largely unregulated extensions of credit. The resulting dangers are all the more serious because of the uncertainties affecting domestic and foreign confidence in the US economy. The vast expansions of international credit encourage and give extensive opportunities for speculation, and the use of these opportunities is facilitated by shifts in the factors giving rise of uncertainties about the profitability of investments in the USA, as well as about stability and growth in the world economy. Comprehensive regulation of the internationalised financial markets is thus becoming more and more imperative. This however is difficult to achieve, because of diverging perceptions of interests, a lack of leadership, and the orientation of US policy.

In the present context of largely inconclusive interactions over monetary, fiscal, and other forms of economic cooperation, national administrations in the major industrialised states appear to prefer loose minimal *ad hoc* regulatory endeavours to the more extensive and more structured arrangements that could result from commitments to achieve global financial order. In such arrangements the rises in policy interdependence would evidently be unwelcome. The USA would have to make compromises and accept measures of accountability that would restrict its freedom of choice. The other large democracies would tend to fear applications of US bargaining leverage. US and other preferences of course are influenced by the representation of national financial interests, and these generally reflect desires to preserve the freedom enjoyed in the present setting, despite awareness of systemic needs for effective regulation.[14]

While the internationalised financial markets remain largely unregulated and continue to grow with the expansion of credit the implementation of sound fiscal and monetary policies by the leading industrialised democracies becomes more necessary for the stability and development of the global economy. Since the required policy learning and motivation is not in prospect, however, except in the European Community and Japan, there is a danger that remedial measures will not be adopted in the largest Trilateral state unless they are forced by a serious crisis. There is also a danger that the adverse effects of such a crisis will be extensive and rapid in the internationalised financial markets before the USA's macromanagement problems can be resolved. For the present these problems include burdens assumed because of failures by domestic financial institutions that have been insufficiently regulated in the recent past. Large increases in the chronic deficit financing have been caused by those burdens, and business confidence has been adversely affected.

Financing mergers and acquisitions in the European Community, especially by US firms already active in Western Europe, is tending to become a major activity in international financial markets.[15] Destabilising speculation may result before the Community becomes sufficiently united to impose effective common financial regulations. These have been needed for many years to safeguard the interests of Community firms, and their absence while full market integration is being attained is a serious vulnerability. If excessive speculation does lead to instability in European financial markets the resulting strains could be worsened by, and could adversely affect, stresses in American financial markets. The global financial system would then be severely affected. The importance of evolving a strong Community financial regulation system therefore has to be stressed, and it is clear that this will have to be accompanied by the development of a vigorous European role working for regulation at the global level. Administrative and corporate preferences unduly influenced by the rather deceptive advantages of the present internationalised system may well be more susceptible to learning in the Community setting if the inferior competitiveness of Community firms in their own market is sufficiently understood.

Opportunities in global financial markets are drawing into their operations more and more US and other banks.[16] Vast profits can be made rapidly, through virtually unregulated activities, and strong positions gained in those intensely competitive markets, while defended and extended as much as possible, can assist growth in the home economy, and help to reduce tax exposure. Overall systemic risk is evidently tending to increase because of the competitive pressures causing operations to expand well in excess of prudent limits which national regulatory authorities wish to introduce if their governments can be motivated to make the necessary commitments. For the present, it must be stressed, the development of a strong political will in the USA to promote international financial regulation is not in prospect. The European Community, moreover, will have to make substantial advances toward economic union before it will be able to build up an adequate regional financial regulatory system.

Linkages

The integration of financial markets on a global scale has opened up vast possibilities for the efficient allocation of investment funds, but on a short term basis, and with a competitive ethos insensitive to welfare considerations. This competitive ethos is leading to a growth of oligopoly power, in which Japanese banks are well positioned because of their mutual ties and links with their home administration, but in which other multinational banks operating more on an individual basis are exposed to serious risks. The competitive pressures to gain oligopoly power lead to ambitious extensions of credit which have to be managed through rapid large scale interbank lending. The credits are extended to governments and large corporations. Their availability facilitates deficit financing, which, depending on its scale, necessitates monetary restraint by the borrowing government, causing differences in national interest rates and exchange rates which are then exploited in the financial markets. The lending to large corporations, meanwhile, facilitates their expansion and acquisition of oligopoly power, leading to the formation of larger global concentrations of industrial strength. The evolution of these factors influences and is influenced by national policy mixes, with significant contrasts between those of the more integrated and the less integrated national political economies.

Differences in the quality of macromanagement, and generally inadequate attempts at fiscal and monetary cooperation, as well as failures in financial cooperation, are basic sources of the opportunities which drive competition between international financial organisations. The competitive extensions of credit contribute to the volatility in exchange rates which they exploit. At the same time functional requirements to promote and combine financial, monetary, and fiscal cooperation, on a basis of general qualitative macromanagement improvements, become stronger and more urgent. Unregulated global financial markets make effective monetary cooperation more and more difficult, and such cooperation is also hindered by failures in fiscal cooperation.

The growth objectives of fiscal policy are not adequately served by international financial markets because, except for the activities of Japanese and German banks, these do not fund industries sufficiently. The pyramiding of financial transactions on a small base of real activity generates vicious cycles of speculative operations which, although spreading risks, entail serious vulnerability. The instability which threatens has the general effect of motivating financial managers to remain involved in the interbank lending, and, apparently, to oppose the introduction of regulatory measures which would tend to shift advantages to the less cooperative states but which could reduce the scale of the operations causing systemic risk. Meanwhile the domestic regulation of financial activity tends to become more difficult, except in the more integrated national political economies, as financial institutions become more deeply involved in global operations that escape national jurisdiction. Fiscal policies moreover are affected, not only because tax exposure can be reduced through international operations but also because industrial enterprises moving into global ventures are given opportunities for financial management that can reduce home and host country taxation. These opportunities in effect supplement those through which taxes can be limited by transfer pricing and by assigning profits to subsidiaries and branches functioning in low tax areas.

The large scale expansion of credit in international financial markets generates inflationary pressures which affect all states, especially the less integrated ones which are not protected by close collaboration between administrative agencies, industrial enterprises, and financial institutions. Since these less integrated states experience political competition that drives them into deficit spending, moreover, the systemic inflationary pressures operate in conjunction with the domestic inflationary pressures associated with that spending. Monetary restraint for inflation control can thus be severe and yet relatively ineffective. The promotion of growth in these states, meanwhile, tends to be hindered by the influence of inflationary trends on the location and production decisions of transnational enterprises, especially because operations in countries with low inflation become more attractive. Export substitution through overseas production and reductions of exports due to the effects of inflation on production costs can thus contribute to trade deficits which in turn affect exchange rates. At the same time, interest rates, exchange rates, inflation, and growth, can be strongly affected by the international borrowing associated with deficit spending. All these problems are evident in the current experience of the USA, and they have serious consequences for the international political economy because of the size of the United States and the large interdependencies which link it with that economy.[17]

The European Community, as it becomes established as a zone of monetary stability and fiscal discipline, under German leadership, will be able to work for the development of more order in global financial markets. Stable institutionalised commitments to establish such order may well be fostered by German economic policy decision makers. The community's growth prospects will be adversely affected because of rising systemic risks associated with American macromanagement problems if the necessary order in financial markets is not attained. Cooperation by Japan would make the achievement of international financial discipline more probable, of course, and much will depend on whether the importance of securing such cooperation will be grasped by community decision makers.[18]

The development of more order in global financial markets would help to correct their current bias toward short term higher growth speculative activities rather than industrial expansion. Real economic functions would then benefit while systemic risk was reduced. The magnitude of that risk is tending to increase while the speculative bias continues, but despite this the risk is clearly underestimated, especially by interested parties and decision makers in the USA. American financial interests are focussing on opportunities for deeper involvement in global financial markets and for larger oligopolistic domination of the domestic market as it is further deregulated.[19] For the US administration, meanwhile, access to the uncontrolled global financial markets is highly important while heavy deficit spending continues.

Policy Options

The utility of attempting fiscal and monetary cooperation is questioned in some of the policy literature because of the danger that governments will collude in the adoption of expansionary policies to further their political interests, that cooperative arrangements will tend to facilitate efforts by a large expansionary state to impose its preferences on other governments, and that opportunities for cooperation will tend to divert the attention of governments from the tasks of sound domestic management. Linked with these points, in some cases, are assertions that the USA, although the largest industrialised democracy, cannot be a reliable partner in economic cooperation because of the lack of integration in its political system.[20] The significance of all these negative comments of course depends on the gravity of the macromanagement problems in the states that could be expected to lead ventures in macroeconomic cooperation, and on the degrees to which they would be inclined to pressure smaller states into compliance with unsound proposals. The criticisms are persuasive, but they reflect excessive pessimism about the potential roles of international economic organisations.

The need for international monetary and financial order, sustained in part by sound coordinated fiscal policies, has to be affirmed. The development of trade and transnational production tends to be hindered by monetary and financial stresses and by the effects of diverging fiscal policies. In a more holistic perspective, the potential for collaborative orchestration of economic growth, through industrial cooperation, now requires extensive fiscal, monetary, and financial collaboration. This need, which concerns the realisation of high order international public goods, has to be affirmed with understandings of the importance of building strong international institutions. Such institutions will have to restrain politically motivated expansionary tendencies by participating governments, and protect smaller states against leverage on macroeconomic issues. The weakening of global economic organisations over the past two decades indicates that the building of strong international institutions for macroeconomic cooperation will be difficult, but does not invalidate the logic of the rationale for their establishment.

Cooperation for fiscal discipline developing in the European Community, in conjunction with monetary cooperation, illustrates the importance of strong institutions. The fiscal collaboration is a process of convergence motivated by commitments to the European Monetary System, and the logic of strengthening this system for the development of a European monetary union has gained widening acceptance because of understandings of the need for a European zone of monetary stability and even more importantly for monetary arrangements that will facilitate full market integration. The fiscal discipline is to a degree helping to reverse a long standing expansionary trend in Community members that has hampered their economic growth.[21] The increasing macroeconomic cooperation in the Community has derived impetus from the drive for deepening integration promoted by the European Commission with the support of business elites, and has contributed to a consensus on the need for institutional integration at a higher level. The operative perceptions of integration logic have been limited to the European context, but the global significance of the endeavour has become increasingly apparent.[22] Important leadership options, therefore, can be seen for the Community, especially with reference to macroeconomic cooperation with Japan and the development of global institutions that would promote Trilateral fiscal discipline.

Since monetary cooperation is politically more feasible than fiscal cooperation, however, and yet can help activate such cooperation, European and Japanese monetary options deserve special consideration. Questions of Euro–Japanese monetary cooperation are less complex and potentially more manageable than those in the Atlantic context or in US–Japan relations. The international role of the US dollar is affected by strong conflicting pressures not only because of the macromanagement problems which require heavy government borrowing and discourage business confidence but also because of the balance of payments consequences of large scale transnational production, limiting export revenue and tax revenue, while the US dollar remains the main target of speculative activity in financial markets. The sources of dollar volatility, clearly, can be overcome only in the long term, but the dimensions of this volatility and its systemic effects can be reduced through Euro–Japanese monetary cooperation and wider international use of the Yen and the Mark. Although Japanese and German monetary authorities have been reluctant to see extensive international use of their currencies, because of the risks of losing elements of monetary sovereignty, they do have institutional capacities which could be used in concert to establish greater order in international financial markets. Formal arrangements for Japanese partnership with the European Monetary System would be a major step toward collaboration for increased order and security in the global monetary and financial systems.

7. Trade, Direct Investment, & Industrial Cooperation

For growth with equity in the international political economy, fiscal, monetary, and financial cooperation must be combined with trade, direct investment, and industrial cooperation. Growth is achieved by increasing gains from trade, through specialisation, economies of scale, and entrepreneurship, in contexts provided by the integration of markets, the promotion and regulation of commerce and direct investment, the orchestration of industrial expansion, and collaborative technological progress. Government failures and enterprise failures in these contexts hinder growth and cause it to become imbalanced.

In liberal perspectives the integration of markets can appear to be sufficient, as it will allow much liberty for the international operations of firms, and competition between them will increase the gains from trade. Governments, however, can prefer only partial market integration, on terms attainable through bargaining, in line with the requests of domestic interests. In the partially liberalised and in any fully integrated markets oligopoly power can be acquired, with or without administrative assistance. The resultant elements of market failure may not be recognised, because of unwillingness to modify liberal beliefs, or may be tolerated because of the domestic political importance of the firms which benefit.

Economic nationalist perspectives, which can be strongly influenced also by the expectations of large domestic interests, focus on the commercial competitiveness between states and on the interactions between their bargaining strategies over questions of sectorally liberalised or managed trade. Theoretical appreciation of the potential benefits of market integration tends to be qualified by beliefs that governments tend to concentrate on enhancing terms of trade for their enterprises through discriminatory commercial measures, to the extent that these can be supported by available bargaining leverage. States which fail to act aggressively for the advancement of their commercial interests are thus expected to be disadvantaged. Trade bargaining, however, depending on relative degrees of leverage, requires identification of compatible interests, since in conditions of structural interdependence preferred trade arrangements cannot be simply imposed.

Questions about the regulation of commerce have to be considered with understandings of the terms on which it has evolved. Large states tend to discriminate against the trading interests of small states, and the regulation of the commerce which develops tends to reflect inequalities in the relationships. If with increasing goodwill trading relationships become more cooperative, however, joint or multilateral regulation can serve common interests, through general increases in growth with equity. Yet the contributions of arm's length trade to growth are of declining importance because of the expansion of transnational production and the increasing volume of intrafirm trade. Problems concerning the regulation of foreign direct investment thus have to be considered. General openness to such investment can offer vast prospects for growth, but can facilitate the emergence of oligopoly power much greater than that likely to result from the liberalisation of arm's length trade. As host governments, national administrations have interests in regulating foreign direct investment, especially when there is pressure from domestic firms and communities, but as home governments they tend to favour minimal foreign regulation of the overseas operations of their firms. Interactions over foreign direct investment issues, like those over trade, tend to result in outcomes reflecting differences in bargaining power, the uses of which are restrained by unequal interdependencies. Common interests in balanced and equitable growth, then, may not be served.

Industrial and technology measures can enhance the competitiveness of firms engaged in arm's length trade and transnational production. There can be enlightened concern to balance competitive forces with forms of cooperation, because of the common interests in fostering harmonious structural interdependencies, but the discriminatory demands of powerful domestic firms and business associations may be compelling. The business practices of international firms, moreover, can introduce other considerations that obligate discriminatory policies.

Trade Cooperation

The USA, the European Community members, and Japan, observe trade liberalisation measures negotiated under GATT rounds that have brought tariffs down to low levels and restricted the use of nontariff barriers. There is also general observance of GATT principles and norms obligating nondiscriminatory trade liberalisation on a basis of reciprocity. There are considerable violations of the principles, norms, and negotiated measures, however, and altogether a large proportion of the commerce between the advanced market economy states is managed, instead of resulting from the free operation of market forces. The volume of managed trade is tending to increase, because deficit states experiencing a lack of competitiveness resort to protectionist arrangements, due to the pressures of domestic interests. Surplus states, meanwhile, endeavour to profit more from their competitiveness by direct and indirect methods of sheltering their domestic industries. The USA is endeavouring to give leadership for the development of a more liberal world trading system, but potent domestic pressures and instances of industrial decline have virtually forced adoption of protectionist devices. Many of these may be terminated if negotiations for a more open global trading system are successful, but some may be maintained although they are unilateral measures that disregard GATT rules.[1] Similar criticisms can be made of the trade restriction practices of the European Community and Japan.

Trade liberalisation arrangements negotiated under successive GATT rounds had resulted in considerable advances toward integration of the markets of the industrialised democracies by the 1970s, but disparities in the spread of gains from the freer commerce tended to become more pronounced. Differences in national competitiveness between the more integrated states under higher quality macromanagement and the less integrated states under less effective macromanagement widened, and the divergences increased under the pressures caused by oil price rises. The vulnerabilities of rising structural interdependence meanwhile activated industries disrupted by competing imports in the less integrated states. Protectionist demands were then expressed in measures which mainly utilised nontariff barriers to shelter the less competitive firms. The adoption of these measures encouraged further protectionist advocacy, which was aided by the dynamics of political competition. Meanwhile more informal methods of protecting internal markets were effective in the more integrated states.

After the 1970s of course the pattern of strained trading relations was altered by heavy fiscal expansion and serious monetary contraction in the USA. This mix was responsible for large scale government borrowing and drastic currency appreciation that caused serious trade imbalances. Issues in the global trading system became more closely linked with questions of fiscal and monetary management in all the major industrialised democracies, and the USA began to seek increased access to the markets of its principal trading partners. The trade deficits which were being experienced were becoming unsustainable, but no significant efforts were made to reduce the appreciation of the dollar until 1985. The appreciation caused exports to slow and decline, while indirectly facilitating export substitution through overseas production, and while increasing imports on a scale that disrupted domestic industries.

US efforts to secure increased access to other advanced country markets became more active after the dollar depreciation in 1985.[2] Pressures from the legislature for executive leverage against trading partners were strong because the flow of imports was not significantly reduced and the recovery of exports was slow, in part because of the continuing effects of increases in overseas production by US firms. Greater direct investment in the European Community was being encouraged by its commitment to full market integration: there were strong incentives to gain large shares of the integrating market before advances toward further political unification could enable the Community to introduce common industrial and foreign direct investment policies.

Questions of international trade cooperation are now being posed in an extraordinary context that has been shaped mainly by the USA's evolving policy mixes. Compatibilities and identities of interest relating to trade liberalisation are inevitably linked with similarities and differences of interest relating to the management of fiscal, monetary, and financial policies, and to trends in transnational production. All these interconnections are sources of multiple uncertainties about the evolution of structural and policy interdependencies that have to be reckoned with by decision makers in the large industrialised democracies. The general effect of these uncertainties is to enhance the significance of national potentials for adjustment to external shocks and for competitive involvement in the international political economy with an emphasis on self reliance that can reduce vulnerabilities. Considerations along these lines, linked with the political significance of domestic groups with active trade policy interests, tend to have potent effects on the perspectives of administrative leaderships. Understandings of the basic rationale for trade liberalisation, with reference to its potential growth effects, thus tend to assume secondary importance.[3] Theorising about the possible achievements of strategic trade policies has accordingly been having some influence in the policy communities of the less competitive states experiencing trade deficits. Vigorous exporting by the surplus states is attributed to competitive advantages gained by their firms from industrial policies intended to support deep sectoral penetration of foreign markets.[4]

In multilateral interactions within GATT, leadership for general trade liberalisation is undertaken by the USA, while its principal concern is to reach a broad settlement with the European Community. The main obstacles, *viz* European reluctance to negotiate reductions in nontariff barriers, to modify the Community's Common Agricultural Policy, and to support liberalisation of services trade, evidence well established interests. The USA has been pressing for the elimination of nontariff barriers (broadly defined) by the Community, Japan, and some of the Newly Industrialising Countries, as well as drastic reductions of the Community's agricultural protectionism, and large scale elimination of impediments to trade in services. The US interest in services, while reflecting awareness that many US firms have competitive advantages in this trade, also evidences appreciation that their activities tend to expand as US manufacturing enterprises extend their overseas operations. Incentives to compromise appear to have only modest influence in Community policy, because of perceptions that West European growth will be aided more by full market integration and Eastern enlargement than by likely increases in commerce with the USA.[5] The large scale manufacturing by US firms within the Community moreover is undoubtedly expected to expand, ensuring American shares of the Community market much larger than Community shares of the US market through trade and overseas production.

The USA has some incentives to compromise because of the Community's increasing significance as its principal trading partner, and because strains over trade issues may affect the interests of the US firms operating in the Community. There are strong internal pressures to extract trade concessions from the Community, however, and these could result in counterproductive attempts at leverage. The Community has numerous complaints about discriminatory US trade measures which restrict its exports, and has condemned, as violations of GATT principles, the US 1988 Omnibus Trade Bill which virtually obligates unilateral retaliation against trading partners deemed to be unfair.[6] The main trade interests shared with the USA are of moderate significance: there is considerable agreement about the scope for further tariff reductions that will benefit Atlantic trade in manufactured products and capital goods, and about the desirability of securing reductions of the protectionist measures employed by Japan and some of the Newly Industrialising Countries.[7]

The dynamics of Atlantic trade interactions may lead to temporary bargained agreements that will reduce barriers to commerce with overall symmetries, but European perspectives will be influenced by concerns about the competitive positions of Community firms in their own market, and about the health of the US economy as well as the stability of the dollar. Commitments made to trade liberalisation may thus be tacitly qualified, on the basis of assumptions that measures may have to be introduced to limit intrusions into the integrating market. The Community is being obliged to evolve an effective competition policy for regulation of its market, and the scope of this policy is not likely to be negotiable.

Trade cooperation that leads to substantially open markets, as has happened through the reduction of tariffs to low levels in commerce between the industrialised democracies, brings into prominence issues regarding competition policy, industrial policy, and foreign direct investment policy. One state's toleration of restrictive business practices may not be acceptable to another, and a state which enforces a relatively effective competition policy may condone restrictive business practices by its firms in overseas markets. Competition policy measures are mostly associated with industrial policy, which seeks to aid improvements in the competitiveness of national firms, and may directly or indirectly discriminate against foreign enterprises. How competition policy operates of course depends very much on the presence or absence of social cohesion between the managements of national firms, as well as within a foreign corporate presence. In the Atlantic trading relationship the USA does not have strong leverage to press for relaxation of the numerous informal and formal ties between business groups and national administrations which tend to enhance the effects of European competition policies.[8] Such leverage, however, is used against Japan. Yet Japan has little need of a formal competition policy directed against foreign enterprises because of the very strong links between its national firms and between those firms and its administration. American demands for market access seek to overcome what can be identified as legal measures limiting foreign penetration, but at the cost of arousing economic nationalism which reinforces the informal business solidarity and strengthens the motivations of Japanese firms to cooperate with their administration.

The outcomes of arrangements for trade liberalisation or managed trade are affected by all the factors in national policy mixes which influence changes in the competitiveness of firms, as well as by the various decisions of international and national managements to produce and market their products. These decisions, it must be stressed, tend to assume more significance than the trade policy measures adopted by administrations. The large issues which are emerging for trade policy makers are the global production and market sharing ventures between international firms, which affect trade flows and the evolution of national industry structures, depending on the degree of integration in each national political economy and the quality of its macromanagement. Those international firms are variously placed to influence trade, industrial, and direct investment policies, especially by revealing their ranges of global options. Relative degrees of integration in national political economies thus assume great significance as determinants of the scope for independent decision making by corporate managements that may diverge from or conflict with national administrative preferences regarding growth, employment, and inflation.[9]

Foreign Direct Investment

Trade cooperation between industrialised democracies, depending on its terms and scope, facilitates cross investment, leading to export substitution through transnational production. At the same time the persistence of tariff and nontariff barriers encourages direct investment, resulting also in export substitution, although host government attitudes may be less favourable than those toward foreign direct investment attracted in a friendly trading relationship. Managements of international firms develop their strategies with emphasis on maintaining production facilities within major national markets while maximising the use of location advantages on a global scale. As production becomes more substantial within a national market advantages may be gained from any degrees of protection it is given by restraints on imports, but such restraints may also hinder the procurement of inputs from outside sources. Home and host government foreign direct investment policies influence corporate choices, and may indicate greater interest in supporting outward direct investment or attracting foreign direct investment than in liberalising or restricting trade.

Questions of cooperation in the management of foreign direct investment policies are posed because of the large volumes of transnational production that are replacing exports between the advanced market economy states. While the USA implements and advocates general adoption of a liberal foreign direct investment policy, the more integrated national political economies, notably Japan and Germany, seek in varying degrees to guide each foreign corporate presence into an appropriate role within the national economic structure, especially to ensure overall efficiency and competitiveness.[10] Cooperation in foreign direct investment policies may amount to shifts in a liberal direction, or compromises between liberal and directive approaches, or the harmonising of directive approaches. Governments with similar or diverging orientations may compete, explicitly or in effect, by offering different location advantages that attract international firms. Administrative capacities to offer dynamic and orderly environments however tend to diminish if liberal foreign direct investment policies are implemented. Growth, employment, inflation, and trade are increasingly affected by the independent activities of transnational enterprises. Substantial numbers of national firms are driven into declines or taken over. Large revenues are lost as the transnational enterprises use accounting methods to reduce tax exposure. Rising costs of government, meanwhile, due to welfare burdens caused by the failures of national firms, obligate heavier taxes, which can cause the transnational enterprises to relocate more production processes in lower cost countries. Because of anticipations of these problems, then, liberal foreign direct investment policies are often implemented with reservations, and of course can be affected by the representations of domestic groups whose interests are threatened.[11]

Compromises between governments whose policies are in varying degrees liberal or directive tend to reflect relative bargaining strengths and the condition of their trading relationships. In the Atlantic context the mainly liberal orientation of US foreign direct investment policy encounters varying degrees of European emphasis on guiding or directing foreign involvement in national economic systems, while US bargaining leverage, which has been superior, is declining. The contrast in policy orientations is tending to become stronger as the European Community market becomes fully integrated and the question of evolving a common Community foreign direct investment policy becomes more urgent, especially because of the increasing involvement of US firms in shaping the industrial capacities of member states.[12] The sharpest contrasts in policy orientations and the most significant issues of efficiency and equity, however, are posed in the US–Japan relationship. In this setting, moreover, the use of American leverage is affected by the high level of financial interdependence. On the Japanese side administrative compromises to permit easier US direct investment are necessary mainly because the USA has become the principal host country for large scale Japanese direct investment. Incoming US firms however have strong incentives to develop joint ventures and linkages with Japanese enterprises, as these are deeply integrated into the host economy and have strong ties with the host government. Hence there are possibilities for indirect guidance of the US enterprises into roles according with the overall pattern of organised enterprise in Japan. Japanese firms operating in the USA, however, have rather wide scope for independent competitive expansion, with or without selective use of American partners. The liberal US foreign direct investment policy has a stable foundation, and Japanese firms in the USA are advantaged by Yen appreciation as well as by their links with each other and with their home government.[13]

Questions about cooperation to guide or direct foreign direct investment are being raised in the European Community because European transnational enterprises, the European Commission, and member governments confront issues concerning the standardisation of national policies within the grouping, for the benefit of Community firms and the regulation of American, Japanese, and other foreign enterprises. The development of a common policy for the guidance or regulation of outside firms is becoming necessary not only to protect Community enterprises but to eliminate competition between some of the member states to attract American or Japanese companies.[14] The development of such a common policy however will not be possible unless there are major advances toward the establishment of an economic union. Pending such advances, governments in the less competitive countries can be expected to seek direct investment by strong outside firms that can promise enhancement of the national economic structures. Over time, moreover, this external involvement, adding to the significance of foreign corporate presences already established, will tend to make a policy consensus on the treatment of these outside enterprises more and more difficult to attain.

The standardisation of national policies on cross investment within the Community is being sought on a liberal basis. This entails dangers for less competitive firms in the less advanced states, and, as these firms are driven into declines, political cohesion within the Community may be strained. In the absence of a common industrial policy, which would require a consensus attainable only in the long term, restructuring possibilities for such firms will depend on national measures, and the effective scope for these will be limited. The liberal orientation of the drive for complete market integration restricts administrative support for industries, and strong European as well as outside firms will have opportunities to defeat the purposes of restructuring endeavours in the less advanced member states.

For balanced growth within the Community, which will be necessary if it is to attain greater political unity, a common policy on cross investment between member states will have to provide guidance in line with a common industrial policy. Freely operating market forces in the grouping will not produce balanced growth: the benefits of full market integration will be spread unevenly, due to large differences in the competitiveness of firms, the competitiveness of member countries, and the qualities of macromanagement.[15] Politically, the introduction of a common industrial policy would require the resolution of conflicts of interest between the more competitive and the less competitive member states that are likely to be sharpened by full market integration. If a policy were introduced under German leadership its effects could be considered unsatisfactory by the less competitive states. A more broadly representative industrial policy however could be implemented on terms that might be considered onerous by the Germans. While the Community functions on a confederal basis majority leverage against Germany is largely precluded, but it could become feasible with advances toward the establishment of a federal structure.

If a common policy on guiding cross investment is evolved the degree of consensus that may sustain this could assist the development of a policy for the guidance of direct investment by outside firms. Any shifts by the Community or its members toward such a policy however would be opposed by the USA. The United States could threaten restrictions on Community direct investment in its economy. Of the larger Community members Britain would be the most seriously affected, because of the large volume of British direct investment in the USA. British opposition to Community measures that could restrict US direct investment in Europe would no doubt be vigorous because of concerns about the investments in the United States and also because of interests in continuing to attract US direct investment into manufacturing ventures in Britain for the Community market. Differences between Britain and many other members of the Community over the treatment of US, Japanese, and other direct investment from outside may increase as the involvement of the external firms becomes more active in the integrating Community market.

There is a potential for Community cooperation with Japan in the guidance of cross investment within that relationship. While the Community would benefit through joint ventures and linkages that would help to upgrade the efficiency of its firms, and through entries of its transnational enterprises into the Japanese economy, Japanese international firms would have wider and more secure access to the Community market. In the absence of a Community policy informal collaboration on a bilateral basis is developing between Japan and some Community states. The most significant opportunities for Japanese firms are in Germany, because of its large advanced industrial structure, and because German goodwill can be especially important in Community decision making on trade issues.[16] Yet the benefits gained by Germany could well be a source of reluctance to facilitate Japanese direct investment cooperation with the entire Community – if that became feasible because of further deepening of the integration process and the development of a broad Community consensus on the need for Japanese inputs into the upgrading of Community firms.

The USA's liberal foreign direct investment policy is being questioned in American public affairs literature dealing with losses of competitiveness by US firms and the persistence of US trade deficits. Substantial regulation of inward direct investment is urged in the principal challenges to mainstream liberal thinking, and this advocacy is often linked with prescriptions for an active industrial policy that will enable US firms to compete against foreign rivals aided by their governments. The concerns about inward direct investment relate to the competitiveness of Japanese firms working in collaboration and with the support of their administration. The negotiation of changes in Japanese business practices and policy is not considered practical, and an active industrial policy is expected to ensure technological advances and productivity gains which firms would not achieve unless given administrative support and guidance.[17] Mainstream liberal thinking rejects that conclusion, arguing principally that US firms must be challenged by market forces to enhance their own competitiveness. This position is given some support by observations that the implementation of an active industrial policy and a policy for guiding foreign direct investment would be strongly influenced by the demands of interest groups, and therefore would fail to achieve its intended objectives.

While consensus is difficult, especially because of the weaknesses of aggregating structures in the American polity, the liberal policy orientation remains in effect with a weakened foundation in elite attitudes and is modified by *ad hoc* measures. These include restraints on inward direct investment in defence related industries, and the adoption of research and procurement projects that can be covered under the general heading of international security policy. Altogether the benefits for US firms, outside the aircraft industry, are small, and overall offer few incentives for firms to produce in the USA rather than overseas, where more profitable operations can finance research and development on a large scale. There is little policy debate about the established liberal orientation toward outward direct investment from the USA and the continuing endeavour to seek liberal treatment of that investment by host governments. While this endeavour benefits from competition between European Community members to attract outside firms it also benefits from the US potential for leverage on trade issues, because of the size of the American market although that potential is decreasing as the Community expands and advances toward higher stages of integration. If those advances continue, of course the competition between community members to attract US and other outside firms will be brought under collective restraint.[18]

Industrial Cooperation

Basic questions about harmonising foreign direct investment and trade policies have to be considered in conjunction with issues of industrial cooperation. For states committed to liberal trade policies, industrial policies are to be eliminated rather than coordinated, but concerns with national competitiveness, as has been noted, tend to erode liberal objections to industrial policy measures, and as this happens there are opportunities for interest groups to press for the introduction of such measures on a larger scale. In addition, the functional significance of those measures tends to be given more recognition in policy making. Meanwhile the rationale for industrial policy remains significant for administrations that have achieved successes through endeavours to orchestrate advances in competitiveness by national firms, in line with concepts of national competitiveness. For harmonious interdependent growth, then, advanced states must endeavour to promote convergence between their industrial policies. Such convergence could be envisaged simply through contractions of the measures used in strongly interventionist states and expansions of those utilised in the more liberal states, but a more fundamental process of policy integration can be advocated. The objective would be collective management of industrial growth.

The functional dimension of industrial policy, although it may be obscured by politically motivated favours to interest groups, can foster cooperation between managements in line with national growth objectives recognised through interplays between corporate learning about macro issues and administrative learning about corporate planning. The most significant example of this integrative dimension is the extensive and very active Japanese process of industrial consultations under administrative guidance.[19] This illustrates that corporate policy learning interacting with administrative expertise in organising corporate plans on a macro scale can produce a highly functional macro-management culture, conducive to community formation. The German model, in which industrial policy functions are in effect assumed by national banks, is inferior because the opportunities for corporate learning on macro issues are relatively smaller, and because there is considerable administrative remoteness from corporate decision making.[20] The degree of integration attained in the German system however indicates a major potential for industrial cooperation with Japan.

Whether the integrative logic of industrial policy can be actualised in strongly pluralistic states is uncertain. Individualistic cultures in those states hinder social cooperation and tend to be sources of problems of governance more serious than those in the more integrated states. Political favours to support groups tend to impart dysfunctional biases to policy that perpetuate an atmosphere of aggressively competitive interest representation. Where industrial policy measures are adopted there is emphasis on providing subsidies to firms, even without significant growth prospects, rather than on fostering cooperation between firms. Debates on industrial policy, moreover, tend to focus on the utility of subsidies instead of on the potential for promoting a higher level of integration in the business community. The rationale for subsidies is significant, as has been evident from their use in the initial stages of Japan's export drive, and from the advantages gained indirectly through defense contracts by American aircraft companies, but there are examples of wasted subsidies. For harmonious trade cooperation, moreover, administrative avoidance of subsidies is, in general, desirable. The alternative tends to be administrative competition in the provision of grants that cause strains in trading relationships and that increase political favouritism in national policies.[21]

The significance of subsidies is generally understood with reference to the competitive aspects of industrial policy, and these are also evident where there is emphasis on the efficiency effects of business cooperation promoted through such policy. Problems of market failure however can be open to resolution through industrial policy measures. These can provide certain types of public goods that are not to be expected from the operation of market forces in totally competitive environments. Administrative promotion of cooperation between firms and of the vertical learning processes between government agencies and corporations can result in the public good of a social partnership. Information costs and transaction costs and risks that would tend to hinder diverse forms of collaboration between firms are thus substantially reduced, while encouragement is given to managerial innovation. To the extent that business cooperation develops in conjunction with corporate policy learning and responsiveness to administrative guidance, moreover, there can be restraints on the growth and exploitation of oligopoly power, with respect for the interests of small and medium sized firms, as has been evident in the Japanese pattern of industrial, banking, and marketing structures. Greater understanding of these public goods aspects of industrial policy could well activate endeavours by corporate and administrative leaders in the strongly pluralistic states to promote broad acceptance of the rationale for government sponsored business collaboration, but with emphasis on the general rejection of subsidies as methods of administrative support.

The public goods aspects of industrial policy at the national level point to international public goods attainable through industrial cooperation. The potential for a common industrial policy is evident in the European Community, despite the problems that affect its political feasibility, and on a more ambitious scale Trilateral industrial cooperation can be envisaged. The basic activity would be consultative, linking the national processes of cooperation through international business associations and structures for cooperation between governments. Complementary concepts of optimum national economic structures and optimum structural interdependencies could thus begin to guide planning by clusters of corporations and the concerting of administrative endeavours. There would be dangers of bias because of the leverage available to large states and the influence that could be exerted by transnational enterprises, but these dangers could be reduced by the formation of international structures to engage with the larger tasks of comprehensive collective management.

Tasks of industrial restructuring, necessitated by technological progress, would be undertaken more effectively with the wide ranging industrial co-operation that can be advocated with a public goods perspective. Restructuring requirements are considered only as competitive necessities in much of the policy literature, but in a public goods perspective broadly cooperative industrial restructuring can be seen as a process which can enhance general growth prospects, in a context of international community formation, through consensually planned complementarity.[22] Ongoing competition, in such a setting, would be managed cooperatively, as has become possible to a significant degree in Japan, without loss of the thrust for achievement that competition can provide, and with the addition of the impetus for performance that task oriented cooperation can generate.

Technology Cooperation

Questions of technological cooperation are linked with issues of industrial collaboration, because integrative efforts to coordinate if not harmonise industrial policies will require supporting research and development endeavours, and present competitive trends in the management of industrial policies are causing greater competition between governments to promote and diffuse technological advances for the benefit of their national and international firms. In this technological competition the more integrated political economies, notably Japan and Germany, have advantages because the cohesion in their administrative–industrial complexes is conducive to innovation and to the retention of advanced technology that would otherwise spread rapidly to trading rivals. Such states can negotiate from relatively strong positions on questions of technology sharing, and their firms can be similarly advantaged in arranging joint ventures and linkages with foreign enterprises. Of the less integrated advanced states however the USA benefits from superior capacities for fundamental research, despite slower processes for the commercial utilisation of new technology, and lower overall levels of investment in nonmilitary research and development.[23]

Advanced technologies for industrial use are being introduced mainly by transnational enterprises. Through intensive large scale research and development, made possible by their vast resources, their competitive advantages are being enhanced, to the detriment of firms virtually confined to operations in smaller markets, although in Japan and Germany their disadvantages are less serious than those of such firms in the USA. Joint ventures and linkages between transnational enterprises result in considerable technology sharing, on terms reflecting negotiating strengths and calculations about potential benefits. Administrative influence exercised from the home economy is evident mainly in the activities of Japanese multinationals. There is little official US involvement, except for defense related reasons, because of the liberal emphasis on aloofness from industry and commerce.

The importance of advanced technology for competitiveness causes managements of international firms to guard against diffusion of the results of their research and development. These tend to be shared only under carefully negotiated arrangements with enterprises of equivalent standing, in terms of industrial advancement and market strength. As international legal mechanisms for enforcement are lacking the negotiated arrangements are conditioned by uncertainties about good faith and future performance. If a firm belongs to an integrated political economy in which there is active administrative guidance however it can operate with security, as any partner in a joint venture or linkage will lose credit with a very large community of organisations if it defaults. The advantages enjoyed by a firm identified with an integrated political economy, moreover, will tend to be cumulative. The development and utilisation of advanced technology, aided by broadly collaborative research, facilitate further research and development, and benefit from increased market shares gained through enhanced productivity. For an international enterprise operating out of a less integrated political economy the benefits of technological progress will of course also be cumulative, but less substantial and less secure. The retention of advanced technology is more difficult, because of generally lower levels of enterprise loyalty, and the funding of long term research and development tends to be hindered by pressures to maximise profits from one short term to the next. Those pressures necessitate continual productivity gains, but these are sought with relatively less reliance on technological advances and more on economising in labour costs.[24]

The contrasts in technological potential are evident mainly between Japan and the USA, but in the Trilateral pattern there are larger contrasts between these two states and the European Community. Technologically the Community as a whole lags behind the two leading industrialised democracies, and this affects the competitiveness of its firms in world markets and in its own market.[25] The capacity of the Community to play a leading role in the global political economy is thus in doubt because of uncertainties about its industrial growth as well as because of its difficulties in advancing toward the establishment of a stronger system of collective management. The need for a strong common industrial policy and a vigorous common technological endeavour is indeed urgent. Within the Community the superior German technological role will thus have to be transformed into a leading force for research and development throughout the grouping.

Market fragmentation in the Community, caused by nontariff barriers, has been the main reason for the technological lag.[26] Country specific factors have included the effects of the individualism in the French political economy, which has hindered the formation of sufficiently large firms and the development of a German style social partnership. Ideological cleavages have complicated the effects of this individualism and an outcome of the ideological conflicts has been the establishment of a large inefficient public sector. Britain's serious industrial decline has also contributed to the technological lag, and has been all the more detrimental because it has provided some of the motivation for British reluctance to support the drive toward European integration, and has thus tended to make the introduction of a common technology policy more difficult. German technological achievements have not been sufficiently diffused in the Community to compensate for the lack of progress in France, Britain, and the more backward member states. The large American corporate presence in the Community, moreover, has been a source of only moderate technological diffusion, in part because of the reluctance of many US firms to enter into joint ventures.[27] The expansion of the American corporate presence in response to full market integration is not altering the preferences of US managements for wholly owned subsidiaries, and to the extent that it drives weaker Community firms into declines it will slow the pace of overall European technological progress.

For efficiency and welfare in the international political economy, Trilateral technological cooperation is needed, with US and Japanese emphasis on assisting European research and development. This requirement need not conflict with expression of the Community's entitlement to a leading political role in the structuring of new forms of global economic cooperation. The US and Japanese contributions, moreover, need not hinder the development of a strong German technological leadership role within the Community. The opportunity for the Community is to evolve a comprehensive design for

Trilateral technological collaboration with features that will adequately reward US and Japanese firms in return for substantial contributions to industrial upgrading by European enterprises.

Without Community promotion and management of a comprehensive technological design European firms and member states will continue to make independent and uncoordinated responses to the challenges of US and Japanese firms in the Community market and outside. Because of the superior organisational, financial, and technological advantages of the US and Japanese enterprises the overall gap in competitiveness will tend to increase. As this becomes evident the Europeans may resort to protectionist measures and take discriminatory actions against foreign direct investment, without, however, developing the political will to implement common industrial and technology policies.[28] Trilateral technological cooperation will then be very difficult to promote. Since the Community's need for this is very great, and since its political leadership will be essential, there is a challenge to undertake long range planning that can provide a basis for Community initiatives as soon as possible. The longer a comprehensive Community response is delayed the greater will be the technological lag that will have to be remedied, and the greater will be the danger that Atlantic frictions over trade and direct investment issues will become more serious. The European Commission and managements of the larger European transnational enterprises have begun to recognise the dimensions of the technology problem, and have helped to initiate modest cooperative research and development endeavours, but have not yet attempted comprehensive engagement with the tasks of upgrading the capacities of Community firms.

The encouragement of Japanese technology cooperation and direct investment in the Community, which would accord with the immediate interests of European firms, would have to be given prominence in a Community sponsored Trilateral technological design. This should be emphasised because of the willingness of Japanese managements to enter into joint ventures and also because of the need for European firms to learn from Japanese methods of introducing new technology into industrial processes at a fast pace. With more active Japanese corporate involvement in the European economy it would be possible for Community decision makers and managers to learn more about processes of administrative guidance that have aided aided growth in Japan. Business and official support for the development of a common Community industrial policy could then increase.

Functional Linkages

Efforts by governments to cooperate with each other on trade, foreign direct investment, industrial, and technology matters have direct and indirect consequences that spread across these areas and that accordingly oblige consistency. The independent activities of firms however can thwart consistent policy mixes, and this possibility increases the significance of relative degrees of integration in national political economies, to the extent that management cooperation with administrative preferences is fostered. For a strongly pluralistic state that allows wide scope for corporate autonomy consistency across areas of economic policy – if it can be attained – may not promise satisfactory results. Agreements to cooperate, then, can be entered into with reservations.

The functional linkages are especially apparent with respect to trade and foreign direct investment, since transnational production substitutes for exports. Some of the major objectives of protectionist trade measures can be obstructed by a liberal foreign direct investment policy. An industrial policy intended to support the growth purposes of a protectionist trade policy will have to be aided by a restrictive foreign direct investment policy, yet this may hinder expected technology transfers. In the absence of industrial and technology policies firms may be disadvantaged in a liberal trade setting, and their lack of competitiveness may open the way for sectoral penetration by outside enterprises taking advantage of a liberal foreign direct investment policy.

Consistency within a mix of trade, foreign direct investment, industrial, and technology policies depends on the coordination of policy communities. In this respect Japan and West Germany are significantly advantaged, because of levels of integration and qualities of macromanagement. Aggressive penetration of foreign markets, with restraints on imports, is facilitated by industrial and technology measures supporting national firms, and these measures in varying degrees discriminate against inward foreign direct investment. National firms, especially in the Japanese case, tend to respond to administrative wishes, and foreign firms that have located in these states have incentives to respond also. Difficulties of policy coordination in the USA, however, allow foreign firms to overcome its protectionist barriers by manufacturing in the United States, while in effect permitting national firms to respond very actively to opportunities for export substitution, thus contributing to trade imbalances.[29] Industrial and technology measures, because of a military bias, are of little aid to American firms with limited resources that must serve overseas markets through exports, although the activities of these firms are especially significant for the trade balance.

Consistency in the context of cooperation between states is difficult to achieve, especially where integrated policies interact with less consistent policies that have differing orientations. The most serious problems in developing a coherent pattern of cooperation between a national group of integrated policies and a national group of less consistent policies have been evident in the Japan–US relationship, and there the incompatibilities have tended to motivate increasing use of bargaining leverage by the United States, as the disadvantaged party. This leverage has not fostered policy convergence and has not been accompanied by endeavours to attain greater consistency in the USA's policies.[30] The strains that have been caused, moreover, have added to uncertainties resulting from the interplay of the two differing groups of policies.

Institutionalised pressure for consistency operates in the European Community, through the activities of the European Commission, to the extent that its advocacy role is given support by the member states through the Council of Ministers. Consistency between and within national economic policies is required increasingly under the Commission's coordinating functions as market integration continues, and is generally accepted because of endorsement of the rationale for integration. Disparities in the spread of gains from full market integration can be expected to pose problems at a later stage as member governments seek to protect and strengthen the positions of national firms. Conflicts between national measures and what have been common policies will then have to be resolved, and there may be inconsistencies in the national measures because of administrative efforts to cope with diverse demands from affected industries. If the Community's structures are able to foster the development of sufficiently integrated and broadly functional trade, foreign direct investment, industrial, and technology policies, however, dynamic growth will be possible.

The absence of sufficiently functional linkages between the USA's trade and foreign direct investment policies is a source of destabilising problems in Atlantic and also Pacific relations. The growth objectives of US trade policy are hindered by the very strong emphasis which firms place on export substitution, in response to clearly excessive incentives for outward direct investment. US policy communities will probably not engage with this problem, because of the extent to which US international firms can influence legislators. The European Community will thus have to face continued pressures from the United States for increased market access while American firms devote greater resources to export substitution in response to the Community's opportunities for foreign direct investment. The US trade pressures, as at present, will be accompanied by demands for liberal Community treatment of American firms operating in Europe. At the same time the USA's rather obscured fiscal problems caused by the revenue losses associated with export substitution will continue to have adverse indirect effects on Atlantic trade relations, especially by obligating efforts to earn trade surpluses through which US foreign debts can be repaid. In the Pacific context, meanwhile, the size of the US overall trade deficit will probably contribute even more to the growth of hostility toward Japan, although the persistence of that overall deficit will be due, increasingly, to export substitution in the Atlantic context, as well as to Japanese competitiveness, and also to the greater share of exports, rather than transnational production, in Japan's foreign economic relations.[31]

The systemic significance of the USA's macromanagement problems is very great, because of the size of the US economy, the degree to which its firms are becoming footloose multinationals, and the extent to which these firms are engaged in transnational production processes that have growth, employment, and inflation effects over which the US and foreign governments have little control. The global trade and production shares of these firms are increasing, especially because of their expansion in the European Community. Because of their great efficiencies, but also because of their capacities to gain oligopolistic strength in world markets, these firms can induce cooperation from governments and profit from rivalry between governments. Their managerial, technological and financial capacities however make them appropriate partners for governments, in so far as governments have responsibilities for national and international public goods. The extent to which these firms are shaping and linking national economic structures, and altering structural interdependencies, moreover, obligates comprehensive cooperation between national administrations, hopefully with many firms in supportive roles.[32]

Japanese international firms, as the principal rivals of the American multinationals, have systemic significance relating to trade and foreign direct investment policies which makes collaborative macromanagement all the more necessary. Because these firms constitute a rather well integrated global corporate presence that is rapidly expanding, the imperatives for cooperation between host governments are in some respects more evident than they are in the cases of US firms. The superior competitive strengths of the Japanese enterprises threaten host country firms, but Japanese managements, while more open to joint ventures, are more oriented toward stable long term relationships with host economies. The continuous tasks of restructuring and adjusting to strains, necessary in each advanced state, tend to be managed more effectively by Japanese firms, especially because of the adaptability resulting from managerial bonds with their work forces and responsiveness to host country public policy concerns.[33] Host governments can compete in offering inducements to attract Japanese direct investment, but collaboration between these governments and the Japanese administration is needed to ensure a significant degree of collective accountability that can match the expanding Japanese integrated corporate presence.

Increasing nationalism in trade, foreign direct investment, industrial and technology policies is in general a force for consistency at the state level but by hindering cooperation between governments it tends to cause vicious circles in which resentments at failures in cooperation increase expressions of nationalism in policy and thus cause further resentments, while having negative growth effects which increase domestic pressures for more nationalistic policies. This danger is commonly recognised in literature on trade policy, but the enlightened prescriptions for trade liberalisation which are then made usually ignore questions of cooperation on foreign direct investment, and on industrial and technology issues. What is required, however, raises very fundamental questions about the domestic dimensions of the cooperation that is needed, and the extent to which these have to be linked transnationally, for broadly representative and functional collaboration. Internationalised interest representation is necessary, through a system of corporatism operating above the state level, so that cooperation between governments will be responsive transnationally, as well as mutually. In the absence of a system of international corporatism Governments will tend to remain responsive only to their domestic patterns of interest representation, and these, while not being responsive to similar patterns in other states, can frequently be dominated by producer interests seeking administrative favours at the expense of foreign economic groups. Domestic solutions to this problem are possible, but it is likely to be more serious, and more difficult, when the vulnerabilities of interdependence are felt because of imports that are especially competitive.

Questions of harmonising foreign direct investment policies and making them compatible with trade cooperation demand attention because intrafirm trade and trade related to multinational linkages is a large and increasing proportion of the commerce between advanced states.[34] While domestic political demands on trade issues tend to be more forceful than those on foreign direct investment matters, moreover, the substitution of transnational production for exports continues on a large scale, in line with corporate decisions influenced by administrative measures shaped in policy processes more elitist than those dealing with trade matters. Foreign direct investment policy can thus diverge more from trade policy, and the kinds of divergence *between* foreign direct investment policies can evidence competition to attract international firms – competition that may be aided or hindered by trade policy. Cooperation to liberalise trade can be accompanied by endeavours to guide or restrict foreign direct investment. Such endeavours may be restrained by and mixed with efforts to attract such investment. Yet to the extent that national firms are seen to be facing competition through trade and transnational production there are likely to be attempts to enhance the capacities of those firms through industrial and technology policies.

Within the European Community, before the current drive for complete market integration, the vulnerabilities of interdependence after the initial processes of trade liberalisation activated producer groups to press for industrial and technology measures that would increase national competitiveness. The same general tendency is apparent in the international political economy, where governments respond to internal demands by attempts to help upgrade the capacities of their firms in a less and less liberal world trading system, thus in effect balancing modified trade cooperation with microeconomic competition. With the continuing rises in structural interdependencies, however, imperatives to realise the international public good of harmonising if not integrating industrial and technology policies become more evident. This is required for equity in the spread of gains from trade. It is also required for equity in the spread of gains from transnational production, and in this respect the importance of linking cooperation on foreign direct investment issues with trade and industrial and technology collaboration deserves special emphasis.

8. Planning Comprehensive Collective Management

Exploration of the complex structural and policy as well as systemic inter-dependencies between the major industrialised democracies indicates that the vast transnational spread of benefits and costs from commerce and transnational production is internationalising the basic responsibilities of governments, although these obligations are not being sufficiently accepted. The logic of organised specialisation to increase gains from trade is applied on a vast scale by enterprises, especially those operating globally, but the results, although substantially beneficial, evidence inefficiencies and inequities due to imbalances between cooperation and competition, between managements, and between managements and governments. Failures in cooperation between governments, and failures by governments in domestic management, are also involved. Large scale requirements to improve, concert, and integrate policies can be seen, together with imperatives to enlist the collaboration of managements. If these needs can be met, high order international public goods will be provided, hopefully through global and regional institutions that will sustain their production.

Recognition of the logic of integration which has begun to operate in the international political economy however is generally not strong enough to have a major influence on policy. Understanding of this logic tends to be hindered by literature for political leaders and managers which stresses tasks to enhance national competitiveness, and the need to give priority to sound domestic management. The literature urging measures for increased competitiveness is especially significant in the United States, because of widespread concerns about losses of shares in world markets by American exporting firms, and about foreign penetration of the domestic market. Administrative and legislative attitudes thus tend to focus on what are seen as endangered US interests. Within the European Community there are also concerns about national competitiveness, and, although these are given much less publicity, they reflect awareness of problems more serious than those of US decision makers. Policy advice urging sound domestic management receives less publicity and attention, in both the USA and the European Community members, but it has some influence, especially because of the emphasis by economic advisors that international economic cooperation may amount to collaborative manipulation of political business cycles by governments seeking reelection.

The literature on competitiveness includes warnings that states can cheat and otherwise violate international commitments, especially when their admin-istrations have strong links with their national firms. The emphasis on potential gains from greater competitiveness, meanwhile, appeals to the petty nationalism often cultivated by politicians. This nationalism is also encouraged by some political scientists who, claiming to be realists, argue that each state seeks only to increase its power and wealth – although this is often stated without implying that all government leaders are authoritarian personalities. The petty nationalism can be manipulated in political business cycles, especially by linking interest group and constituency concerns with national ambitions for larger roles in global commerce.

Petty nationalism is a factor in the larger context of *problems of advanced political development*. In the leading industrialised democracies the most important of these problems is the dependence of ruling groups on political exchange processes that in varying degrees conflict with requirements for sound domestic management and international economic cooperation. Persistent failures to observe fiscal responsibility in the USA are the most prominent examples of problems of advanced political development. International economic co-operation however cannot be deferred until problems of advanced political development are overcome. Although these are fundamental difficulties, co-operative ventures have to be launched, in view of the large interdependencies that demand management. The ventures have to be planned to activate new forms of neofunctional logic, drawing on the current experience of the European Community. They can be planned, moreover, in ways that increase learning experiences, elite socialisation processes, and external accountability, in line with the real international and transnational responsibilities that governments have to accept.

Forecasting

On present indications, the structural, policy, and systemic interdependencies in the upper layers of the international political economy will continue to increase, principally because of the independent activities of multinational firms.[1] Governmental involvement in this process, through forms of administrative guidance and support, will be evident mainly in the more integrated national political economies, especially Japan and Germany, and in those cases will reflect neomercantilist orientations. More remote and less active administrative involvement, in effect allowing wider scope for the activities of international enterprises, will remain a feature of the USA's foreign economic relations. American firms that move into international operations will continue to become footloose, while by substituting overseas production for exports, on a large scale, they will contribute to further US trade deficits and losses of tax revenue.

Imperatives for collaborative management of the growing interdependencies can be expected to become more evident, despite concerns with competitiveness, because of increasing strains in the international trading and monetary systems, attributable primarily to unresolved macromanagement problems in the USA. Continued US trade deficits will adversely affect national growth and make repayments of the country's large foreign debts more difficult, while sustaining pressures for the adoption of protectionist measures. Financial markets, meanwhile, will be threatened more seriously by conflicting pressures on the

US dollar, some of which will be related to uncertainties affecting business confidence in the United States.

The responses of the principal industrialised democracies to the imperatives for cooperation will probably be inadequate. The USA will remain entitled to a leadership role, but fulfillment of such a role will tend to be increasingly difficult because of the accumulated effects of macromanagement problems. These give policy processes an inward looking character, increase domestic conflicts, and generate pressures to externalise costs of adjustment. The difficulties of constructive engagement with external tasks become apparent to foreign decision makers and discourage trust. The European Community's deepening integration process will prepare it for global leadership, but meanwhile that process will take up most of the attention of decision makers in its larger states. Japan, meanwhile, will be given little genuine American or European encouragement to provide leadership in the international political economy. The perceived policy orientations of major trading partners will tend to strengthen the economic nationalism at the basis of Japan's neomercantilism.

Similarities in policy styles suggest that there will be significant possibilities for policy learning in Japanese–German interactions, subject mainly to German initiatives, but subject also to French and other European recognition of important economic benefits attainable through cooperation with Japan. Euro–Japanese cooperation, with leadership coming mainly from Germany, could become a potent force for Trilateral economic cooperation, but this would require enlightened moderation of the influence of economic nationalism on each side.

While uncertainties persist about the potential for Euro–Japanese cooperation, stresses in the US–Japan relationship will probably become more serious.[2] While efforts are made to reduce the US fiscal deficit, overall US dependence on Japanese financing of an important part of the nation's borrowing needs will become much larger. The danger of a drastic shift in the preferences of Japanese investors will be an increasing but frustrating constraint on US leverage against Japan for wider market access. At the same time the expansion of Japanese commerce with and transnational production in the European Community and in Third World areas may gradually reduce Japanese vulnerability to US pressures based on controlled access to the US market. Meanwhile gains in competitiveness by Japanese firms will tend to make resolution of the bilateral trade problems more difficult. The marked contrasts in policy styles, moreover, will continue to hinder the development of understanding and goodwill. Mutual accountability and socialisation factors that can aid cooperative policy learning in the Atlantic context will remain less significant in this Pacific relationship. Crude political journalism in the USA will no doubt assist the efforts of politicians advocating increased restrictions on Japanese imports.

The lack of cooperation between the leading industrialised democracies will adversely affect Third World growth prospects. The East Asian Newly Industrialising Countries, heavily dependent on the US market, will encounter difficulties in their efforts to diversify their trade because of European and Japanese protectionism. The larger debt burdened Latin American states will have to cope with Trilateral trade barriers that will hinder export expansion needed for the repayment of outstanding foreign loans. Their efforts to shift from import substituting to export oriented industrialisation will be affected, and the stresses in their foreign economic relations will limit opportunities for collaboration through which European and other Trilateral assistance could be given for improvement of their administrative functions. In the rest of the Third World, and especially in Africa, growth financed through commodity exports will remain slow, and the development of manufacturing for export, while hampered by dependence on the sales of primary products, will continue to be hindered by Trilateral protectionism.

Economic reforms in the East European states and the USSR, and the integration of these nations into the international political economy, will not be aided sufficiently while the principal industrialised democracies fail to cooperate to the degree required by their interdependencies. By in effect restricting each other's growth and remaining absorbed in their trade and investment disputes the major Trilateral administrations will continue to limit their resources for constructive Eastern policies. The reforming Socialist states will be challenged to bargain, with weak assets, for consideration of their trading interests by the competing Trilateral states, instead of being offered broad collaboration for rapid rehabilitation and development. Since there is a danger that power in the USSR may shift to conservative elements determined to restabilise its system the importance of evolving an integrated and comprehensive Trilateral design for cooperation with the reforming Socialist states deserves much emphasis.

Principles of Cooperation

In view of what can be projected from current policy orientations and failures to collaborate, contributions to the streams of advice for decision makers in the leading Trilateral states must stress principles which obligate international economic cooperation. These are principles of *extended accountability*, as governments have to accept transnational responsibilities because of the effects of their policies on foreign producers and consumers, on account of the proliferation of structural interdependencies. The public goods of sound domestic management have to be linked with the international public goods of sound collective management. Formal accountability to domestic communities tends to obscure the moral obligations of extended accountability, although governments move increasingly into informal relationships with international firms that involve exchanges of understandings and commitments relating to terms of entry and expansion, as well as to trade and infrastructure development. The concept of extended accountability goes beyond this area of transnational interaction to refer to externalities affecting entire communities.[3] It also covers responsibilities to domestic groups whose interests are closely linked with foreign producers and consumers.

The concept of extended accountability is implicit in reform oriented international political economy literature. This literature is mostly ignored by national decision makers, because of its weak influence on public opinion, but the concept is at the basis of moral imperatives for cooperation whose neglect has extensive domestic and foreign effects. Questions of equity are involved, because communities lacking transnational interest representation have to accept the consequences of decisions by foreign governments. Efficiency issues are also involved, because policies influenced by economic nationalism amount to rejections of opportunities for collaborative specialisation. The questions of equity and efficiency however are complicated by the operations of firms. There has to be accountability to national and international enterprises that have become dependent on established policies, but corporate responsiveness also has to be considered, especially where high levels of autonomy are being gained through the avoidance of host and home country regulatory measures.[4]

Extended accountability is a government responsibility resulting from the evolution of integration logic, and becomes a responsibility for guiding that evolution. Integration logic applied in enterprises, through vertical and horizontal expansion as well as through diversification, imposes stable organised specialisation with administered prices in place of contracts between separate agents, thus changing numerous market functions and providing comprehensive new market functions with greatly increased market power. To maximise profits, however, market power can be used to restrict output, raise prices, and obstruct the entry of other firms. Market power may thus be increased, reducing overall efficiency and equity. Alternatively, there may be prolonged and indecisive competition between firms, involving increases in efficiency and perhaps in equity but with inefficiencies and inequities related to restrictive business practices. A further possibility is that the competition may be subjected to administrative regulation, with or without a supporting consensus among the managements of firms. The regulatory process may aim simply at a rough balance between contending enterprises, or it may be intended to build a diversified and integrated national economy, an optimum national economic structure. Enhanced competitiveness in global markets may be in view, or there may be a higher purpose, related to the provision of high order international public goods.

Improving the quality of organised specialisation at the national level is tending to become less and less feasible without international cooperation, because of the extent to which firms have implemented the logic of integration on a global scale. National administrations are beginning to lack the economic sovereignty necessary for the building of optimum economic structures, despite the pressures to increase national competitiveness. National economic identities are being blurred, and any industrial sector intended to benefit from measures for enhanced competitiveness is likely to include subsidiaries of foreign enterprises as well as local firms operating in linkages with such enterprises. The trend however is uneven, and it is less evident in states which had become highly integrated political economies before the contemporary large scale internationalisation of business. In such states, and especially in Japan, the level of integration tends to be sustained by cultural and political factors, although it also tends to be weakened by joint ventures and linkages entered into by national firms moving into global operations. It can be argued that the less integrated national political economies need international economic cooperation more than the highly integrated states, especially as these are able to operate with greater competitiveness. These higher performing states, however, depend on the willingness of the former states to keep their economies relatively open.

Questions of economic cooperation between governments are now becoming more urgent because integration logic at the enterprise level is being implemented at a more advanced stage through multinational consortia, for collaborative domination of global markets. These consortia greatly increase the dimensions of issues encountered by governments in their concerns with competitiveness and the building of optimum national economic structures.[5] The economic sovereignty of the more integrated states is affected as well as that of their less integrated trading partners. The appropriate response may seem to be more active expression of economic nationalism, through strategies for enhanced competitiveness. Imperatives to serve the international common interest, however, in line with the concept of extended accountability, have to be affirmed.

The high order international public goods that must be provided are understanding, trust, and goodwill between governments, for comprehensive collective management. Providing these goods requires considerate treatment of the interests of other states, in the context of structural interdependencies, with emphasis on collaborative regulation of the activities of international firms. The necessary building of trust can be viewed as an international replication of the social organisation of trust in the Japanese political economy.[6] The development of goodwill, through reciprocal affirmation of shared values related to extended accountability, is essential for the building of an international community of political and economic elites. In such a community, a political culture for the support of international economic structures can be established. The importance of developing such a culture must be stressed because the necessary collective management must be comprehensive, on account of the dimensions of each state's structural interdependencies, and must also be discretionary. A further reason is that there must be unity of purpose between government leaders, with mostly generalist skills, and officials, as well as representatives of interest groups, whose roles as specialists tend to set them apart from the generalists.

In a perspective which relativises or excludes considerations of international justice and other moral concerns governments can be seen simply as ruling groups striving to consolidate their power through political exchange methods that maximise benefits for influential sections of their constituencies. The functional needs of an industrialised state however cannot be met without certain moral qualities at the macromanagement level. There is a need, a public interest requirement, for high level decision making directed toward public goods, and not merely the retention of office for private benefit. This type of obligation has been affirmed in policy literature opposing the common tendency for political leaders to seek broad popular support through distributional measures that increase government debt burdens for future generations. A new dimension of extended accountability can thus be seen. In this context, the requirement to institutionalise restraints on deficit spending has been emphasised by some political economists, in terms which have implied moral obligations to observe those restraints even though their rejection could be politically beneficial for a ruling political groups seeking to retain power.[7]

The principles of comprehensive collective management relate to problems of development in the international political economy. These are matters of political integration, in which loyalties that have moved in the past from parochial to national levels must now move to regional communities and global institutions. With this kind of international political advancement there must be solutions for problems of participation in collective management. These solutions clearly must be based on processes of transnational interest aggregation, and on arrangements for the involvement of national administrations as equals, rather than on the basis of relative bargaining strengths. This can be affirmed with reference to the importance which equality of participation has assumed for the integration process of the European Community.

For participation in collective decision making and implementation there must be institutions. While these will have to be structured to ensure adequate representation, they will also have to be functional, for the exercise of collective administrative expertise. The two needs can be met through provisions for transnational interest representation and for the establishment of common bureaucratic structures patterned on the European Commission. Regionalised, Trilateral, and global institutions for transnational interest aggregation are needed. Through interactions with these, bureaucratic organisations at the same levels would be able to relate effectively to the cooperating governmental leaders, providing guidance for collective decision making. While this guidance would have a representative quality, it would also be functional, in line with general interests, as has become possible to a considerable extent in the operations of the European Commission.

Balance between the differing levels of collective management would be essential, especially to prevent overloading of the global structures. The formation of regional communities of states will be a primary requirement, and for the development of these much leadership can be hoped for from the European Community. Collective management at the regional level is the most extensive way in which the logic of integration can be implemented by governments, to correspond with the application of that logic by firms. Regulation of the global operations of firms will require cooperation between regional systems of collective management, and collaboration at the global level that can give support and guidance to the processes of cooperation between regions.

Structuring Cooperation

Political designing in line with the main principles of international economic cooperation can derive guidance from the experience of the European Community, and from the achievements of the more integrated national political economies, principally Japan and Germany. The European experience has indicated the importance of consensus in elite networks, the necessity of transnational interest representation, the need for intergovernmental inter-actions, and the vital roles that can be played by institutions for collective decision making.[8] The Japanese and German political economies have demonstrated how cooperative orientations in national cultures can facilitate interest aggregation with a strongly functional orientation, the building of effective institutions, and the organisation of systems of guided cooperative capitalism.

The formation of elite communities united across national boundaries on principles of international economic cooperation becomes possible with frequent conferences, and can be given impetus by collaborative ventures expressing the logic of integration. The initial drive to form the European Community came from a network of dedicated elites who intended the successes of an elementary stage of integration to lead to the development of a community with a strong basis in societal loyalties. A reciprocal relationship thus developed between economic integration processes and societal integration processes. The dominant commitments concerned high order public goods, and similar commitments will be required in future regional, Trilateral, and global networks of elites working for comprehensive collective management. Such elites will not be mediocre rational utility maximisers or economic nationalists of the kind depicted in 'realist' literature on international affairs. The collaborative ventures to be planned will have to offer the benefits of initial stages of economic integration, but with consensus that these must lead to further advances if destabilising inequalities are to be prevented.

Transnational interest aggregation will have to be planned for, as a source for guidance of the collaborative ventures, to give a representative character to the neofunctional logic which they will express. Transnational interest aggregation can help give institutional expression to the concept of extended accountability, so that cooperating governments will be responsive not only to their domestic constituencies but also to patterns of interest representation extending across national boundaries. The development of regionalised interest groups in the European Community and their interactions with the European Commission have indicated how extended accountability can help to orient governments more toward integrative cooperation. Broader transnational interest representation however can be possible through a regional elected assembly, as has been demonstrated by the European Parliament, despite its current limitations, which will have to be overcome as the European integration process continues.[9]

For the structuring of international economic cooperation under the leadership of the major industrialised democracies some arrangements for Trilateral interest aggregation will have to be planned. An organisation comprising representatives of Trilateral Chambers of Commerce and delegates from the European Parliament, the US Congress, and the Japanese Diet can be suggested. If a Pacific Economic Community is established, comprising the market economy states of East Asia and North America, with Australia and New Zealand, the Trilateral arrangements could be broadened into a partnership between the European and Pacific groupings. Representatives from these two regional communities could then constitute the formative elements of a new system of global economic institutions.

The promotion of Trilateral intergovernmental interactions would appropriately complement the development of transnational interest aggregation on a Trilateral scale, to broaden the perspectives of officials and increase their understandings of extended accountability, as well as to bring working level expertise to bear on issues of economic cooperation. Intergovernmentalism can assist the growth of transnational elite networks and processes of transnational interest aggregation. It can also contribute to policy learning at the executive level, through the upward transmission of ideas and advice that narrow departmentalism would otherwise exclude. All these benefits have been evident in the European Community, but there has been little development of intergovernmentalism through matching interactions between government agencies in the Atlantic context, or in US–Japan relations. The growth of intergovernmental exchanges can be aided when officials are drawn into the conferences of elite networks, but depends very much on encouragement from each executive level. In the European Community its growth was for a considerable period the result of misguided efforts by member governments to bypass the European Commission. The strengthened role of the Commission in the current drive toward a higher level of integration however has given new impetus and direction to intergovernmental consultations.

In the Trilateral context, and hopefully at a later stage in a Euro–Pacific context, linking the European Community with a Pacific Community, the most important intergovernmental exchanges would be between Germany, the USA, and Japan. The quality of these exchanges would to a considerable extent influence the degrees to which integrative approaches to cooperation would develop at the highest levels. The presence of a large number of transient political appointees in the upper branches of the US administration however would tend to limit the longer term potential of the interchanges, and would make their utility depend to a significant degree on presidential initiative. On the Japanese side the presence of permanent officials at all bureaucratic levels would be a great advantage, as it would be in Germany, and the strong influence of the senior personnel in policy making would add to the utility of the intergovernmental exchanges. Intense and somewhat narrow departmental task orientations would affect the participation of the Japanese officials, but these personnel would profit from learning experiences incidental to the intergovernmental consultations.

Planning for the establishment of collective decision making structures would have to be linked with the designing of community forming processes intended to develop through intergovernmentalism, transnational interest aggregation, and elite networks. The decision making structures could be set up progressively, with an initial stage at which a common advisory body could be formed. This could be a Trilateral Council of Economic Advisors, charged with presenting proposals for economic cooperation to the Council of Ministers in the European Community, the US administration, and the Japanese Cabinet. After the establishment of a Pacific Economic Community a reconstituted Council of Economic Advisors could relate to a Euro–Pacific Ministerial Council.

A Trilateral Council of Economic Advisors, planned to evolve into a Euro–Pacific Council, could assist the formation of, and begin to relate to, Trilateral Chambers of Commerce. Proposals to the Trilateral governments, and, later, to a Euro–Pacific Ministerial Council, would thus assume a representative quality. The Trilateral governments therefore would not interact only on the basis of their own perceived interests in economic cooperation but would be challenged to respond to the proposals of the economic advisors, advanced on the basis of common interests. Of course the Council of Economic Advisors could be ineffectual because of internal disputes or weak task orientation, or because of the unwillingness of governments to accept it in an advocacy role. The members of the Council would probably have to be appointed by the national administrations, in concert, but not all the decisions might be made in good faith. The activities of the Trilateral Chambers of Commerce and other groups however could help to strengthen the capabilities and the commitments of the Economic Advisors. This can be suggested in view of the cooperation between European business groups and the European Commission in the current drive for deepening integration within the European Community, although the European Commission has a much stronger role than that which can be envisaged for a Trilateral Council of Economic Advisors.[10]

Over the longer term, the proposed group of advisors could evolve into a structure similar to the European Commission. This would require the development of strong commitments to cooperation by the participating governments, and sustained pressure from the various organisations involved in transnational interest representation. The attitudes of the participating governments would no doubt depend mainly on the benefits derived from collaborative ventures related to market integration and complementary industrial development. The characteristics of the structure evolved for collective decision making by those governments would also be a factor. A Ministerial body with a unanimity rule would seem to be appropriate, but more important than this rule would be the kind of political culture that would sustain the collective decision making. Integrative rather than aggressively bargained cooperation would be needed to ensure equitable distribution of the benefits from trade, industrial, and investment cooperation.

At the global level, the Trilateral structures, evolving hopefully into Euro–Pacific structures, would have to assume North–South dimensions. The formation of regional economic communities in Third World areas would have to be encouraged, despite the failures of such ventures thus far. Strong influence would have to be exerted by the major Trilateral states to foster reform in the numerous corrupt, incompetent, and oppressive authoritarian Third World regimes, and to promote cooperation between those which have been restructured. The virtual imposition of external accountability, through economic pressures and inducements, is necessary in the interests of their peoples, especially as these peoples can do little to free themselves from exploitation. Collusion between the oppressive regimes and foreign firms, especially to violate the rights of workers, will have to be eliminated, and remedial action through Trilateral Chambers of Commerce will hopefully assist this task. Debt relief will have to be offered to many of the Third World regimes, especially the heavily burdened ones in Latin America, but without external pressure for political reform considerable portions of the aid will simply increase administrative corruption and facilitate purchases of foreign military equipment.

Sufficiently representative Third World regional economic organisations will have to be offered cooperation by the leading Trilateral states in structures designed to function above the regional level. Initially, an enlarged and more active Organisation for Economic Cooperation and Development (OECD) could become the principal structure, fostering consultations between representatives of the European, Pacific, and Third World regional systems. The consultations could prepare the way for collective decision making on supraregional issues. The Trilateral and later Euro–Pacific structures that have been suggested could assist the expansion of OECD and the development of Third World regional communities to participate in the OECD's new global role.[11]

Multilevel Structures

With the formation of a Pacific and then Third World regional economic communities, commerce between members of those organisations would be managed through their collective decision making mechanisms. The General Agreement on Tarrifs and Trade could thus become a forum for trade negotiations between regional communities. For a more effective role in the evolving system of regional and global management however GATT could be transformed into a collective decision making organisation, with a strong secretariat that could assume independent surveillance and advocacy functions. Restraint could thus be imposed on the use of crude bargaining leverage for the settlement of trade issues between the regional communities. There would be a potential, moreover, for correcting sectoral bias introduced into trade negotiations by the pressures of interest groups in major states within the regional communities. The concerns of Third World regional communities could thus be given better consideration. Under the present GATT system all Third World countries are disadvantaged by exposure to the bargaining leverage of the large industrialised democracies, and by use of that leverage in ways that restrict export opportunities for their low technology manufactures.[12] Sympathy for the Third World states may be less than warranted, because of their serious political deficiencies, but political reforms in these states would still leave them vulnerable to trade discrimination by the advanced nations.

A reconstituted GATT in a regionalised world economy could function under an enlarged OECD. This would be desirable because the restructured OECD would have assumed broad responsibilities for collective management at the global level. But the collective regulation of trade – between regions – would have to be accompanied by collective management of the transnational production relationships which are assuming greater significance than arm's length trade as linkages between states, and which must be expected to have much significance as linkages between future regional communities. The restructured GATT could assume responsibility for promoting cooperation between regions on foreign direct investment issues. To take into account the interests of firms the GATT secretariat could interact extensively with international business associations that hopefully would be represented in the restructured OECD. Within the regional economic communities harmonised if not integrated industrial and foreign direct investment policies would ensure management of transnational production issues, thus allowing the new GATT to focus on the larger problems of cooperation resulting from cross regional direct investment. Firms implementing global production and marketing strategies would have to adjust to the combined concerns of regional decision making organisations about the development of optimum patterns of industrial capacity and optimum types and levels of structural interdependence in their communities. The collaboration which hopefully would result between managements, regional decision making organisations, and GATT, would be a high order international public good, conducive to general development, equity, and stability.

Monetary and financial cooperation within and between regional economic communities would be a further vital element in the emerging system of comprehensive collective management. The development of a system of monetary and financial management in the European Community could be followed by a similar system for the Pacific, and others for the Third World regional communities to be promoted under Trilateral sponsorship. The degree to which financial markets have already been globalised makes regional monetary and financial management all the more desirable, although it will be difficult. The present pattern of largely unregulated globalised financial markets, it must be stressed, has to be replaced by a more orderly system with a sound basis. A regionalised system coordinated under a global structure can be advocated, with a rationale founded in part on lessons to be drawn from the success of the European Monetary System in establishing a zone of monetary stability.[13] Because of the gravity of the problems of dollar instability and turbulence in world financial markets the regulatory structure that is needed will have to have a broad and secure foundation in the future regional communities, and their collaboration will have to be firmly established under an effective global organisation. This could be a reconstituted International Monetary Fund, operating with voting power shared equitably between the European Community, the United States, Japan, and representatives of the Third World regional communities. The US and Japanese participation could be replaced by that of a Pacific Community if such a grouping were established. The restructured IMF could function under the overall direction of the enlarged OECD.

Representative hierarchical expression of the logic of integration by collaborating governments is an inescapable international public goods requirement, in view of the increasing structural interdependencies of the world economy, especially those that are being shaped mainly by independent firms. The building of regional communities has to be provided for, to ensure that collective management processes will be sufficiently in touch with local realities and that such processes at the global level will not be overloaded.[14] Within the regional communities the structuring of collective decision processes will restrain the use of bargaining leverage by larger states and help to promote integrative collaboration. Through membership of regional communities, moreover, small states will be relatively protected against leverage by large states outside their communities, as well as by multinational firms seeking to exploit the needs of host countries.

Above the regional level structures for global collective management will be needed, to promote transregional cooperation, while representing the aggregated interests of regional communities. The collective decision making systems of these communities, then, will give expression to the concept of extended accountability upwards to the global level and downwards to their member states. The entire pattern, however, will be critically dependent on advances in political development at the national level, especially in the larger industrialised democracies. As these become postindustrial societies they may experience changes that increase their problems of advanced political development. The most dangerous changes are losses of commitment to what are often called traditional moral values, and the adoption of instrumental values, expressed in permissive life styles and manipulative political behaviour. The abuse of public office through political exchange practices that add heavily to government debt and necessitate crushing taxation are common effects of the social changes.[15] Urgent questions, therefore, have to be asked about the effects of education systems and general socialisation patterns on the influence of values in the advanced national political economies.

Elites working for a well structured system of collective management however can provide new forms of inspiration to government leaders while drawing them into multilevel processes of international economic cooperation. Inspiration that is both moral and functional can be effective across national boundaries, as was evident, it must be reiterated, in the initial drive to establish the European Community. The launching of regional economic communities, while dependent on motivations deriving from goodwill toward neighbours and understandings of potentials for the realisation of common benefits, can place governments in new settings of accountability, with socialisation processes and learning experiences, in which openness to further inspiration is encouraged.

Ideally, the multilevel pattern of collective management would operate with some of the qualities of the German system of cooperative federalism, fostering broad social partnerships to sustain interdependent national systems of organised social market capitalism. The contemporary German model deserves recognition because replication of its basic operating principles at the international level would provide high order public goods, while helping to reorient political cultures in the more pluralistic states burdened with problems of governance. German nationalism, of course, would have to be combined with a new internationalist spirit in the projected system of collective management. The current evolution of German nationalism in the European Community context encourages optimism that an international dimension appropriate for global management can be added.[16]

Japan represents another model, giving more intense expression to the logic of integration, with emphasis on the social organisation of trust. The Japanese emphasis on achieving consensus, building trust through goodwill, fostering autonomy at the working level, and establishing a firm social basis for economic and political interaction, could provide very valuable contributions to the building of international political cultures to sustain regional and global systems of cooperation.[17] Recognition of the international potential of the Japanese model tends to be hindered, especially in the USA, by the effects of crude anti-Japanese political agitation, but the model will have to command attention in the United States, as well as from elites in the European Community who see their organisation assuming responsibilities for promoting economic cooperation on a global scale.

Consideration of the Japanese model, even more than the German one, can help to correct perspectives derived from much current policy literature concerned exclusively with hard bargaining approaches to economic cooperation. With such perspectives, the building of structures for integrative collaboration may seem impossible. It must be emphasised, however, that requirements for comprehensive collective management which are set by large scale complex interdependencies will not be met by states seeking maximum use of their leverage and insisting on maintaining freedom of action. The prospects for effective and sustained cooperation would be no better than those for building a social partnership in a strongly pluralistic state, where interest groups, legislators, government agencies, and executive figures are in almost constant conflicts. With integrative cooperation, similar to that between groups in Japan, the multi-level structure necessary for regional and global collective management could function very efficiently instead of being threatened with pluralistic stagnation by aggressive representations of national interests.

Transition Problems

The current lack of cooperation in the international political economy, the strains resulting from attempts to extract collaboration through leverage, and the efforts of certain major states to impose costs of adjustment on trading partners, all dramatise imperatives for collective management. But problems of transition to a well structured system of collective management are evident, especially because of the macromanagement problems affecting the USA, which have weakened its potential for global leadership and discouraged cooperation with it by other states. Alternative sources of leadership have to be considered, and special consideration has to be given to the potential role of the European Community, although it is still in transition to a higher stage of integration and has not yet evolved an integrated foreign policy through its system of Political Cooperation.[18]

The development of a regionalised world awaits replication of the European Community's achievements, especially through the formation of a Pacific Community in which the USA would be associated with Japan and the high growth developing East Asian market economy states. The building of such a community is warranted because of the structural interdependencies that are developing rapidly in this area. Because of its geographic and social distances, however, and the severe contrasts between the Japanese and US policy styles, as well as because of the weak bargaining positions of the developing market economy East Asian states, active European Community involvement in the development of Pacific regional economic cooperation will be highly desirable.[19] If such involvement is undertaken it will aid collaboration between the two major regional systems, thus helping to establish a basis for partnership at the global level and in the sponsoring of regional cooperation throughout the Third World. With collaboration by the Pacific grouping, moreover, the European Community would be able to cope more effectively with the tasks of aiding the Soviet Union's integration into the international political economy.

The importance of Pacific Community formation in a planned transition to comprehensive collective management must be stressed because such a community can provide a setting for resolution of the issues between the USA and Japan and for their development of more constructive orientations toward questions of global economic cooperation. US and Japanese collaboration, moreover, will be needed by the European Community if it is to play the global leadership role that is warranted by its successes in collective management. For the USA, Pacific Community formation offers the prospect of evolving more complementary commercial relationships with the high growth East Asian states, and possible compensation for any losses of competitiveness in the European Community if its governments and firms collaborate more actively to realise the benefits of full market integration. For Japan, Pacific regional economic cooperation would also open up possibilities for more complementary trade relationships with the developing market economy East Asian countries. Prospective reductions of their protectionist measures would benefit both the USA and Japan, although Japan's gains, judging from current trends, would probably be greater.[20]

Substantially increased international use of the Yen would be an important consequence of Pacific regional economic cooperation. A Pacific Community would make this possible by providing a framework for general expansion of Japan's trade and direct investment links with the area, and by intensifying competition between Japan and the USA, although hopefully at the governmental level more integrative cooperation would develop between these two states. The wider international use of the Yen would be significant for the global economy because it would introduce more stability into world financial markets. For the present these remain extremely vulnerable to shocks because of continued large scale use of the US dollar. The benefits in terms of overall stability could be greater if the European Community were deeply involved in the Pacific because there would also be wider use of the German mark, and, later, a European currency unit. Problems of exchange rate management, for the USA, and for the major industrialised democracies as a group, could thus be reduced to dimensions more suitable for engagement at the global level. At the same time the more limited role of the US dollar could oblige the United States to moderate its emphasis on monetary autonomy and accept the need for monetary cooperation with Japan and the European Community.

The USA's trade and fiscal deficits, which are especially serious sources of strain in the world economy, could be overcome more rapidly after the formation of a Pacific economic community because of the increased scope for gains from commerce, although existing incentives for export substitution through outward direct investment would have to be reduced. There could be pressures from business associations to increase those incentives, because of Japanese competition, but their reduction would be necessary to overcome the chronic trade imbalance and to secure greater tax revenues. European involvement in the Pacific regional system meanwhile would be an important source of pressure on the USA for fiscal discipline. This could become more significant if that involvement led to greater understanding and cooperation between the European Community and Japan.

The development of a regional economic community for Latin America would be a further significant process in the transformation of global economic relations. This would require very intensive engagement by the European Community, identifying with Latin American aspirations for collectively more self reliant industrialisation, and for more diversified external economic relations, as well as for the relief of current debt burdens. Well intentioned political entrepreneurs, unrelated to threats of economic domination, would be necessary to overcome all the antipathies and distrust that have obstructed Latin American regional economic cooperation schemes thus far. The increased growth to be expected from Latin American regional cooperation would help US export expansion and thus indirectly assist reductions of the US fiscal deficits, while further moderating strains in the international political economy and removing obstacles to cooperation at the global level.[21]

For harmonious transition to a comprehensive collective management system some ventures in industrial cooperation could be undertaken. These need not entail commitments to adopt industrial policies, which are likely to remain subjects of unresolved controversies in the USA. Collaboration between industry groups within and across the boundaries of regional communities could be promoted by governments sponsoring sectoral development conferences. These could attract representatives of firms and governments for the discussion of infrastructure plans, market trends, complementarity in direct investment projects, and financing methods. Corporate planning could thus become more cooperative, in a more stable and more supportive environment, with the assistance of greatly increased information flows.

The European Community has evolved a favourable setting for industrial cooperation, supported by member governments, and this cooperation may well be intensified to cope with external competition in the fully integrated Community market.[22] If this cooperation becomes more active the experience gained could enable the Community to sponsor conferences on industrial cooperation in the Pacific, and in Latin America, with concerns larger than those now operative in the European context. Such entrepreneurship, as it led to practical results, could be especially significant for community formation, through the extension of elite networks, and through encouraging confidence in the benefits of collaborative private planning with collective administrative support. Trade flows would be influenced, and could become more balanced because of the complementarity that could be fostered through the cooperative private industrial planning. Rivalry between governments for the development of competitive national economic structures would be moderated, with overall benefits, in terms of growth and stability, made possible by the continuing increases in complementarity.

Altogether, then, ventures in regional cooperation could reduce the number and dimensions of issues on the agenda for global collective management. At this level, enlargement of the OECD's functions would be made politically more feasible because of the expansion of cooperation in the emerging regional communities as well as because of the more manageable agenda for decision making on global issues. Questions of harmonising the fiscal policies of the leading industrialised states, which figure prominently in literature on global economic problems, would become less urgent because there would be less reliance on fiscal expansion for economic growth, due to the vigor that could be anticipated because of the industrial planning conferences, and to the gains from regional trade liberalisation. Any major issues of fiscal harmonisation would also be resolved more easily because of the spirit of cooperation developing in the regional communities.

Complex problems about the reciprocal effects of fiscal expansion and contraction in the leading industrialised democracies during phases of stress in the world economy and stages of political business cycles would be more amenable to solution. The most prominent problems during the past two decades have been attributable in a large measure to US fiscal and monetary policies managed without sufficient regard for the interests of other industrialised democracies or for the welfare of the US economy.[23] The external pressures for improved macromanagement in a Pacific system of regional cooperation, with European involvement, it must be stressed, could have considerable influence on US decision makers. Collective adaptability to economic stresses, moreover, which could be expected to develop in the Euro–Pacific regional partnership, could facilitate engagement with the problems of fostering evenly distributed growth.

Contrasts in competitiveness and performance between the more integrated and the less integrated industrialised democracies, which are tending to become sharper and more disruptive in the present global system, would become less significant with the suggested extensions of regional cooperation. In addition to the pressures for improved macromanagement in each regional community, the multiple growth effects of regional cooperation would tend to have levelling consequences, especially with increasingly intensive industrial cooperation. The development of collective decision making structures for the Pacific region could enhance the effectiveness of its industrial cooperation processes, as has happened in the European Community. In Europe the contrasts in competitiveness between Germany and the other members have certainly been intensifying in the recent past, especially because of macromanagement failures in France and Britain, but deepening integration in the Community does offer prospects of more evenly spread growth, in part because of greater pressures on France and Britain for improved macromanagement.

Political Entrepreneurship

To initiate processes of cooperation oriented toward more and more comprehensive collective management there must be some activation of neofunctional logic, through which collaborative ventures will generate results that will motivate collaboration on a larger scale. Hopes for such increases in cooperation can be based on the economic benefits in prospect, but have to be sustained by trustful relationships developing in the course of cooperation. Where social commitments to these relationships are strong there can be confidence that difficulties in realising satisfactory benefits from future cooperation will be overcome. The collaboration can thus be stable, the cooperating states can relate to each other as members of a community, and the sharing of common purposes can be highly productive.

Political entrepreneurship for the promotion of international economic cooperation must be functional, in line with sound designs for collaboration that will produce equitably shared benefits, in increasing abundance. But if it is assumed that the participating states will be led, and will continue to be led, only by economic nationalists, the requirements for devising functional processes of cooperation become very exacting, and prospects for continuing the cooperation when there are unanticipated strains become very uncertain. The community building aspect of the promotional entrepreneurship thus deserves special attention: it is especially important where the intended cooperation will be complex, and where it must be adaptable. The significance of complexity has to be stressed because of the range and the dimensions of the structural interdependencies requiring management, and because of the large numbers of international firms that must be drawn into association with that management process. Adaptability must be stressed also because of uncertainties posed in the context of any initial cooperative endeavours, and the prospect of continuing uncertainties even if the expanding collaboration produces more order and stability.

Sustained reciprocal affirmations of values, given practical expression through integrative cooperation, are necessary for community formation. International political entrepreneurship to promote such affirmations of values and mobilise support for substantial cooperation has to begin with conferences in elite networks. This, it must be repeated, is the lesson to be drawn from the European experience. What has to be stressed, however, is that for the building of a Pacific Community, a Euro–Pacific partnership, Third World regional communities, and new global institutions, the European Community will have to become a source of political entrepreneurship as it moves toward a higher level of integration. This has to be emphasised because of several factors affecting the considerable American potential for international leadership. In the present American system the executive is burdened by domestic overload, hampered by an assertive Congress, and inefficiently served by its transient political appointees in the higher levels of the bureaucracy. The accumulated effects of some three decades of macromanagement failures have set very demanding requirements for adjustment and reform, while contributing to severe stresses in the global trading and financial systems.

Political entrepreneurship by the European Community, and by private groups within the Community, can affirm its principles of cooperation as a basis for regional collaboration in the Pacific. An important opportunity for Pacific involvement is provided by the Community's links with the Association of Southeast Asian Nations.[24] These can be strengthened, through commerce, direct investment, and developmental aid, while encouragement and political support can be given for an active ASEAN role in discussions with the USA and Japan on the establishment of a Pacific economic association. Several ASEAN governments have been reluctant to consider membership in a community that could be dominated by the USA and Japan, but with strong European support they could be confident of benefitting from such involvement. European participation in official and unofficial conferences on

Pacific regional cooperation, meanwhile, can prepare the way for formulation of a doctrine of regional and transregional cooperation. The US administration could be reluctant to accept such European participation, but should bargaining become necessary the European Community would have considerable leverage, especially because of its size and prospects for expansion.

In the USA, private groups with regional vision could assist the European endeavours. Thus far such groups have given little attention to the relevance of the European experience for the Pacific, and have tended to favour only low level collaboration in that area, because of its diversity, but the dimensions of the interdependencies that need to be managed in the Pacific oblige adoption of a more holistic perspective. This, to a degree, has been made evident by the attempts of the Bush administration to negotiate some fundamental changes in the US–Japan trading relationship. Atlantic oriented groups in the USA could strengthen those working for Pacific cooperation, if sufficiently motivated by awareness of the need for a Euro–Pacific partnership.

The promotion of conferences to strengthen and activate elite networks would have to emphasise attracting representation from firms. The European Community's main officially sponsored business organisation could play a very important role, reaching out to American and Japanese economic associations, and preparing the way for Pacific and Euro–Pacific industrial planning discussions. In these, European contributions could be of vital importance for the development of collaboration between firms and governments, along lines compatible with aggregated economic interests, and for the maintenance of socially desirable balances between the roles of multinationals and small and medium sized enterprises. The need for such balances has to be recognised because of the continuing expansion of international firms and their tendencies to acquire oligopoly power. The social and economic benefits of maintaining substantial roles for small and medium sized firms have been well illustrated in Japan. The significance of the Japanese model can be stressed, although advocacy of the principle involved will have to be largely a European function. This can be affirmed because of the anti-Japanese bias that persists in much of the Trilateral context. The bias, hopefully, will be overcome by European political and business leaders.

Promotional enterpreneurship will have to stress that business representation in conferences on regional economic cooperation, especially with reference to industrial collaboration, would open up new opportunities for policy learning by managements, and for learning about corporate strategy by officials, while encouraging the development of stronger and more active national and regional business associations. The administrative and corporate learning, it could be indicated, would develop in settings in which governments would be able to shape coordinated policies on the basis of each other's interests and plans, and with considerable knowledge of the projected operations of firms. Matching advantages for managements which could be given prominence would be enhanced comprehension of policy trends and administrative preferences, as well as of the revealed plans of many enterprises offering possibilities of cooperation and competition. Altogether, information processing costs, negotiation costs, and overall operating uncertainties would be greatly reduced. National administrative responsiveness to domestic forms of interest representation would be altered, to the general advantage, by the expanded external responsiveness. The transnational aggregations of business interests, moreover, although changing, could be expected to display considerable continuity, and thus could have a somewhat stabilising influence on policy choices.[25]

Diffuse neofunctional logic could be activated through the promotion of sustained interaction between firms and regionally cooperating governments. Innovative exploration of opportunities for more and more ambitious collaboration would be encouraged. There could be increasingly broad acceptance of the need to advance through the intermediate stages of regional economic integration toward the formation of systems for comprehensive collective management. The danger of selective collaboration between governments and firms for party, group, and sectoral benefits however would have to be recognised in the promotional entrepreneurship. A credible method of protection against political exchange bias that could jeopardise regional cooperation would have to be offered. The need for greatly expanded policy review functions in national legislatures could be indicated, and the policy appraisal activities of the enlarged OECD could be stressed.

Prospects

The development of a pattern of regional and global cooperation for comprehensive collective management is to a considerable extent predicated on deepening integration in the European Community, and the evolution of a strong Community leadership role in world affairs.[26] The Community's continued progress toward economic union depends very much on stability of purpose in the Franco–German partnership, and this may well be sustained, despite the danger of disunity in France, which could be caused by a succession struggle in the Socialist Party. On the German side stability of purpose seems quite probable, but could be adversely affected by the emergence of a coalition of Southern Community members seeking to exert more influence in the shaping of Community policies. The development of a Community international leadership role will require considerable progress in institutional integration, and preservation of the Franco–German partnership, as well as the evolution of a more outward orientation in that partnership. German and French political groups still have strong inclinations to focus on intra-Community matters, and this focus tends to be stronger than it would be otherwise partly because of British reluctance to identify with the drive toward economic union.

American cooperation with a European Community leadership role would be helpful, but is uncertain. Pressures deriving from acute macromanagement problems will probably tend to become more severe in the USA, affecting the orientation and political capabilities of the executive. The dynamics of popular choice, moreover, may be responsible for the emergence of a president with inferior administrative skills and little capacity for the direction of foreign relations. Any European initiatives, then, may not be encouraged, although they may well be utilised as occasions for gestures aimed at the domestic audience. The persistence of serious macromanagement problems will generate further pressures for unilateral methods of solving difficulties in foreign economic relations, especially for the purpose of forcing reductions in large trade imbalances. The imbalances will probably remain substantial because of the strong incentives for firms to produce abroad rather than export from the USA. Quests for free trade agreements, especially in Latin America, will no doubt reflect the unilateral trend, rather than an interest in fostering regional economic cooperation. The development of US policy in the Pacific can be expected to evidence such an orientation. The growth of a strong elite network seeking to promote wide ranging Pacific cooperation however will remain possible, and could be given leadership from within US business and academic circles.

Because of the strains in the US–Japan relationship, and the danger that US pressures against Japan will increase, the development of a more active Japanese global and regional leadership role will depend very much on European initiatives. The European Community's concerns with the competitiveness of its firms in their own market and with the advantages of US enterprises in that market will probably become more intense, and accordingly interest in economic cooperation with Japan may develop among European firms seeking dynamic foreign partners that do not threaten hostile takeovers. European protectionist measures directed against Japanese products could be relaxed, and European diplomacy could seek to give Japan greater status in the international political economy. If a Japanese advisory group were appointed to the European Commission the way would be open for a rapid expansion and diversification of collaborative ventures. Even without this option, however, the logic of working for collaboration through sponsorship of industrial planning conferences may well become more evident to Community decision makers.

Pragmatic and incremental moves by the leading industrialised states to increase their economic cooperation may be envisaged, in view of the uncertain prospects for promotional political entrepreneurship on the scale needed for collective management. Pragmatic incrementalism however can disappoint the neofunctional expectations which it tends to arouse. This can happen because the distrust of planning associated with pragmatism results in a focus on prospective short term gains, and because the cooperation attempted is on a provisional basis. Since it is without commitments to community formation moreover it is likely to be undertaken with an emphasis on domestic benefits according with each government's current constituency concerns. Mutual perceptions of pragmatic and incremental approaches to cooperation tend to motivate cautious and risk reducing behaviour, with little confidence in the willingness of partners to make binding commitments. Pragmatic incrementalism thus favours informal, flexible, *ad hoc*, rather than institutionalised cooperation.

Failures in collective management, it must be stressed, are in prospect because of current policy orientations in the leading industrialised states, and because of stresses in the international political economy caused by those policies and by differences in national competitiveness which tend to increase because of inadequate cooperation. National processes of elite socialisation are producing few internationally minded leaders, and those gaining office tend to be the ones most adept at responding to domestic pressures generated by macromanagement problems. The logic of integrative cooperation for comprehensive collective management, however, is becoming more persuasive, because of the increasing dimensions of the interdependencies linking national political economies, and the growing costs of the stresses affecting them. These are causing the developmental problems of the international political economy to become more urgent.

New contributions to the policy literature, especially in Europe but also in Japan and the USA, may well enhance understandings of the moral and functional imperatives to manage interdependencies. Such contributions are needed to introduce more holistic perspectives, and to inspire stronger commitments among elites working for increased economic cooperation. Much of the current policy literature tends to obscure the potential for orchestrating and accelerating growth in the international political economy through comprehensive collective management. There is emphasis on the need for cooperation to reduce or eliminate the negative external effects of economic policies, particularly those of the larger states, especially as these influence stability in product and money markets. There is also emphasis on the degrees to which international collaboration can increase the effectiveness of national policies, as these tend to be weakened by rises in interdependence. State-centric perspectives in the elaboration of these themes convey impressions that governments independently seeking to promote noninflationary growth will derive benefits from cooperation, but hinder awareness that the growth achieved is, increasingly, an international process, with asymmetries due to the activities of firms and governments. The fundamental collective responsibility for building a more fully integrated world political economy, with symmetries of efficiency and equity, is not recognised.

If obligations to the development of the international political economy are not given substantial recognition, through elite policy learning and moral development, strains in the trading and financial systems will probably increase. Ventures in pragmatic and incremental cooperation will continue, on terms negotiated according to relative bargaining strengths, but the overall levels of the unequally bargained collaboration will probably decline, due to the combined effects of differences in national competitiveness and levels of macromanagement. Collaborative endeavours will lack commitments that could ensure concerted adaptation to stresses in mutual relations and in the global economy. Vicious cycles of noncooperation and macromanagement failures will have to be expected, as indeed can be projected from recent history. All these problems, moreover, may well be severely aggravated by the global effects of a US depression. This danger is serious because of the heavy burden of American government debt; the extent to which this slows growth; the disruptive consequences of excessive domestic speculation; and the continuing development of industrial capacity at overseas locations rather than in the home economy.

All the options for reforming political entrepreneurship thus deserve much emphasis. Tasks much greater than the building of the European Community must be taken up, with the Community itself as an initial model. Understanding the Community makes enormous demands on contextual analysis, but its achievements in activating neofunctional logic, despite vast patterns of particularistic loyalties, have global significance. A vital element in its integration process has been the moderation of historic Franco–German antagonisms through the proliferation of structural interdependencies. This achievement has potential significance for management of the strained US–Japan relationship. If far sighted political entrepreneurship recognises the opportunities for transforming that relationship in the context of an emerging Pacific Community linked with the European Community a foundation may be established for global collective management. Such a system would give wide expression to the concept of extended accountability. Hopefully, it would also reflect general awareness of the importance of transcendental accountability.

Notes

Chapter 1

1. See Robert E. Lane, 'Market Justice, Political Justice', *American Political Science Review*, 80, 2, June 1986, 383–402.
2. See, for example, Peter J. Katzenstein (ed.) *Industry and Politics in West Germany* (Ithaca, N.Y.: Cornell University Press, 1989).
3. See comments on US fiscal policies in Vito Tanzi, 'International Coordination of Fiscal Policies', *Journal of Public Policy*, 8, 2, April–June 1988, 111–124.
4. For general comments on the concept of an optimum national economic structure see John H. Dunning (ed.), *Multinational Enterprises, Economic Structure, and International Competitiveness* (New York, N.Y.: John Wiley & Sons, 1985).
5. See Takashi Inoguchi and Daniel I. Okimoto (eds), *The Political Economy of Japan* (Stanford, California: Stanford University Press, 1988)
6. Same.
7. Same.
8. On the striving for competitiveness see Ronald Dore, Jean Bounine-Cabale and Kari Tapiola, *Japan at Work: Markets, Management, and Flexibility* (Paris: OECD, 1989).
9. See reference to problems of the US economy in Martin Feldstein (ed.) *The United States in the World Economy* (Chicago: University of Chicago Press, 1988).
10. See Katzenstein, cited.
11. See Gerhard Fels and Hans-Peter Froehlich, 'Germany and the World Economy: a German View', *Economic Policy*, 4, April 1987, 178–205, and Elke Thiel, 'West Germany's Role in the International Economy: Prospects for Economic Policy Coordination', *Journal of International Affairs*, 42, 1, Fall 1988, 53–74.
12. See Bernhard Heitger, Grant Kirkpatrick, Gernot Klepper, and Frank D. Weiss, *Trade Policy in West Germany* (Boulder, Colorado: Westview Press, 1988).
13. On economic issues in Germany see Martin Hellwig and Manfred S.M. Neumann, 'Economic Policy in Germany: was there a turnaround?', *Economic Policy*, 5, October 1987, 103–146.
14. Same.
15. See Katzenstein, cited.
16. See Lane, cited.
17. On the USA's problems of governance see Joseph A. Pika, 'Management Style and the Organizational Matrix: Studying White House Operations', *Administration and Society*, 20, 1, May 1988, 3–29; Joseph J. Hogan, 'Analysing Recent US Presidential–Congressional Relationships', *Political Studies*, XXXIII, 1, March 1985, 122–128; Thomas Gais, Mark A. Peterson, and Jack L. Walker, 'Interest Groups, Iron Triangles, and Representative Institutions in American National Government', *British Journal of Political Science*, 14, 2, April 1984, 161–186; and Jo Freeman, 'The Political Culture of the Democratic and Republican Parties', *Political Science Quarterly*, 101, 3, 1986, 327–356.
18. See Richard Portes and Alexander K. Swoboda (eds), *Threats to International Financial Stability* (New York, N.Y.: Cambridge University Press, 1987), especially Appendix on USA, and James M. Buchanan and others, *Reaganomics and After* (London: Institute of Economic Affairs, 1989).
19. On the effects of variations in Presidential capacities and preferences see Pika,

cited.

20. See Alice M. Rivlin, 'Economics and the Political Process', *American Economic Review*, 77, 1, March 1987, 1–10, and Michael M. Atkinson and William D. Coleman, 'Strong States and Weak States: Sectoral Policy Networks in Advanced Capitalist Economies', *British Journal of Political Science*, 19, 1, January 1989, 47–67.

21. See I.M. Destler, *American Trade Politics: System under Stress* (Washington DC: Institute of International Economics, 1986).

22. See review of dynamics of US monetary policy in I.M. Destler and C. Randall Henning, *Dollar Politics: Exchange Rate Policymaking in the United States* (Washington DC: Institute of International Economics, 1989).

23. See Jeremy Richardson (ed.), *Policy Styles in Western Europe* (London: George Allen & Unwin, 1982)

24. See Kent Matthews and Patrick Minford, 'Mrs Thatcher's Economic Policies, 1979–1987', *Economic Policy*, 5, October 1987, 57–102.

25. See Michael E. Porter, *The Competitive Advantage of Nations* (New York, N.Y.: Free Press, 1990), ch. 9.

26. The comparative strength of these incentives is reflected in statistics in *International Direct Investment and the New Economic Environment* (Paris: OECD, 1989)

27. See Pater Hall, *Governing the Economy* (New York, N.Y.: Oxford University Press, 1986), Part III.

28. Same.

29. Same, and see John R. Freeman, *Democracy and Markets* (Ithaca, N.Y.: Cornell University Press, 1989).

30. See Yves Meny, 'The National and International Context of French Policy Communities', *Political Studies*, XXXVII, 3, September 1989, 387–399.

31. See Juliet Lodge (ed.), *The European Community and the Challenge of the Future* (New York, N.Y.: St Martin's Press, 1989), ch. 12.

32. See Alberto Alesina, 'Politics and Business Cycles in Industrial Democracies', *Economic Policy*, 8, April 1989, 55–98.

33. See Dunning, cited, and Porter, cited.

34. See *Industrial Policy Developments in OECD Countries, Annual Review* (Paris: OECD, 1989).

35. See *International Direct Investment and the New Economic Environment*, cited, and Gavin Boyd, 'European Management of Trilateral Interdependencies', in Michael S. Steinberg (ed.), *The Technical Challenges and Opportunities of a United Europe* (London: Pinter Publishers, 1990), 91–112.

36. See *American Trade Politics*, cited, and Douglas Nelson, 'Domestic Political Preconditions of US Trade Policy: Liberal Structure and Protectionist Dynamics', *Journal of Public Policy*, 9, 1, Jan–March, 1989, 83–106.

37. See *Millennium*, 17, 2, Summer 1988, symposium on Philosophical Traditions in International Relations.

38. See Dunning, cited.

39. See Dieter Helm (ed.), *The Economic Borders of the State* (Oxford: Oxford University Press, 1989) and Michael Calingaert, *The 1992 Challenge from Europe: Development of the European Community's Internal Market* (Washington DC: National Planning Association, 1988).

40. See *The Political Economy of Japan*, cited, and Gavin Boyd, 'Japan in the Pacific Policy Environment for Strategic Planning', in Peter Nemetz (ed.), *The Pacific Rim: Investment, Development, and Trade* (Vancouver: University of British Columbia Press, 1990).

41. See *Germany* (Paris: OECD, 1989).

42. See Dunning, cited.
43. See comments on direct investment trends in *International Direct Investment and the New Economic Environment*, cited, and in Dunning, cited.
44. See comments by W. Michael Blumenthal in Martin Feldstein (ed.), *International Economic Cooperation* (Chicago: Chicago University Press, 1988), 45.

Chapter 2

1. See *Germany* (Paris: OECD, 1989).
2. See John H. Dunning (ed.), *Multinational Enterprises, Economic Structure, and International Competitiveness* (New York, N.Y.: John Wiley & Sons, 1985), and John Dunning, *Multinationals, Technology and Competitiveness* (London: Unwin Hyman, 1988).
3. On Atlantic cross investment see Roy H. Ginsberg, 'US–EC Relations' in Juliet Lodge (ed.), *The European Community and the Challenge of the Future* (New York, N.Y.: St Martin's Press, 1989), ch. 14; and *International Direct Investment and the New Economic Environment* (Paris: OECD, 1989); and Robert E. Lipsey 'Changing Patterns of International Investment in and by the United States', in Martin Feldstein (ed.), *The United States in the World Economy* (Chicago: University of Chicago Press, 1988), ch. 8.
4. See *Multinationals, Technology and Competitiveness*, cited.
5. See Jeffrey A. Frankel, 'International Capital Flows and Domestic Economic Policies' in Feldstein, cited, ch. 9.
6. See *Multinationals, Technology, and Competitiveness*, cited.
7. See Frankel, cited.
8. See Vito Tanzi, 'International Coordination of Fiscal Policies', *Journal of Public Policy*, 8, 2, April–June 1988, 111–124.
9. See Shijuro Ogata, Richard N. Cooper, and Horst Schulmann, *International Integration: The Policy Challenges* (New York, N.Y.: Trilateral Commission, 1989).
10. See I.M. Destler, *American Trade Politics: System under Stress* (Washington DC: Institute for International Economics, 1986).
11. See *Multinational Enterprises, Economic Structure, and International Competitiveness*, cited.
12. See Alice M. Rivlin, 'Economics and the Policy Process', *American Economic Review*, 77, 1, March 1987, 1–10.
13. See Tommaso Padoa–Schioppa and others, *Efficiency, Stability, and Equity* (Oxford: Oxford University Press, 1987).
14. See Frances McCall Rosenbluth, *Financial Politics in Contemporary Japan* (Ithaca, New York: Cornell University Press, 1989).
15. See Michael Devereux and Thomas A. Wilson, 'International Coordination of Macroeconomic Policies: A Review', *Canadian Public Policy*, XV, special supplement, February 1989, 20–34.
16. See Raymond J. Waldmann, *Managed Trade: The New Competition between Nations* (Cambridge, Mass: Ballinger, 1986).
17. See references to Japan and Germany in Martin Feldstein (ed.), *International Economic Cooperation* (Chicago: Chicago University Press, 1988).
18. See for example Destler, cited.
19. See Frankel, cited.
20. See Robert Solow, 'The Conservative Revolution: a Roundtable Discussion', *Economic Policy*, 5, October 1987, 181–200.
21. See Destler, cited.

22. See *Multinational Enterprises, Economic Structure, and International Competitiveness*, cited.
23. For a study of business organisations that reflects cultural differences see W. Coleman and W. Grant, 'The Organizational Cohesion and Political Access of Business: a Study of Comprehensive Associations', *European Journal of Political Research*, 16, 5, September 1988, 467–488.
24. See reflections by James M. Buchanan in James M. Buchanan and others, *Reaganomics and After* (London: Institute for Economic Affairs, 1989).
25. See comments by Christian von Weizsacker in 'The Conservative Revolution: A roundtable Discussion', cited, and Ralph C. Bryant and others (eds), *Macroeconomic Policies in an Interdependent World* (Washington DC: Brookings Institution, 1989).
26. See Paul R. Krugman (ed.), *Strategic Trade Policy and the New International Economics* (Cambridge, Massachusetts: MIT Press, 1986).
27. See *Multinational Enterprises, Economic Structure, and International Competitiveness*, cited.
28. See Thomas D. Willett, 'National Macroeconomic Policy Preferences and International Coordination Issues', *Journal of Public Policy* 8, 3&4, July–December 1988, 235–264.
29. See *Efficiency, Stability, and Equity*, cited.
30. See Ronald W. Jones and Anne O. Krueger (eds), *The Political Economy of International Trade* (Cambridge, Massachusetts: Blackwell, 1990).
31. See Destler, cited, and *The United States in the World Economy*, cited.
32. See reflection of US concerns in Michael Calingaert, *The 1992 Challenge from Europe* (Washington DC: National Planning Association, 1988).
33. See Takashi Inoguchi and Daniel I. Okimoto (eds), *The Political Economy of Japan* (Stanford, California: Stanford University Press, 1988).
34. See Michael E. Porter, *The Competitive Advantage of Nations* (New York, N.Y.: Free Press, 1990) and DeAnne Julius, *Global Companies and Public Policy* (London: Royal Institute of International Affairs, 1990).
35. See Porter, cited.
36. See Gavin Boyd, 'Japan in the Pacific Policy Environment for Strategic Planning' in Peter Nemetz (ed.), *The Pacific Rim, Investment, Development, and Trade* (Vancouver: University of British Columbia Press, 1990).

Chapter 3

1. See Sidney Golt, *The GATT Negotiations 1986–90: Origins, Issues, and Prospects* (London: The British–North American Committee, 1988).
2. The requirement can be indicated with reference to the growth of linkages between international firms. See Richard W. Moxon, 'Multinational Consortia in Manufacturing', *Research in International Business and International Relations*, 3, 1989, 11–28.
3. See T. Ozawa, 'Can the Market Alone Manage Structural Upgrading? A Challenge Posed by Economic Interdependence' in John H. Dunning and Mikoto Usui (eds), *Structural Change, Economic Interdependence, and World Development* (New York, N.Y.: St Martin's Press, 1987) 45–62.
4. See suggestions in same by Jack N. Behrman, 'International Industrial Integration through Multinational Enterprises', 63–76.
5. For a wide ranging survey of these problems see Gerald K. Helleiner, 'The New Global Economy: Problems, Prospects, and Priority Research Requirements', *Journal of Development Planning*, 17, 1987, 19–35.

6. See Vito Tanzi, 'International Coordination of Fiscal Policies', *Journal of Public Policy*, 8, 2, April–June 1988, 111–124.
7. See James M. Verdier, 'Advising Congressional Decision Makers', *Journal of Policy Analysis and Management*, 3, 3, 1984, 421–438.
8. See Jeffrey A. Frankel, 'Obstacles to International Macroeconomic Policy Coordination', *Journal of Public Policy* 8, 3&4, July–December 1988, 353–374.
9. Same, and see Ralph C. Bryant and others (eds), *Macroeconomic Policies in an Interdependent World* (Washington DC: Brookings Institution, 1989).
10. See Paul Taylor, 'The New Dynamics of EC Integration in the 1980s', in Juliet Lodge (ed.), *The European Community and the Challenge of the Future* (New York, N.Y.: St Martin's Press, 1989) 3–25.
11. See Cesare Merlini (ed.), *Economic Summits and Western Decision Making* (New York, N.Y.: St Martin's Press, 1984) and Jocelyn Horne and Paul R. Masson, 'Scope and Limits of International Economic Cooperation and Policy Coordination', *IMF Staff Papers*, 35, 2, June 1988, 259–296.
12. See review of issues between the major industrialised states in C. Randall Henning, *Macroeconomic Diplomacy in the 1980s* (Paris: Atlantic Institute for International Affairs, 1987)
13. Reference however should also be made to the reluctance of the Thatcher administrations to support advances toward deeper integration in the Community. See Paul Taylor, cited.
14. See Golt, cited, and Juergen B. Donges, 'Whither International Trade Policies: Worries about Continuing Protectionism', in Kimberly Ann E. Elliott and John Williamson (eds), *World Economic Problems* (Washington DC: Institute for International Economics, 1988) 57–92.
15. See Paul Taylor, cited.
16. See Albert Bressand's comments on the global significance of deepening integration in the European Community in Albert Bressand, 'Beyond Interdependence: 1992 as a Global Challenge', *International Affairs*, 66, 1, January 1990, 47–66.
17. See review of trade issues for the USA in *Proceedings of the Academy of Political Science*, 37, 4, 1990 – symposium on *International Trade: the Changing Role of the United States*.
18. These observations are based on Tommaso Padoa Schioppa's review of the European Monetary System in 'Policy Cooperation and the EMS Experience', in Willem H. Buiter and Richard C. Marston (eds), *International Economic Policy Coordination* (New York, N.Y.: Cambridge University Press, 1985) 331–365.

Chapter 4

1. See *Proceedings of the Academy of Political Science*, 37, 4, 1990 – Symposium on International Trade: the Changing Role of the United States.
2. See Raymond Vernon, 'European Community 1992: Can the US Negotiate for Trade Equality?' in same, 9–16.
3. Same.
4. See Albert Bressand, 'Beyond Interdependence: 1992 as a Global Challenge', *International Affairs*, 66, 1, January 1990, 47–66.
5. See John H. Jackson, *Restructuring the GATT System* (London: Royal Institute of International Affairs, 1990).
6. See C. David Finch, *The IMF: the Record and the Prospect* (Princeton: Essays in International Finance 175, September 1989, Department of Economics, Princeton University).

7. Same, and see discussion of IMF aid to Third World countries in Dragoslav Avramovic, 'Developing Country Debt Revisited: Facts, Theory, and Policy' in Kimberly Ann Elliott and John Williamson (eds), *World Economic Problems* (Washington DC: Institute for International Economics, 1988) 107–148.
8. See Rachel McCulloch, 'The United States–Canada Free Trade Agreement', in *Proceedings of the Academy of Political Science*, cited, 79–89.
9. See Vernon, cited.
10. Same
11. See Stephen D. Cohen, 'United States–Japan Relations' in same.
12. See Finch, cited.
13. See Nicholas Bayne, 'Making Sense of Western Economic Policies: the Role of the OECD', *The World Today*, 43, 2, February 1987, 27–30.
14. See Robert Kuttner, 'Managed Trade and Economic Sovereignty' in *Proceedings*, cited, 37–53, and Sidney Golt, *The GATT Negotiations 1986–90: Origins, Issues, and Prospects* (London: British–North American Committee, 1988).
15. See Jagdish Bhagwati, 'The United States and Trade Policy: Reversing Gears', *Journal of International Affairs*, 42, 1, Fall 1988, 93–108.
16. Same.
17. See Kuttner, cited, and Vernon, cited.
18. See Stephen D. Cohen, 'United States–Japan Trade Relations', in *Proceedings*, cited, 122–136.
19. See Finch, cited, and Rudiger Dornbusch, 'The Dollar and the Adjustment Options', in *Proceedings*, cited, 54–66
20. See *International Capital Markets: Developments and Prospects* (Washington DC: International Monetary Fund, 1989) and Christopher Allsopp and K. Alec Chrystal, 'Exchange Rate Policy in the 1990's', *Oxford Review of Economic Policy*, 5, 3, Autumn 1989, 1–23.

Chapter 5

1. See *Economic Policy*, 5, October 1987 – symposium on Conservative goverments.
2. See Juliet Lodge, 'The European Parliament – from 'assembly' to co-legislature: Changing the institutional dynamics', in Juliet Lodge (ed.), *The European Community and the Challenge of the Future* (New York, N.Y.: St Martin's Press, 1989) 58–82.
3. See Gavin Boyd, 'European Management of Trilateral Interdependencies', in Michael S. Steinberg (ed.), *The Technical Challenges and Opportunities of a United Europe* (London: Pinter Publishers, 1990) 91–112.
4. See Stephen D. Cohen, 'United States–Japan Trade Relations' *Proceedings of the Academy of Political Science*, 37, 4, 1990 – symposium on International Trade: the Changing Role of the United States – 122–136.
5. See Albert Bressand, 'Beyond Interdependence: 1992 as a Global Challenge', *International Affairs*, 66, 1, January 1990, 47–66.
6. See Takashi Inoguchi and Daniel I. Okimoto (eds), *The Political Economy of Japan* (Stanford, California: Stanford University Press, 1988).
7. See Robert E. Baldwin, *The Inefficacy of Trade Policy* (Princeton: Essays in International Finance, Department of Economics, Princeton University, 1982).
8. See Juliet Lodge, *'European Political Cooperation: towards the 1990s'*, in Lodge, cited, 223–240
9. See Boyd, cited.
10. See Martin Hellwig and Manfred J. M. Neumann, 'Economic Policy in Germany: was there a turnaround?', *Economic Policy*, 5, October 1987, 103–146.

11. See *Germany* (Paris: OECD, 1989).
12. See Cohen, cited.
13. See Jack H. Knott, 'The Fed Chairman as a Political Executive', *Administration and Society*, 18, 2, August 1986, 197–231
14. See James R. Hines and R. Glenn Hubbard, *Coming Home to America: Dividend Repatriations by US Multinationals* (Princeton: Discussion Papers in Economics, Woodrow Wilson School, 1989).
15. See Rudiger Dornbusch, 'The Dollar and the Adjustment Options', in *Proceedings*, cited, 54–66.
16. See Kiyoshi Kojima and Terutmo Ozawa, *Japan's General Trading Companies* (Paris: OECD, 1984).
17. See Young–Kwan Yoon, 'The Irony of Plenty: Japanese Foreign Direct Investment and Productivity', paper given at 1987 annual meeting of the American Political Science Association, Chicago, September 3–6, 1987.
18. See Howard W. Wachtel and Jochen Lorentzen, 'Preconditions for International Economic Cooperation', paper given at International Studies Association annual meeting, London, March 1989.
19. See Cohen, cited, and Thomas A. Pugel and Robert G. Hawkins (eds), *Fragile Interdependence* (Lexington, Massachusetts: D. C. Heath, 1986).
20. See Jacques de Larosiere, 'Monetary Policy in the Community', *European Economic Review*, 34, 4, June 1990, 721–723, and Tommaso Padoa Schioppa, 'Policy Cooperation and the EMS Experience', in Willem H. Buiter and Richard C. Marston (eds), *International Economic Policy Coordination* (New York, N. Y.: Cambridge University Press, 1985) 331–355.
21. On the possibilities for US policy learning see Alice M. Rivlin, 'Economics and the Political Process', *American Economic Review*, 77, 1, March 1987, 1–10; James W. Verdier, 'Advising Congressional Decision-Makers: Guidelines for Economists', *Journal of Policy Analysis and Management*, 3, 3, 1984, 421–438; and Robert H. Nelson, 'The Economics Profession and the Making of Public Policy', *Journal of Economic Literature*, XXV, 1, March 1987, 49–91.
22. See Bressand, cited.
23. Technology cooperation in the Trilateral pattern has evolved mainly on the basis of shared external security concerns, but is being affected increasingly by technological competition, in which Japanese enterprises are making significant advances. See Jill Hills, 'Foreign Policy and Technology: The Japan–US–Britain and Japan–EEC Technology Agreements', *Political Studies*, XXXI, 2, June 1983, 205–223.

Chapter 6

1. See Vito Tanzi, 'International Coordination of Fiscal Policies', *Journal of Public Policy*, 8, 2, April–June 1988, 111–124.
2. Suggestions in same that countries could benefit from concerted fiscal expansion have to be criticised because of the difficulties of assessing equivalence in cross national comparisons and also because of uncertainties about the growth effects of increases in infrastructure spending that can normally be considered productive.
3. Same.
4. See Alberto Alesina, 'Politics and Business Cycles in Industrial Democracies', *Economic Policy*, 8, April 1989, 55–98.
5. See reflections on the Bonn Summit of 1978 – which committed Japan and

Germany to increased public spending – in *Why Economic Policies Change Course: Eleven Case Studies* (Paris: OECD 1988) chs 3&4, and in David A. Currie, Gerald Holtham, and Andrew Hughes Hallett, 'The Theory and Practice of International Policy Coordination: Does Coordination Pay?', in Ralph C. Bryant and others (eds), *Macroeconomic Policies in an Interdependent World* (Washington DC: Brookings Institution, 1989) 14–46.

6.   Further significant contrasts are that the German policy orientation is dominated by concerns to prevent inflation, while the US policy orientation has swung between expansionary and contractionary extremes. See Thomas D. Willett, 'National Macroeconomic Policy Preferences and International Coordination Issues', *Journal of Public Policy*, 8, 3&4, July–December 1988, 235–264.

7.   See Christopher Allsopp and K. Alec Chrystal, 'Exchange Rate Policy in the 1990s', *Oxford Review of Economic Policy*, 5, 3, Autumn 1989, 1–23.

8.   See comments on post 1985 pressures affecting the dollar in same.

9.   See R. M. Pecchioli, *The Internationalisation of Banking* (Paris: OECD, 1983).

10. See review of fluctuations in value of the dollar in Richard C. Marston, 'Exchange Rate Policy Reconsidered' in Martin Feldstein (ed), *International Economic Co-operation* (Chicago: University of Chicago Press, 1988) 79–136.

11. See Peter B. Kenen, *Managing Exchange Rates* (London: Royal Institute of International Affairs, 1988), ch. 6.

12. See Colin Mayer, 'New Issues in Corporate Finance', *European Economic Review*, 32, June 1988, 1167–1189, especially his observations that the world's most competitive financial markets have been the most deficient in funding their industries.

13. On the industrial funding by Japanese banks see Meyer, cited. See also Randall S. Jones, 'Japan's Expanding Role in World Financial Markets', *Columbia Journal of World Business*, XXIV, 3, Fall 1989, 3–9, and comments on US banks in Dan Khambata, 'Off-Balance Sheet Activities of US Banks: an Empirical Evaluation', *Columbia Journal of World Business*, XXIV, 2, Summer 1989, 3–13. See, in addition, C. Randall Henning, 'Finance–Industry Linkages and Exchange Rate Policy in the USA, Japan, and Germany', paper for annual meeting of the International Studies Association, Washington DC, April 11, 1990.

14. On the influence of national business interests see Henning, cited.

15. See Jonathan Fuerbringer, 'US Acquisitions Surge in Europe', *New York Times*, February 8, 1990, D2, and Robert Lipsey, *American Firms Face Europe: 1992* (Cambridge, Massachusetts: National Bureau of Economic Research working paper 3293, 1990).

16. See Khambata, cited.

17. See Rudiger Dornbusch, 'The Dollar and the Adjustment Options', *Proceedings of the Academy of Political Science*, 37, 4, 1990, 54–66, and Kenen, cited.

18. This observation is based on the rationale for a global European role set out in Albert Bressand, 'Beyond Interdependence: 1992 as a Global Challenge', *International Affairs*, 66, 1, January 1990, 47–66.

19. See Khambata, cited.

20. See Martin Feldstein, 'Rethinking International Economic Cooperation', *Oxford Economic Papers*, 40, 2, June 1988, 205–219.

21. See Giuseppe Tullio, 'Long Run Implications of the Increase in Taxation and Public Debt for Employment and Economic Growth in Europe', *European Economic Review*, 31, 3, April 1987, 741–780.

22. See Bressand, cited.

Chapter 7

1. See European Community complaints in 'EC Releases 1989 Report on US Trade Barriers', *European Community News*, 13/89, May 3, 1989.
2. See Douglas Nelson, 'Domestic Political Preconditions of US Trade Policy: Liberal Structure and Protectionist Dynamics', *Journal of Public Policy*, 9, 1, January–March 1989, 83–105; Edward John Ray, 'The Impact of Rent Seeking Activity on US Preferential Trade and World Debt', *Review of World Economics*, 125, 3, 1989, 619–636; Robert E. Baldwin, *Trade Policy in a Changing World Economy* (Chicago: University of Chicago Press, 1988); and Jagdish Bhagwati, 'The United States and Trade Policy: Reversing Gears', *Journal of International Affairs*, 42, 1, Fall 1988, 93–108.
3. See *Oxford Review of Economic Policy*, 3, 1, Spring 1987 – symposium on *International Trade and Commercial Policy*, and Nelson, cited.
4. See Timothy Wendt, 'Strategic Trade: Protecting American Economic and Political Interests' in *Proceedings of the Academy of Political Science*, 37, 4, 1990, 165–180; J. David Richardson, 'The Political Economy of Strategic Trade Policy', *International Organisation*, 44, 1, Winter 1990, 107–135; and 'Statement by Forty Economists on American Trade Policy', *The World Economy*, 12, 2, June 1989, 263–265.
5. On the US interest in trade in services see Rachel McCulloch, 'International Competition in Services', in Martin Feldstein (ed.), *The United States in the World Economy* (Chicago: University of Chicago Press, 1988, 367–406. On European perspectives see Raymond Vernon, 'European Community 1992: Can the US Negotiate for Trade Equality?' in *Proceedings*, cited, 9–16.
6. See *European Community News*, cited.
7. See Vernon, cited.
8. On the industrial involvement of EC members see Ulrich Hilpert, 'Techno–Industrial Innovation, Social Development, and State Policies', *International Political Science Review*, 11, 1, January 1990, 75–86. On EC competition policy see Manfred J.M. Neumann and others, 'The Appropriate Level of Regulation in Europe: local, national, or community-wide? A Roundtable Discussion', *Economic Policy*, 9, October 1989, 467–481.
9. See 'The IntraCompany Trade of US Multinationals', *World Economic Monitor* (Conference Board) 1, 4, Fall 1986, 1–4; John Dunning (ed.), *Multinational Enterprises, Economic Structure, and International Competitiveness* (New York, N. Y.: John Wiley & Sons, 1985); and Yves Doz, *Strategic Management in Multinational Companies* (Elmsford, N. Y.: Pergamon Press, 1986).
10. See Dunning, cited.
11. Same, and see arguments for regulation in Simon Reich, 'Roads to Follow: Regulating Foreign Direct Investment', *International Organisation*, 43, 4, Autumn 1989, 543–584.
12. See Robert Lipsey, *American Firms Face Europe: 1992* (Cambridge, Massachusetts: National Bureau of Economic Research, Working Paper 3293, 1990).
13. See Reich, cited, and Dunning, cited.
14. See John H. Dunning and Peter Robson, 'Multinational Corporate Integration and Regional Economic Integration', *Journal of Common Market Studies*, XXVI, 2, December 1987, 103–126.
15. Same.
16. See references to centers of innovation in same.
17. See Reich, cited, and Stephen D. Cohen, 'United States–Japan Trade Relations', *Proceedings*, cited, 122–136.

18. See observations on Community foreign direct investment policies in David Greenaway, 'Intra-Industry Trade, Intra-Firm Trade and European Integration: Evidence, Gains, and Policy Aspects', *Journal of Common Market Studies*, XXVI, 2, December 1987, 153–170.

19. See Takashi Inoguchi and Daniel I. Okimoto (eds), *The Political Economy of Japan* (Stanford, California: Stanford University Press, 1988).

20. See Peter J. Katzenstein (ed.), *Industry and Politics in West Germany* (Ithaca, New York: Cornell University Press, 1989).

21. The administration of subsidies has to cope with increasing complexities regarding corporate nationality because of the expansion of linkages between international firms. See John M. Kline, 'Trade Competitiveness and Corporate Nationality', *Columbia Journal of World Business*, XXIV, 3, Fall 1989, 25–31.

22. See *Economies in Transition: Structural Adjustment in OECD Countries* (Paris: OECD, 1989) for a discussion of the mainly competitive aspects of industrial policy.

23. See Frank Press and others, *A High Technology Gap: Europe, America, and Japan* (New York, N.Y.: Council on Foreign Relations, 1987) and Jill Hills, 'Foreign Policy and Technology: The Japan–US, Japan–Britain and Japan–EEC Technology Agreements', *Political Studies*, XXXI, 2, June 1983, 205–223.

24. See Peter Enderwick, 'Multinational Corporate Restructuring and International Competitiveness', *California Management Review*, 32, 1, Fall 1989, 44–57.

25. See *A High Technology Gap: Europe, America, and Japan*, cited.

26. See Dunning and Robson, cited, and Tommaso Padoa–Schioppa and others, *Efficiency, Stability and Equity: A Strategy for the Evolution of the Economic System of the European Community* (Oxford: Oxford University Press, 1987).

27. See general comments on preferences of US firms in Anant R. Negandhi, 'Management Strategies and Policies of American, German, and Japanese Multinational Corporations', *Research in International Business and International Relations*, 3, 1989, 29–50.

28. US concerns about EC discrimination are reflected in Michael Calingaert, *The 1992 Challenge from Europe: Development of the European Community's Internal Market* (Washington DC: National Planning Association, 1988).

29. See references to problems of consistency in the USA by Vernon, cited.

30. See Cohen, cited.

31. Same, and, on Atlantic relations, see Vernon, cited.

32. See J.N. Behrman, 'The Future of International Business and the Distribution of Benefits', *Columbia Journal of World Business*, XX, 4, 1986, 15–22.

33. See Ronald Dore, Jean Bounine-Cabale and Kari Tapiola, *Japan at Work: Markets, Management, and Flexibility* (Paris: OECD, 1989).

34. See *World Economic Monitor*, cited, and Richard W. Moxon, 'Multinational Consortia in Manufacturing', *Research in International Business and International Relations*, cited, 11–28.

Chapter 8

1. See Richard W. Moxon, 'Multinational Consortia in Manufacturing', *Research in International Business and International Relations*, 3, 1989, 11–28, and Ellen R. Auster, 'International Corporate Linkages: Dynamic Forms in Changing Environments', *Columbia Journal of World Business*, XXII, 2, Summer 1987, 3–6.

2. See Stephen D. Cohen, 'United States–Japan Trade Relations', *Proceedings of the Academy of Political Science*, 37, 4, 1990, 122–136.

3. The concept of extended accountability can be derived from the significance of externalities as sources of market failure and therefore as factors obligating international cooperation. See Richard N. Cooper, 'Economic Interdependence and the Coordination of Economic Policies', in Ronald W. Jones and Peter B. Kenen (eds), *Handbook of International Economics* (New York, N.Y.: North-Holland, 1985) 1196–1231.

4. See J.N. Behrman, 'The Future of International Business and the Distribution of Benefits', *Columbia Journal of World Business*, XX, 4, 1986, 15–22.

5. See Moxon, cited, and John H. Dunning (ed.), *Multinational Enterprises, Economic Structure, and International Competitiveness* (New York, N.Y.: John Wiley & Sons, 1985).

6. See Ronald Dore, *Taking Japan Seriously* (Stanford, California: Stanford University Press, 1987).

7. See James M. Buchanan and others, *Reaganomics and After* (London: Institute of Economic Affairs, 1989).

8. See Juliet Lodge (ed.), *The European Community and the Challenge of the Future* (New York, N.Y.: St Martin's Press, 1989) Pt 1; Wayne Sandholtz and John Zysman, '1992: Recasting the European Bargain', *World Politics* XLII, 1, October 1989, 95–128; and Dieter Helm and Stephen Smith, 'The Assessment: Economic Integration and the Role of the European Community', *Oxford Review of Economic Policy*, 5, 2, Summer 1989, 1–20.

9. See Lodge, cited.

10. On the relationships between business groups and the European Commission see Sandholtz and Zysman, cited.

11. On the current role of the OECD see David Henderson, 'The State of International Economic Cooperation', *The World Today*, 44, 12, December 1988, 212–215.

12. See especially Edward John Ray, 'The Impact of Rent Seeking Activity on US Preferential Trade and World debt', *Review of World Economics*, 125, 3, 1989, 619–637.

13. See Tommaso Padoa Schioppa, 'Policy Cooperation and the EMS Experience' in Willem H. Buiter and Richard C. Marston (eds), *International Economic Policy Coordination* (New York, N.Y.: Cambridge University Press, 1985) 331–355.

14. On the logic of regional economic integration see John H. Dunning and Peter Robson, 'Multinational Corporate Integration and Regional Economic Integration', *Journal of Common Market Studies*, XXVI, 2, December 1987, 103–126

15. See concerns expressed by Buchanan, cited.

16. See Emil J. Kirchner, 'West German Policy and Deepening Integration in the European Community', paper for annual meeting of the International Studies Association, Washington DC April 10–14, 1990.

17. See Dore, cited.

18. See David Allen and Michael Smith, 'Western Europe's Presence in the Contemporary International Arena', *Review of International Studies*, 16, 1, January 1990, 19–37, and Albert Bressand, 'Beyond Interdependence: 1992 as a Global Challenge', *International Affairs*, 66, 1, January 1990, 47–65.

19. See Gavin Boyd, *Pacific Trade, Investment, and Politics* (London: Pinter Publishers, 1988).

20. Same.

21. On US economic relations with Latin America see Sebastian Edwards, 'The United States and Foreign Competition in Latin America', in Martin Feldstein (ed.), *The United States in the World Economy* (Chicago: University of Chicago Press, 1988) 9–63.

22. See Sandholtz and Zysman, cited, and DeAnne Julius, *Global Companies and Public*

Policy: The Growing Challenge of Foreign Direct Investment (London: Royal Institute of International Affairs, 1990).

23. See Thomas D. Willett, 'National Macroeconomic Policy Preferences and International Coordination Issues, *Journal of Public Policy*, 8, 3&4, July–December 1988, 235–264.
24. See Boyd, cited.
25. These considerations are based on observations in Behrman, cited.
26. On the EC potential for a leadership role see Bressand, cited.

Index

LIP